INTO UNKNOWN ENGLAND

Peter Keating was born in London in 1939 and educated at the University of Sussex. From 1968 to 1972 he was lecturer in English at the University of Leicester, and is at present Lecturer in English Literature at the University of Edinburgh He is the author of *The Working Classes in Victorian Fiction* (1971), and studies of a number of Victorian writers including George Gissing Arthur Morrison, Robert Browning and Matthew Arnold.

Into Unknown England

1866–1913

SELECTIONS FROM THE SOCIAL EXPLORERS

Edited by Peter Keating

Fontana/Collins

This selection first issued in Fontana 1976
Copyright © in the editor's introduction and
this selection Peter Keating 1976

Second Impression September 1978

Made and printed in Great Britain by
William Collins Sons & Co Ltd, Glasgow

A hardback edition of this book
is published by Manchester University Press
by arrangement with Fontana.

Contents

Contents

Contents

Preface

The items in this anthology have been chosen to illustrate a characteristic type of nineteenth- and twentieth-century literature. Some of the extracts are justly famous, others are less familiar. Considered together they make up a substantial, wide-ranging, and varied tradition which is of real importance for any understanding of class relationships in modern democratic society. It is a tradition that is best defined in terms of the language which the writers themselves used to describe their activities. Acting as representatives of upper- or middle-class life, they cast themselves as 'explorers', entering, for the good of society as a whole, a world inhabited by the poor and destitute. The reports they send back from their exploratory trips are interesting from various points of view (the historical, literary, and sociological) but they possess also a value that transcends such academic distinctions. Above all, it is a frame of mind that is offered here, a way of looking at and describing society that undergoes frequent change yet is continuous in both its attitudes and the nature of its concerns.

The period covered by the anthology is the late nineteenth and early twentieth centuries, with James Greenwood's *A Night in a Workhouse* (1866) adopted as a starting point. This has meant excluding some major early Victorian examples of social exploration, most notably Engels's *The Condition of the Working Class in England* (1845) and Henry Mayhew's *London Labour and the London Poor* (4 vols. 1861). It would also, of course, be possible to go farther back in time to Cobbett's *Rural Rides* (1830), the reports of Royal Commissions in the 1830s and 40s, or even farther back to Defoe's *A Tour Thro' the Whole Island of Great Britain* (1724–7). In the present context the most important omission seems to me to be Mayhew, but selection in his case has in the past been damaging to a true recognition of his achievement, and complete editions of his works are now readily available.

The more positive justification for concentrating on the late Victorian and Edwardian periods is that it is here we find an important turning point, with the older tradition of personal exploration blending into the newer techniques of sociological analysis. It is one of the main aims of *Into Unknown England* to demonstrate some early stages in this change as well as a special response to it that leads to a characteristically modern kind of social explorer.

I would like to express my gratitude to the following for allowing me to reprint material of which they hold the copyright: The Joseph Rowntree Charitable Trust for B. S. Rowntree's *Poverty: A Study of Town Life*; the Estate of C. F. G. Masterman for *From the Abyss*; G. Bell & Son Ltd for Mrs Pember Reeves's *Round About a Pound a Week*; and Edward Arnold (Publishers) Ltd for Lady Bell's *At the Works*. Every effort has been made to trace copyright holders but in a few cases this has proved impossible. The publishers would be interested to hear from any copyright holders not here acknowledged.

PETER KEATING

Introduction

'Wealth has accumulated itself into masses,' wrote Carlyle in 'Characteristics' (1831), 'and Poverty, also in accumulation enough, lies impassably separated from it; opposed, uncommunicating, like forces in positive and negative poles.' Of all the social problems faced by the Victorians, this perception, that society was becoming rapidly divided into classes of people separate from and hostile to each other, was felt to be the most fundamental. For Carlyle England seemed an 'enchanted' land, cursed by the gods, flowing with wealth from improved agriculture and industrial invention yet unable to solve, even perhaps incapable of comprehending, the terrible problem of poverty that such wealth had brought with it:

> To whom, then, is this wealth of England wealth? Who is it that it blesses; makes happier, wiser, beautifuler, in any way better? . . . We have more riches than any Nation ever had before; we have less good of them than any Nation ever had before. Our successful industry is hitherto unsuccessful; a strange success, if we stop here! In the midst of plethoric plenty, the people perish; with gold walls, and full barns, no man feels himself safe or satisfied.

By the time these words were published in *Past and Present* (1843), Carlyle's message was well understood and being widely echoed. Two years later it was to receive a memorable formulation in Disraeli's *Sybil*, where the rich and the poor are described as: 'Two nations between whom there is no intercourse and no sympathy; who are as ignorant of each other's habits, thoughts, and feelings, as if they were dwellers in different zones, or inhabitants of different planets.' And in 1848 Marx and Engels made the same point, though with a very different emphasis, in terms which have become even more famous:

> The modern bourgeois society that has sprouted from the ruins of feudal society has not done away with class

antagonisms. It has but established new classes, new conditions of oppression, new forms of struggle in place of the
old ones. Our epoch, the epoch of the bourgeoisie, possesses,
however, this distinctive feature : it has simplified the class
antagonisms. Society as a whole is more and more splitting
up into two great hostile camps, two great classes directly
facing each other : Bourgeoisie and Proletariat.[1]

Marx and Engels welcomed the division of society into two
easily-definable hostile forces as a crucial stage in the eventual
and inevitable destruction of capitalism by class conflict, while
Carlyle and Disraeli, whose views were far more representative
of mainstream Victorian thought, urged the need for action to
alleviate poverty and to bridge, at all costs, the gap between
the classes. But while action of some kind was necessary, it
was by no means clear what form it should take. Both writers
stress that this new society has emerged in a largely haphazard
way, unwatched, uncared for, and unknown : the sense of
shock in drawing attention to it is an important part of their
approach, as also is their sense of the urgent need to know
more about it. In 'Characteristics' Carlyle proclaims that,
considering the state of matters, a true answer to the question
'What is the actual condition of Society?' is almost the 'one
thing needful' : and the heroes of Disraeli's novels move
between the two nations, horrified at what they find yet
confident that social harmony can be achieved.

Throughout the 1830s and 40s while Carlyle thundered and
Disraeli dreamed of transforming the country through a re-
vitalised Tory party, politicians, social reformers, statistical
societies, Royal Commissions, and philanthropists, were actively
gathering the information needed to answer the question 'What
is the actual condition of Society?' and also were hurriedly
introducing legislation to halt some of the earliest abuses of
urban-industrial life. The widespread and varied reform movements of the 1830s represent the first real attempts by government to come to terms with this new and strange society, an
acknowledgement that if both revolutionary threat and humanitarian disgrace were to be avoided then this could be achieved
only through a massive accumulation of detailed information
on the conditions in which people lived and worked.

Out of this concern there develops a distinctive branch of modern literature in which a representative of one class consciously sets out to explore, analyse, and report upon, the life of another class lower on the social scale than his own: the reverse procedure being, of course, not really possible, except in satire. In one obvious sense this is a modern variant of an age-old literary device, the journey undertaken whether aimlessly or with some specific purpose, during which the range and variety of human life is displayed. Where the literature of social exploration departs from this tradition is in its narrowing of social focus; the rigid class relationship it presupposes, and, in many cases, the contribution it makes to social change, either directly through the introduction of reforms, or, more, usually, by the influence it exerts on a public conscience or consciousness.

In its purest form, as it develops throughout the nineteenth century and into the twentieth, it tells the story of one person's journey into an alien culture and offers the detailed results of his findings, but the complexity of the issues it raises forbids total purity. In its early stages it is closely related to the reports published by Royal Commissions, and it later blends into sociology. Looked at from another angle, it is more a frame of mind than a literary form. Many Victorian novelists, in addition to Disraeli, assume the social explorer's characteristic role, or allot it to characters in their novels. Dickens and Mrs Gaskell are both social explorers, conscious and proud of the role, as also, in very different ways, are Mr Jarndyce in *Bleak House* and Margaret Hale in *North and South*. Beyond these examples, there is barely an area of nineteenth-century fictional and non-fictional prose, in which the central attitudes and terminology of social exploration do not appear. It is so pervasive because it expresses perfectly the fears and difficulties of an emergent democratic society.

In his preface to the first volume of *London Labour and the London Poor*, Mayhew employs a classic image of the social explorer. His book 'is curious', he writes: 'As supplying information concerning a large body of persons, of whom the public had less knowledge than of the most distant tribes of the earth . . . and as adducing facts so extraordinary, that the traveller in the undiscovered country of the poor must, like Bruce, until his stories are corroborated by after investigators, be content to lie under the imputation of telling such tales, as travellers are generally supposed to delight in.' Like Disraeli and many other contemporary writers, Mayhew uses the imagery of exploration primarily to draw attention to in-equalities in English society and to force upon the reader an awareness of his social blindness. The poor inhabit a separate 'country' which remains to be discovered by the wealthy, and the way of life in that country is so strange that a leap of imagination is required to believe that it even exists. But these are far from the only connotations to be drawn from the language of exploration: it was its almost inexhaustible adaptability that made it so attractive to writers like Mayhew.

The most obvious irony is that the two nations are really one: the distant tribes live not in Africa or India, but in Soho, East London, Manchester, or Birmingham. The voyage of discovery is, as George Sims points out in *How the Poor Live* (1883): 'Into a dark continent that is within easy walking distance of the General Post Office.' After 'brooding over the awful presentation of life' in the African rain forests by H. M. Stanley, General Booth asks himself and the reader: 'As there is a darkest Africa is there not also a darkest England?' The question is rhetorical, and Booth's book, *In Darkest England and the Way Out* (1890) is built entirely upon the analogy. Some explorers reinforce the fundamental irony by using it ironically, as Jack London does in his admonition to the greatest travel agent of his day:

But O Cook, O Thomas Cook & Son, path-finders and trail-clearers, living sign-posts to all the world, and bestowers of first aid to bewildered travellers – unhesitatingly and instantly, with ease and celerity, could you send me to Darkest Africa or Innermost Thibet, but to the East End of London, barely a stone's throw distant from Ludgate Circus, you know not the way!

The paradox of things being at the same time both near and distant serves to give a genuine exploratory value to what is being revealed while demonstrating that anyone can be this kind of explorer if he will only open his eyes and heart. 'These wonders and terrors have been lying by your door and mine ever since we had a door of our own,' wrote Thackeray in response to Mayhew's revelations in the *Morning Chronicle*. 'We had but to go a hundred yards off and see for ourselves, but we never did.'[2]

A careful balance must, however, be maintained. The social explorer wants to inspire others to follow his example and therefore needs to stress the accessibility of these dark and forbidding places, but if he makes the journey seem too easy then no real challenge is offered and his main purpose is defeated. The answer is to show that the social explorer must be prepared to confront and endure, potentially at least, the same kind of dangers and hardship as his more exotic counterpart. The constant references to 'wandering tribes', 'pygmies', and 'rain forests', help to convey this feeling, though more forceful are the dangers posed by the living conditions of the poor. Terrible diseases are not restricted to tropical climates, as Andrew Mearns indicates in *The Bitter Cry of Outcast London* (1883):

> Few who will read these pages have any conception of what these pestilential human rookeries are, where tens of thousands are crowded together amidst horrors which call to mind what we have heard of the middle passage of a slave ship. To get into them you have to penetrate courts reeking with poisonous and malodorous gases arising from accumulations of sewage and refuse scattered in all directions and often flowing beneath your feet.

James Greenwood, having survived the horrors of a communal bath, gets ready to sleep and finds, 'in the middle of the bed I had selected was a stain of blood bigger than a man's hand'. The explorer's courage in this case, as indeed in so many others, was acknowledged by his readers. Greenwood's willingness to spend one night in a manner similar to that spent by many thousands of his fellow men was described by Sir William Hardman, editor of the *Morning Post*, as: 'An act of bravery . . . which ought to entitle him to the VC.'[3] Before plunging into the unknown world of the East End, Jack London hired a private detective to keep track of him, and other social explorers, if of a less sensational turn of mind, were careful to point out that the investigation of poverty led inevitably to some kind of contact with crime. The language they use to describe even a commonplace event serves to glorify their own special qualities: they seem never to walk or ride into a slum, they 'penetrate' it.

The most spectacular aspect of the explorer's role was not in simply examining and writing about the lives of the poor, but becoming temporarily one of them. This was to be the method employed by George Orwell, the most famous of twentieth-century social explorers, though the long tradition to which Orwell in this respect belongs, is less often remembered. The vogue seems to have started with James Greenwood's *A Night in a Workhouse* (1866). The suggestion that a reporter should spend one night in a London workhouse, disguised as a 'casual' so that he would receive the same treatment as one of the genuine homeless, came from Greenwood's brother Frederick, editor of the recently founded *Pall Mall Gazette*. The articles caused a sensation. They are reputed to have played a large part in boosting the sales of the *Pall Mall Gazette*, were reprinted in full by *The Times*, and gave to Greenwood his early pseudonym 'the amateur casual'. They also established his reputation as a writer specializing in unusual and dangerous investigatory journalism. One surprising result of the articles was that 'Daddy', the kindly deputy in charge of the workhouse, became, according to Sims: 'The talk of the town, and presently the rage of the town. Songs were composed in his honour, songs sentimental, comic, and serio-comic.'[4] Certainly the popularity of Greenwood's voyage of exploration was sufficiently widespread for a broadside to be issued in *his* honour:

> Now a gent, with good intent, to Lambeth workhouse went,
>   The mystery of the place to explore, sir,
> Says he, without a doubt, I shall then find out,
>   What treatment they give the houseless poor, sir.
> So he went through his degrees, like a blessed brick,
>   Thro' scenes he had never seen before, sir,

So good luck to him, I say, for ever and a day,
For bestowing a thought upon the poor, sir.[5]

From reports by contemporary journalists it appears that Greenwood really was a master of disguise, and that he possessed a knowledge of working-class ways and language that made it easy for him to adopt different class roles.

Not all of Greenwood's work was sensational, but he was to be involved in one further celebrated exposé, that concerning an organized fight between a man and a dog in Hanley, an extract of which is included here. It is a brutal scene, described vividly, and built up to by a characteristically low-key discussion of the miners' love of dogs, which provoked questions in Parliament and angry protests when it first appeared in the *Daily Telegraph*. The seriousness with which Greenwood took his role as a 'volunteer explorer in the depths of social mysteries',[6] can be seen by the details he offered the public of his attempts to gather supporting evidence for his story, when the article was reprinted in book form. Whether true, as described, or not, the anger it aroused in the Potteries lingered for many years. More than thirty years later Arnold Bennett, drawing attention to the hospitable nature of the inhabitants of the Five Towns in 'The Death of Simon Fuge', makes Greenwood an exception to the rule: 'The only man who stands a chance of getting his teeth knocked down his throat here is the ingenious person who started the celebrated legend of the man-and-dog fight at Hanbridge. It's a long time ago, a very long time ago; but his grey hairs won't save him from horrible tortures if we catch him.'

The use of disguise did not bring with it a corresponding change in personality, the transformation was largely external; but it added a dash of flair to the explorer's journey, and the felt need to put on, as it were, a uniform in order to enter the life of the poor, carried in itself lessons about class distinctions which the explorers understood and used. Jack London, posing as 'the seafaring-man-who-had-lost-his-clothes-and-money', noted how class status often came simply from wearing the right 'badge and advertisement'. To the working man he immediately became 'mate' rather than 'sir' or 'governor'; on asking a policeman how to get to a certain locality, the query in return is no longer 'Bus or 'ansom, sir?' but 'Walk or ride?' The most perceptive of his observations in this respect is that in crossing crowded streets, vehicles obviously take less care in avoiding him: 'It was strikingly impressed upon me that my life had cheapened in direct ratio with my clothes.' The feeling is widespread that so great is the gulf between classes that some kind of new identity is needed if communication with the poor is to be made on any level other than the philanthropic or patronizing. Attempted disguise is as much an attempt to break from one form of status as it is to adopt the trappings of another. Mary Higgs went on the tramp to find out at first hand about the lives of the destitute women she normally helped, in her role as a minister's wife, in Oldham. Sims, whose Dagonet Ballads were no doubt familiar to many of the poor, pretended he was connected with the School Board, and was always worried in case it was assumed instead that his real connection was with the police. The desire to obtain an inside view as the only way of reaching the truth is also observable in very different kinds of explorer: in the use by Booth and Rowntree of men and women with special local knowledge, and by Masterman and Reynolds who go to live among the poor.

If the imagery of exploration served primarily to indicate material differences between the classes, with references to wandering tribes and natives indicating the lack of stable homes and decent clothing of the poor, it acted also to reveal a sub-culture created by the new industrial and urban way of life. The distance-nearness paradox was employed to describe attitudes and values far removed from those which the Victorians and Edwardians so rigidly codified. Time and again the explorers emphasize that poverty dictates how people behave and that it is meaningless to try to bring to bear easy middle-class morality. This may emerge, as in *The Bitter Cry*, as a challenging proclamation phrased deliberately to shock: 'Incest is common', or in the calmly-repeated report that many 'marriages' among the poor were in name only. The acknowledgement of patterns of behaviour in many respects quite different from their own does bring the role of the social explorers nearer to that of the anthropologist: again and again they suspend moral judgement and their own deeply-held beliefs in the more crucial cause of human understanding and compassion. 'Who are the lost?' asks General Booth, and answers: 'I reply, not in a religious but in a social sense, the lost are those who have gone under.'

General Booth's recognition that the Salvation Army could not hope to succeed in its spiritual campaign unless it concentrated first on the curing of social ills, is representative of a widespread late-Victorian sense of priorities. The very existence of the social explorers presupposes failure on someone's part. Only Greenwood, writing firmly in the mid-Victorian period and early in his career, is satisfied with pointing out that the scene he has described is 'infamous' without being more precise on correctives. All of the other explorers recognize that the problem of poverty has now reached such a magnitude that only State action can be truly effective. 'Without State interference nothing effectual can be accomplished upon any large scale,' Mearns decides, in the process of confessing that the Church he belongs to has done far from enough to help, and the sentiment recurs with increasing force as the nineteenth century draws to a close.

The true significance of this tendency lies as much in what it rejects as in what it advocates. By appealing for the State to take a greater part in social welfare, the explorers reflect a growing discontent with the mid-Victorian faith in the ability of voluntary organizations to solve problems, and are, sometimes explicitly as in the cases of General Booth and Mearns, though more often implicitly, forcing upon their readers an awareness of the failure of some of the most cherished mid-Victorian ideals, the Church, Philanthropy, and Self-Help. Here again the language and imagery of exploration are used aptly to contrast the moral fervour aroused by the plight of the foreign and distant poor with that of the poor at home: variations on the theme of 'telescopic philanthropy' derided so memorably by Dickens in *Bleak House* are to be found everywhere in the literature of social exploration.

General Booth is characteristically blunt on the hypocrisy involved: 'What a satire it is upon our Christianity and our civilisation that the existence of these colonies of heathens and savages in the heart of our capital should attract so little attention! It is no better than a ghastly mockery.' Sims is

indignant in the same way: 'The woes of an Egyptian, or a
Bulgarian, or a Zulu send a thrill of indignation through honest
John Bull's veins; and yet at his very door there is a race so
oppressed, so hampered, and so utterly neglected, that its
condition has become a national scandal.' The irony of England
having played an active part in the abolition of slavery is frequently invoked: 'If chains for slaves are not made here,'
writes Robert Sherard, 'it is doubtless because there are no
slaves in England; or it may be because hunger can bind tighter
than any iron links.' And the high noon of imperialism gave a
new and bitter twist to the imagery, as in Jack London's
description of the East End as a place, 'where the sun on rare
occasions may be seen to rise'. The upsurge of interest in the
East End of London during the 1880s and 90s had at hand a
ready-made contrast between East and West which could be
used to refer simultaneously to both London and the Empire,
and this became so popular that it led to what can almost be
considered a sub-genre of exploration literature, while the
increased activity of the churches at this time in setting up
'missions' and 'settlements' provoked a fresh spate of 'telescopic
philanthropy' images.[7]

But however different the emphasis, the language of exploration in this specific context is still an extension of what had
been common for the previous fifty years. The one image
which, if hardly 'new', is used in a new way at the turn of
the century, is of the working classes and the poor as inhabiting an 'abyss' at the edge of society. An element of class fear,
whether from contagious diseases or revolution, is never
entirely absent from the work of earlier social explorers, but
the repeated use of the word 'abyss' marks a real change of
attitude. It reflects a feeling of despair at worsening social
conditions and at the inability of existing institutions to deal
with the problem; it reflects also a corresponding concern at
the growing militancy of the working-class movement that was
apparent in public demonstrations, politics, and trade union
activity.

An abyss still conveys enough sense of distance to be attractive to the social explorer, but it carries with it an eeriness
which replaces the more exotic associations of travel. You
don't journey *to* an abyss: you descend or fall into it. It is all

very well claiming that a Dark Continent lies at one's doorstep but that metaphorically is more welcome than a gaping hole. And what may walk out of an African rain forest is one thing, what *climbs* out of an abyss is quite another. Its use also implies a change in class relationships with the explorer peering over the edge at, or climbing down to, the massed poor below. The gap between the classes is now 'deep' and terrifying, a matter of delicate balance and subtle gradations, of possibly climbing up or clinging on or falling down, as E. M. Forster indicates, with just this image in *Howards End* (1910): 'The boy, Leonard Bast, stood at the extreme verge of gentility. He was not in the abyss, but he could see it, and at times people whom he knew had dropped in, and counted no more. The main reason for the word's popularity is, however, political, as the inhabitants of the abyss now in theory at least have political equality with the explorer. With the extension of the franchise in 1867 and 1884, political power became for the first time a matter of counting heads, and the late Victorian and Edwardian explorers were fully aware that not only were the people of the abyss virtually a different race, but that there were an awful lot of them.

General Booth and Jack London both use the word 'abyss' but without attaching these specific meanings to it. If it has one particular derivation it comes from H. G. Wells. Jack London admitted that he had taken the phrase 'people of the abyss' from Wells, the reference being to a short story 'In the Abyss'. But of more importance is *The Time Machine* (1895) where we find the concept and its class connotations, if not the actual word. In Wells's allegory of the Capital/Labour conflict, the ruling classes have declined into the effete Eloi who are preyed upon by the subterranean Morlocks. At this level the social message of *The Time Machine* is do something quickly or perish: it was a lesson that C. F. G. Masterman was quick to learn and propagate:

As the Red Indian, putting his ear to the ground, could hear murmurs beyond the horizon inaudible to the bystander, so the trained ear could discern the turmoil of the coming flood and the tramp of many footsteps. Our streets have suddenly become congested with a weird and uncanny people. They have poured in as dense black masses from the eastern railways; they have streamed across the bridges from the marshes and desolate places beyond the river; they have been hurried up in incredible number through tubes sunk in the bowels of the earth, emerging like rats from a drain, blinking in the sunshine.

These are the people from the modern abyss, and, following Wells, they are described in a way that is strikingly new. Earlier explorers had offered graphic studies of individual or family suffering; a wide range of differentiated street characters, and hints of wandering tribes – all small units within a larger whole. Masterman moves from this tradition to concentrate on the mass. The individual case study may be more effective for stirring compassion, but it can no longer serve to describe adequately the sight of tens of thousands of people streaming over the abyss in workmen's specials; walking across the Thames bridges; and being brought out of the abyss by convoys of underground trains. Masterman even mocks the now conventional imagery of exploration, adopting, in order to do so, the voice of the poor:

> We are the subjects of lengthy and acrimonious controversy. Novelists jaded with battues of blacks in unknown lands, select as heroes the denizens of lands still more unknown at their very doors; relate of their travels into our dangerous and desolate regions, of the life and manners and habits of the aborigines.

The mockery expresses Masterman's conviction that a fresh stage in class relations had been inaugurated, and more must be said of him in this context, but even so he adapts the imagery of exploration rather than dispenses with it entirely. His concern, as with all writers in the tradition to which he belongs, must be mainly with the condition of the people, and the true nature of that remains unknown though, it is felt, no longer unknowable. The disguises and assumed identities, rain forests and arid deserts, pygmies and naked savages, are rhetorical devices to be taken literally only in the narrowest of senses, and are truly effective in so far as they reveal human suffering and arouse active compassion for it.

Rider Haggard is alone among the writers represented here in rarely making an emotional appeal on behalf of the poor. Preoccupied with the country itself as much as with the men and women who work in it, obsessed with the depopulation of rural England, openly distrustful of the agricultural labourer's ability to speak for himself, yet forced by rapidly changing circumstances to argue for improvement, Haggard is a rare example of a social explorer who voyages into a land of employers rather than employees, of masters rather than men. In this he stands apart from the others, all of whom would have agreed with Sims that: 'No man who has seen "How the Poor Live" can return from the journey with aught but an aching heart.'

The aching heart removes the paradox from the imagery of social exploration by conveying the nearness and immediacy of the suffering involved and thus obliterating metaphorical distance. Mearns and Sims focus on the appalling housing conditions in London; General Booth on those of the poor who have no homes of any kind and sleep on the Embankment; Sherard on the child workers of Birmingham; Mary Higgs on the girls who drift helplessly into prostitution; Greenwood and Jack London on the indignity of the workhouse and casual ward. The emotive technique most frequently used is the vivid brief vignette: the Birmingham mother and five-year-old child working for six and a half evening hours in the 'hook and eye' trade to earn 4d; the homeless man walking the streets throughout the night so that he will be on hand for any early-morning casual jobs: 'I got a penny yesterday at it, and twopence for carrying a parcel, and today I've had a penny.' Sketches such as these are multiplied with apparently endless ease and expanded outwards to make an overall case. Jack London, the explorer most blatantly in search of copy, turns from a line of men waiting to enter the 'Spike' and portrays a respectable working-class family on the opposite side of the street: 'To them our presence was nothing unusual. We are not an intrusion. We were as natural and ordinary as the brick walls and stone curbs of their environment.' And even Greenwood, more willing than most to pass easy character judgements, is struck by the significance of a typical sound of poverty:

Every variety of cough that ever I heard was to be heard
there: the hollow cough; the short cough; the hysterical
cough; the bark that comes at regular intervals, like the
quarter chiming of a clock, as if to mark off the progress
of decay; coughing from vast hollow chests, coughing from
little narrow ones – now one, now another, now two or three
together, and then a minute's interval of silence in which to
think of it all, and wonder who would begin next.

As individual examples multiply and the aching heart
acknowledges its helplessness in the face of widespread
poverty, it becomes clear that mid-Victorian paternalism has
failed and that different methods must be tried.

In May 1887 Charles Booth read to the Royal Statistical Society
a paper called 'Condition and Occupations of the people of
The Tower Hamlets 1886–7'. In it he gave details of his first
year's work on the survey of poverty in London which had
begun with the East End and was then systematically expanded
to cover London as a whole. The findings were published
irregularly throughout the 1890s, culminating in the seventeen-
volume edition of 1903, *Life and Labour of the People in
London*. In his talk to the Royal Statistical Society, Booth
explains that he began with the East End because here was
generally felt to be the 'focus of the problem of poverty in
the midst of wealth'. He outlines the methods he has adopted,
and describes as his leading idea in undertaking the survey:
'That every social problem, as ordinarily put, must be broken
up to be solved or even to be adequately stated.'

From the beginning Booth's survey aroused a great deal of
interest and became immediately a standard point of reference
not only for other workers in similar areas, but for politicians
and social reformers. Some aspects of the methods employed
by Booth (especially his classification of the working classes,
and the way much of his information was gathered through
School Inspectors) have been severely criticized,[8] but in
historical terms his importance is clear and undeniable. For the
first time an attempt had been made to define what was meant
by poverty, and to develop methods which could be used

reliably to measure the extent to which it existed in London. We have seen how convinced the social explorers were that they were dealing with a problem so large that only State intervention could hope to deal effectively with it. This conviction was confirmed and strengthened by Booth's work.

Life and Labour does not mark, as one might expect, an end to the literature of social exploration, but rather the appearance of a quite different kind of explorer. At the beginning of his survey Booth had expected to be able to disprove the claim by H. M. Hyndman that 25 per cent of the people in London lived in extreme poverty, and in his talk to the Royal Statistical Society he criticized the 'agitators' and 'sensational writers' who 'talk of "starving millions" and . . . tack on the thousands of the working classes to the tens or perhaps hundreds of distress'. Two years later he was less confident of his right to make this sort of distinction, and in the conclusion to the first volume of *Life and Labour* he returned to the point by means of a dramatically posed question:

> East London lay hidden from view behind a curtain on which were painted terrible pictures: Starving children, suffering woman, overworked men; horrors of drunkenness and vice; monsters and demons of inhumanity; giants of disease and despair. Did these pictures truly represent what lay behind, or did they bear to the facts a relation similar to that which the pictures outside a booth at some country fair bear to the performance or show within?

Booth's answer was that not only had he underestimated originally the extent of poverty in London, but so had Hyndman as well. The statistics showed that 35.2 per cent of the East London population lived in poverty, and, what was even more disturbing considering that the East End was supposed to be a special case, later investigation gave the corresponding figure for London as a whole as 30.7 per cent.

The question these figures raised was, if the East End was not as exceptional as was often claimed, then could London itself be regarded as a special case? It was to answer this question that Seebohm Rowntree undertook a similar survey of York, the results of which were published as *Poverty: A*

Study of Town Life (1901). Rowntree openly admitted that his approach owed much to Booth and that his task was considerably simpler. The size of York made it possible for Rowntree to carry out a house-to-house survey of all 11,560 working-class families in the town, and this in turn enabled him to refine Booth's rather vague definition of poverty and offer instead a distinction between degrees of poverty, which Rowntree terms Primary and Secondary. Rowntree further introduced the concept of the 'poverty cycle' which demonstrated disturbingly how a working man was subject to phases of poverty throughout his life and these at the most crucial stages of his physical development.

The survey of York established two undeniable facts which were to be used repeatedly by social reformers. First, Rowntree's figure for those living in poverty in York was 27·84 per cent, which approximated closely to Booth's findings for London, and this in a provincial town of average size at a time of relative prosperity. Secondly, Rowntree also confirmed that poverty was by no means confined to the weak, lazy, and debased, but was the regular condition of a large proportion of decent hard-working families. These findings were offered in a much cooler, more detached, manner than Booth's, nothing being allowed to detract from the final statistical results. As Asa Briggs has written : 'The appeal of the book did not depend on its style, which was workmanlike rather than dramatic . . . the strength of the text rested on its economy of treatment and the steady accumulation and unfolding of evidence.'[9] The wandering Arabs, distant tribes, and rain forests have been replaced by 'poverty cycles' and 'subsistence levels'; the graphic vignette makes way for a statistical table; the individual becomes part of the mass; and the explorer studies not the poor (an appropriate label for the objects of Victorian paternalism) but poverty (the disease itself):

What was the true measure of the poverty in York, both in extent and depth? How much of it was due to insufficiency of income and how much to improvidence? How many families were sunk in a poverty so acute that its members suffered from a chronic insufficiency of food and clothing? If physical deterioration combined with a high

death-rate ensued, was it possible to estimate such results
with approximate accuracy?[10]

It is the twentieth century's particular form of the language
of exploration, as is the vast literature that develops from it.
There remain two nations, as Booth and Rowntree recognize,
but the role of the social explorer (or investigator as he is now
more often called) is taken over by the professional sociologist.
The example set by Booth and Rowntree was followed
immediately by others: Lady Florence Bell's study of the lives
of iron-foundry workers in Middlesbrough, *At the Works*
(1907); Edward Howarth and Mona Wilson's *West Ham* in the
same year; and Mrs Pember Reeves's *Round About a Pound a
Week* (1913), which examined family life in South London.
The country, which had received nothing like the amount of
attention devoted to the city, was now given a similar treatment, by Maude F. Davies, *Life in an English Village* (1909),
and by Rowntree and May Kendall, *How the Labourer Lives*
(1913); while in *Livelihood and Poverty* (1915), A. L. Bowley
and A. R. Burnett-Hurst, pioneered the comparative study of
urban poverty by the new method of random sampling. The
desired pose ceases to be one of passionate involvement and
arduous physical exertion, and is replaced by calm, studied,
'scientific' objectivity, without which help cannot be given and
the problems of society solved. The imagination of the exotic
explorer is needed as much as ever, even in one sense a great
deal more, but he is no longer the courageous, death-defying
individual, but the leader of a team of professional experts who
know how to catalogue, estimate, and quantify everything
from the amount of food it takes to keep a workman working
to the number of times in a year that he or his wife visits the
public library.

Yet the more sophisticated sociological methods did not make
the traditional social explorer obsolete. Instead they acted as a
help and inspiration, providing him with trustworthy information and an up-to-date terminology. General Booth bemoans the
fact that 'the Social problem has scarcely been studied at all
scientifically', and pointing to Booth's work as an honourable
exception, uses figures from the first volume of *Life and
Labour* to estimate the number of poor throughout England,

the famous 'submerged tenth'. It is interesting that General
Booth, writing his own book before the second volume of *Life
and Labour* appeared in 1891, assumes that the East End is an
'exceptionally bad district from which to generalise for the
rest of the country' and to be on the safe side he takes as a
national average half of that given for the East End, thus neatly
combining old and new attitudes. An even more striking
example is provided by Mary Higgs who claimed to have
sought first-hand experience of women's lodging-houses because
of her realization that 'exploration was the method of
science'.[11] She explains : 'Society has now arrived at a point
of development when . . . the whole question of the organisation of humanity must be put on a scientific basis.' Jack
London quotes Booth's statistics, and Rider Haggard uses Rowntree's findings as evidence to show how deluded the agricultural
labourer must be to leave the country for the worse conditions
of the city.

Masterman's response was the most comprehensive. In a
perceptive review of *Poverty* he described the book as 'shatter-
ing the roseate dream' that large-scale poverty was confined to
London and other huge cities. 'Practically "poverty" holds the
same proportion in the city of sixty thousand as in the city of
six million,' he points out, and on the basis of Rowntree's
figures estimates that a total of seven and a half million people
throughout England are living in a state of poverty.[12] But
Masterman's commitment was not basically to statistical
evidence. His exploration of working-class life had its roots in
the settlement movement of the 1880s, the characteristic late-
Victorian stirring of conscience, analysed so brilliantly by
Beatrice Webb in *My Apprenticeship*, that under the influence
of Ruskin, Arnold Toynbee, and Samuel Barnett, had inspired
middle-class men and women to 'settle' in working-class districts. They went as helpers and educators but also as students.
The influence that this experience had on Masterman gives to
his writing a distinctive tone of passionate sympathy held in
check by an astute understanding of the changing pattern of
democratic society. In *From the Abyss* he pretends to speak
as one of the inhabitants but the perceptions are entirely his.
In this pamphlet, as in the later more famous work *The
Condition of England* (1909), there is a rejection of Utopian

fantasies, an urgent desire to confront urban problems (with Masterman's analysis of the class structure of cities being among the most perceptive produced by an age obsessed with the issue) and always the awareness that for democracy one of the critical factors in coming to terms with any social problem was to be the 'numbers' involved, the same concern that inspired the development of empirical sociology.

In one other respect Masterman's response to the poor epitomizes a recurring middle-class trend, a special kind of involvement of which Ruskin must stand as the dominant Victorian figure and Orwell as the classic twentieth-century example. Masterman's exploration was as much inwards as outwards, a laying naked of his own guilty conscience against which the demands and values of working-class life could be constantly tested. Out of this self-probing there develops the desire not simply to visit the poor in disguise, but to effect a cultural transformation, shedding the trappings of the middle-class in order to adopt those of the workers. Masterman's determination to analyse the ills of a whole society held him back from making this final act of commitment, though others willingly surrendered their objectivity.

For Stephen Reynolds it is middle-class not working-class life that is the problem. In rejecting his own background in order to live with the family of a Devonshire fisherman, Reynolds realized the ambiguous nature of his choice. In a letter to Edward Garnett, he wrote: 'What a position I'm in; neither philanthropist nor any sort of worker; simply a sponge to listen and an understander and sympathiser.'[13] More than this in fact. For Reynolds working-class life is better than that of the middle classes; the slum is preferable to the suburb; lack of education more admired than developed intelligence. 'Why live with the poor?' he is asked by friends, and he replies: 'The briefest answer is, that it is good to live among those who, on the whole, are one's superiors.' Here once again, though in a very different form, is the need to seek an inside view – it being accepted by all of the social explorers, of whatever cultural or political persuasion, that the poor and the working class cannot speak for themselves – and while Reynolds does not use the language of social exploration, he is in many senses nearer the anthropologist than Sims or Greenwood, London or General

Booth. He really is exploring a distant tribe, a way of life entirely unlike his own, and the details he notes and reports back on are concerned not with destitution or suffering, hardship or vice, but with the use of language, the closeness of family relationships, with the way a fisherman's wife cooks her husband fish for dinner; all described with an air of dazed admiration. It can be argued that Reynolds represents a new kind of condescension, but sentimentality is the truer word. He believed working-class life to be so superior that he opposed social reform and political action out of a fear that any change would ruin what he admired: 'I wish I could throw myself into Socialism, but the individualist in me makes me fear that every reform now on the carpet will spoil the "lower classes", even in making them more comfortable. Their good qualities have so largely developed from generations of discomfort.'[14]

The distance we have come from the early-Victorian Carlyle, urging some kind of action at all costs, to the Edwardian Reynolds, seeing the need for action yet refusing to countenance it, and both speaking on behalf of the working classes, is striking. As different as the two attitudes appear they should not, however, be treated as polar opposites. Reynolds still shares Carlyle's two-fold concern that society is divided into separate nations, and that the only way to heal the division is for the governing class to know more about the governed. By the time Reynolds was making his particular class gesture the way in which the problem of poverty in the midst of wealth was to be solved seemed clear. The sociologist would determine by 'scientific' methods the nature and extent of poverty, and the politicians, through increased State action, would introduce the necessary legislation: the need for the social explorer with his vague statistics, emotive language, and simple humanitarian appeal, would cease to exist.

But far from dying out, the tradition of social exploration continued, and continues, with, if anything, increased power. Quantification leaves as many problems unsolved and ills vaguely defined as Victorian paternalism, and the complex development of a democratic society seems no longer to be moving towards the formation of one relatively harmonious group. On the contrary, it appears always to be creating new kinds of divisions, groupings, alignments, each of which once forced into prominence, shocks by its 'newness' and 'unknown' nature, and this gives fresh impetus to the spirit, mood, and language, of social exploration. The novel, social-survey, and vivid account of personal experiences, continue as popular media for the social explorer, though supplemented by the inventions of a technological age – film, radio, television, and tape-recorder. No week now passes without the story of some voyage of social exploration being carried into the homes of millions of viewers, including the homes of those being explored. And because the problems have shifted rather than changed, the methods employed to provoke attention are little different from those pioneered by the Victorians and Edwardians.

The fundamental issue remains the division between wealth and poverty, and the desire to move between them is no less strong. 'I have a little spare time, & I feel I *must* tell you about my first adventure as an amateur tramp,' the young George Orwell writes to a friend, revealing the start of a lifetime's obsession. He adds, as explanation: 'Like most tramps, I was driven to it.'[15] Like most social explorers certainly. The imagery recurs, echoing through what is now a very substantial tradition, each voyage old yet new. As recently as 1936 Hugh Massingham could describe himself as 'driven' to live for a while in the East End: 'For years I had been struck by the extraordinary fact that two communities were living side by side, each with its own peculiar customs, superstitions, culture, sex life and to some extent even language, and that each was ignorant of the other.'[16]

Massingham seems barely aware of how many people before him had felt and said exactly the same, whereas, more recently, Ken Coates and Richard Silburn, in *Poverty: The Forgotten Englishman* (1970), draw upon the tradition and use it actively to criticize those who would argue complacently that the Welfare State has solved the problem of poverty. Now there is little point in claiming to 'discover' poverty, the discovery has been 'forgotten' and needs to be 'rediscovered'. The exploration continues and expands. Other groups offer themselves as forgotten or ignored by society. Some (men and women in prisons or mental institutions, or gypsies) have long been the concern of social explorers, but others may suddenly demand our attention, paradoxically, because they seem so much the norm, and we are invited to explore the unknown world of the suburban housewife or white-collar worker. Nothing is normative in social exploration except the need to keep pace with social change and to watch attentively the development of democracy. 'Would you care to go out dancing?' asks a character in Colin MacInnes's novel *City of Spades* (1957). 'Would you like to come into a world where you've never set foot before, even though it's always existed underneath your nose?' That world, distant yet on the doorstep, is inhabited by black immigrants, and the classic image of social exploration used to describe it provides a neat, if in this particular context ironic, illustration of a continuing process and attitude in twentieth-century society.

NOTES

1. Manifesto of the Communist Party, Marx and Engels, *Selected Works* (2 vols. Moscow, 1962), I, 34–5
2. 'Waiting at the Station', first published in *Punch*, XVIII (1850), 93
3. J. W. Robertson Scott, *The Story of the Pall Mall Gazette* (1950), 168
4. *Glances Back* (1917), 245
5. Charles Hindley, *Curiosities of Street Literature* (1871, repr. 1969), 137
6. *The Seven Curses of London* (1869), 47
7. See P. J. Keating, 'Fact and Fiction in the East End' in H. J. Dyos and Michael Wolff (eds.), *The Victorian City: Images and Realities* (2 vols. 1973)
8. See Eileen Yeo, 'Mayhew as a Social Investigator' in Yeo and Thompson (eds.), *The Unknown Mayhew* (1971), and for a contrasting view Gertrude Himmelfarb, 'The Culture of Poverty' in Dyos and Wolff (eds.), *The Victorian City*
9. *Social Thought and Action: A Study of the Work of Seebohm Rowntree* (1961), 31
10. *Poverty* (1901), vi
11. *Glimpses Into the Abyss* (1906), xi
12. 'The Social Abyss', *Contemporary Review*, LXXI, January 1902
13. Harold Wright (ed.) *The Letters of Stephen Reynolds* (1923), 32
14. ibid., 50
15. Sonia Orwell and Ian Angus (eds.) *The Collected Essays, Journalism and Letters of George Orwell* (4 vols. 1968), I, 11
16. *I Took Off My Tie* (1936), 1

James Greenwood

James Greenwood (184?–1929) was the son of a London coach-builder, and the brother of Frederick Greenwood, founder and first editor of the *Pall Mall Gazette*. Little is known of Greenwood's life: reminiscences of him tend to confirm what is already apparent in his writings. He was a master of disguise, sympathetic to the poor, and attracted to the more out-of-the-way aspects of lower-class life. These he explored and wrote up as newspaper articles under the pseudonyms 'The Amateur Casual' and 'One of the Crowd'. He worked first for the *Pall Mall Gazette* (where *A Night in a Workhouse* was originally serialized in 1866) and later mainly for the *Daily Telegraph*. His notorious account of a fight between a man and a dog in Hanley was first published in the *Daily Telegraph*, 6 July 1874, and reprinted with additional material detailing Greenwood's attempts to prove the truth of his story in *Low-Life Deeps* (1876) from which the extract printed here is taken. Although primarily a journalist, Greenwood published novels and short stories, and his work as a whole contains observation of and comment on a wide range of lower-class life, not all of it by any means 'sensational'.

'A NIGHT IN A WORKHOUSE'

I

At about nine o'clock on the evening of Monday, the 8th inst. (Jan. 1866), a neat but unpretentious carriage might have been seen turning cautiously from the Kennington Road into Princes Road, Lambeth. The curtains were closely drawn, and the coachman wore an unusually responsible air. Approaching a public-house which retreated a little from the street, he pulled up; but not so close that the lights should fall upon the carriage door; nor so distant as to unsettle the mind of any one who chose to imagine that he had halted to drink beer before pro-

ceeding to call for the children at a juvenile party. He did not
dismount, nor did any one alight in the usual way; but the
keen observer who happened to watch his intelligent countenance might have seen a furtive glance directed to the wrong
door : that is to say, to the door of the carriage which opened
into the dark and muddy road. From that door emerged a sly
and ruffianly figure, marked with every sign of squalor. He was
dressed in what had once been a snuff-brown coat, but which
had faded to the hue of bricks imperfectly baked. It was not
strictly a ragged coat, though it had lost its cuffs – a bereavement which obliged the wearer's arms to project through the
sleeves two long inelegant inches. The coat altogether was too
small, and was only made to meet over the chest by means of
a bit of twine. This wretched garment was surmounted by a
'birds-eye' pocket-handkerchief of cotton, wisped about the
throat hangman fashion; above all was a battered billy-cock
hat, with a dissolute drooping brim. Between the neckerchief
and the lowering brim of the hat appeared part of a face,
unshaven, and not scrupulously clean. The man's hands were
plunged into his pockets, and he shuffled hastily along in boots
which were the boots of a tramp indifferent to miry ways.
In a moment he was out of sight; and the brougham, after
waiting a little while, turned about and comfortably departed.

This mysterious figure was that of the present writer. He was
bound for Lambeth workhouse, there to learn by actual experience how casual paupers are lodged and fed, and what the
'casual' is like, and what the porter who admits him, and the
master who rules over him; and how the night passes with the
outcasts whom we have all seen crowding about workhouse
doors on cold and rainy evenings. Much has been said on the
subject – on behalf of the paupers – on behalf of the officials;
but nothing by any one who, with no motive but to learn and
make known the truth, had ventured the experiment of passing
a night in a workhouse, and trying what it actually is to be a
'casual'.

The day had been windy and chill – the night was cold; and
therefore I fully expected to begin my experiences amongst a
dozen of ragged wretches squatting about the steps and waiting
for admission. But my only companion at the door was a
decently dressed woman, who, as I afterwards learned, they

declined to admit until she had recovered from a fit of intoxication from which she had the misfortune to be still suffering. I lifted the big knocker, and knocked; the door was promptly opened, and I entered. Just within, a comfortable-looking clerk sat at a comfortable desk, ledger before him. Indeed, the spacious hall in every way was as cheery as cleanliness and great mats and plenty of gaslight could make it.

'What do you want?' asked the man who opened the door.

'I want a lodging.'

'Go and stand before the desk,' said the porter; and I obeyed.

'You are late,' said the clerk.

'Am I, sir?'

'Yes. If you come in you'll have a bath, and you'll have to sleep in the shed.'

'Very well, sir.'

'What's your name?'

'Joshua Mason, sir.'

'What are you?'

'An engraver.' (This taradiddle I invented to account for the look of my hands.)

'Where did you sleep last night?'

'Hammersmith,' I answered – as I hope to be forgiven!

'How many times have you been here?'

'Never before, sir.'

'Where do you mean to go when you are turned out in the morning?'

'Back to Hammersmith, sir.'

These humble answers being entered in a book, the clerk called to the porter, saying, 'Take him through. You may as well take his bread with you.'

Near the clerk stood a basket containing some pieces of bread of equal size. Taking one of these, and unhitching a bunch of keys from the wall, the porter led me through some passages all so scrupulously clean that my most serious misgivings were laid to rest.

Then we passed into a dismal yard. Crossing this, my guide led me to a door, calling out, 'Hillo! Daddy, I've brought you another!' Whereupon Daddy opened to us, and let a little of his gaslight stream into the dark where we stood.

'Come in,' said Daddy, very hospitably. 'There's enough of

you tonight, anyhow! What made you so late?'

'I didn't like to come in earlier.'

'Ah! that's a pity now, because you've missed your skilley (gruel). It's the first night of skilley, don't you know, under the new Act.'

'Just like my luck!' I muttered dolefully.

The porter went his way, and I followed Daddy into another apartment where were ranged three great baths, each one containing a liquid so disgustingly like weak mutton broth that my worst apprehensions crowded back.

'Come on, there's a dry place to stand on up at this end,' said Daddy, kindly. 'Take off your clothes, tie 'em up in your hank'sher, and I'll lock 'em up till the morning.'

Accordingly, I took off my coat and waistcoat, and was about to tie them together when Daddy cried, 'That ain't enough, I mean *everything*.'

'Not my shirt, sir, I suppose?'

'Yes, shirt and all; but there, I'll lend you a shirt,' said Daddy. 'Whatever you take in of your own will be nailed, you know. You might take in your boots, though – they'd be handy if you happened to want to leave the shed for anything; but don't blame me if you lose 'em.'

With a fortitude for which I hope some day to be rewarded, I made up my bundle (boots and all), and the moment Daddy's face was turned away shut my eyes and plunged desperately into the mutton broth. I wish from the bottom of my heart my courage had been less hasty; for hearing the splash, Daddy looked round and said, 'Lor, now! there was no occasion for that; you look a clean and decent sort of man. It's them filthy beggars' (only he used a word more specific than 'filthy') 'that want washing. Don't use that towel – here's a clean one! That's the sort! and now here's your shirt (handing me a blue striped one from a heap), and here's your ticket. Number 34 you are, and a ticket to match is tied to your bundle. Mind you don't lose it. They'll nail it from you if they get a chance. Put it under your head. This is your rug – take it with you.'

'Where am I to sleep, please, sir?'

'I'll show you.'

And so he did. With no other rag but the checked shirt to cover me, and with my rug over my shoulders, he accompanied me to the door at which I had entered, and, opening it, kept me standing with naked feet on the stone threshold, full in the draught of the frosty air, while he pointed out the way I should go. It was not a long way, but I would have given much not to have trodden it. It was open as the highway – with flagstones below and the stars overhead; and, as I said before, and cannot help saying again, a frosty wind was blowing.

'Straight across,' said Daddy, 'to where you see the light shining through. Go in there and turn to the left, and you'll find the beds in a heap. Take one of 'em and make yourself comfortable.' And straight across I went, my naked feet seeming to cling to the stones as though they were burning hot instead of icy cold (they had just stepped out of a bath, you should remember), till I reached the space through which the light was shining, and I entered in.

No language with which I am acquainted is capable of conveying an adequate conception of the spectacle I then encountered. Imagine a space of about thirty feet by thirty enclosed on three sides by a dingy white-washed wall, and roofed with naked tiles which were furred with the damp and filth that reeked within. As for the fourth side of the shed, it was boarded in for (say) a third of its breadth; the remaining space being hung with flimsy canvas, in which was a gap two feet wide at top, widening to at least four feet at bottom. This far too airy shed was paved with stone, the flags so thickly encrusted with filth that I mistook it at first for a floor of natural earth. Extending from one end of my bedroom to the other, in three rows, were certain iron 'cranks' (of which I subsequently learned the use), with their many arms raised in various attitudes, as the stiffened arms of men are on a battle-field. My bed-fellows lay amongst the cranks, distributed over the flagstones in a double row, on narrow bags scantily stuffed with hay. At one glance my appalled vision took in thirty of them – thirty men and boys stretched upon shallow pallets which put only six inches of comfortable hay between them and the stony floor. Those beds were placed close together, every occupant being provided with a rug like that which I was fain to hug across my shoulders. In not a few cases two gentlemen had clubbed beds and rugs and slept together. In one case (to be further mentioned presently) four gentlemen had so clubbed together. Many of my fellow casuals were awake – others asleep or pretending to sleep; and shocking as were the waking ones to look upon, they were quite pleasant when compared with the sleepers. For this reason : the practised and well-seasoned casual seems to have a peculiar way of putting himself to bed. He rolls himself in his rug, tucking himself in, head and feet, so that he is completely enveloped; and, lying quite still on his pallet, he looks precisely like a corpse covered because of its hideousness. Some were stretched out at full length; some lay nose and knees together; some with an arm or a leg showing crooked through the coverlet. It was like the result of a railway accident : these ghastly figures were awaiting the coroner.

From the moral point of view, however, the wakeful ones were more dreadful still. Towzled, dirty, villanous, they squatted up in their beds, and smoked foul pipes, and sang snatches of horrible songs, and bandied jokes so obscene as to be absolutely appalling. Eight or ten were so enjoying themselves – the majority with the check shirt on and the frowsy rug pulled about their legs; but two or three wore no shirts at all, squatting naked to the waist, their bodies fully exposed in the light of the single flaring jet of gas fixed high up on the wall.

My entrance excited very little attention. There was a horse-pail three parts full of water standing by a post in the middle of the shed, with a little tin pot beside it. Addressing me as 'old pal', one of the naked ruffians begged me to 'hand him a swig', as he was 'werry nigh garspin''. Such an appeal of course no 'old pal' could withstand, and I gave him a pot full of water. He showed himself grateful for the attention. 'I should lay over there if I was you,' he said, pointing to the left side of the shed; 'it's more out of the wind than this 'ere side is.' I took the good-natured advice and (by this time shivering with the cold) stepped over the stones to where the beds or straw bags were heaped, and dragged one of them to the spot suggested by my naked comrade. But I had no more idea of how to arrange it than of making an apple-pudding; and a certain little discovery added much to my embarrassment. In the middle of the bed I had selected was a stain of blood

bigger than a man's hand! I did not know what to do now.
To lie on such a horrid thing seemed impossible; yet to carry
back the bed and exchange it for another might betray a
degree of fastidiousness repugnant to the feelings of my fellow
lodgers and possibly excite suspicions that I was not what I
seemed. Just in the nick of time in came that good man Daddy.

'What! not pitched yet?' he exclaimed; 'here, I'll show you.
Hallo! somebody's been a-bleedin'! Never mind; let's turn him
over. There you are, you see! Now lay down, and cover your
rug over you.'

There was no help for it. It was too late to go back. Down
I lay, and spread the rug over me. I should have mentioned
that I brought in with me a cotton handkerchief, and this
I tied round my head by way of a nightcap; but not daring to
pull the rug as high as my face. Before I could in any way
settle my mind to reflection, in came Daddy once more to do
me a further kindness, and point out a stupid blunder which
I had committed,

'Why, you *are* a rummy chap!' said Daddy. 'You forgot
your bread! Lay hold. And look here, I've brought you another
rug; it's perishing cold tonight.'

So saying, he spread the rug over my legs and went away.

I was very thankful for the extra covering, but I was in a
dilemma about the bread. I couldn't possibly eat it; what, then,
was to be done with it? I broke it, however, and in view of
such of the company as might happen to be looking made a
ferocious bite at a bit as large as a bean, and munched
violently.

By good luck, however, I presently got half way over my
difficulty very neatly. Just behind me, so close indeed that
their feet came within half a yard of my head, three lads were
sleeping together.

'Did you 'ear that, Punch?' one of these boys asked.

''Ear what?' answered Punch, sleepy and snappish.

'Why, a cove forgot his toke! Gordstruth! you wouldn't
ketch me a-forgettin' mine.'

'You may have half of it, old pal, if you're hungry,' I
observed, leaning up on my elbows.

'Chuck it here, good luck to yer!' replied my young friend,
starting up with an eager clap of his dirty hands.

I 'chucked it here', and, slipping the other half under the side of my bed, lay my head on my folded arms.

II

It was about half-past nine when, having made myself as comfortable as circumstances permitted, I closed my eyes in the desperate hope that I might fall asleep, and so escape from the horrors with which I was surrounded. 'At seven tomorrow morning the bell will ring,' Daddy had informed me, 'and then you will give up your ticket and get back your bundle.' Between that time and the present full nine long hours had to wear away.

But I was speedily convinced that, at least for the present, sleep was impossible. The young fellow (one of the three who lay in one bed, with their feet to my head) whom my bread had refreshed, presently swore with frightful imprecations that he was now going to have a smoke; and immediately put his threat into execution. Thereupon his bedfellows sat up and lit their pipes too. But oh! if they had only smoked – if they had not taken such an unfortunate fancy to spit at the leg of a crank distant a few inches from my head, how much misery and apprehension would have been spared me! To make matters worse, they united with this American practice an Eastern one: as they smoked they related little autobiographical anecdotes – so abominable that three or four decent men who lay at the farther end of the shed were so provoked that they threatened, unless the talk abated in filthiness, to get up and stop it by main force. Instantly, the voice of every blackguard in the room was raised against the decent ones. They were accused of loathsome afflictions, stigmatized as 'fighting men out of work' (which must be something very humiliating, I suppose), and invited to 'a round' by boys young enough to be their grandsons. For several minutes there was such a storm of oaths, threats, and taunts – such a deluge of foul words raged in the room – that I could not help thinking of the fate of Sodom; as, indeed, I did several times during the night. Little by little the riot died out, without any the slightest interference on the part of the officers.

Soon afterwards the ruffian majority was strengthened by the arrival of a lanky boy of about fifteen, who evidently recognized many acquaintances, and was recognized by them as 'Kay', or perhaps I should write it 'K'. He was a very remarkable-looking lad, and his appearance pleased me much. Short as his hair was cropped, it still looked soft and silky; he had large blue eyes set wide apart, and a mouth that would have been faultless but for its great width; and his voice was as soft and sweet as any woman's. Lightly as a woman, too, he picked his way over the stones towards the place where the beds lay, carefully hugging his cap beneath his arm.

'What cheer, Kay?' 'Out again, then, old son!' 'What yer got in yer cap, Kay?' cried his friends; to which the sweet voice replied, 'Who'll give me part of his doss (bed)? —— my —— eyes and limbs if I ain't perishin'! Who'll let me turn in with him for half my toke (bread)?' I feared how it would be! The hungry young fellow who had so readily availed himself of half *my* 'toke' snapped at Kay's offer, and after a little re-arrangement and bed-making four young fellows instead of three reposed upon the hay-bags at my head.

'You was too late for skilley, Kay There's skilley now, nights as well as mornins.'

'Don't you tell no bleeding lies,' Kay answered, incredulously. 'Blind me, it's true! Ain't it, Punch?'

'Right you are!' said Punch, 'and spoons to eat it with, that's more! There used to be spoons at all the houses, one time. Poplar used to have 'em; but one at a time they was all nicked, don't you know.' ('Nicked' means 'stolen', obviously.)

'Well, I don't want no skilley, leastways not tonight,' said Kay. 'I've had some rum. Two glasses of it; and a blow out of puddin' – regler Christmas plum puddin'. You don't know the cove as give it me, but, thinks I this mornin' when I come out, Blessed if I don't go and see my old chum. Lordstruth! he *was* struck! "Come along," he ses, "I saved you some puddin' from Christmas." "Whereabouts is it?" I ses. "In that box under my bed," he ses, and he forks it out. That's the sort of pal to have! And he stood a quarten, and half a ounce of hard-up (tobacco). That wasn't all, neither; when I come away, ses he, "How about your breakfus?" "Oh, I shall do," ses I. "You take some of my bread and butter," he ses, and he cuts me off four chunks buttered thick. I eat two on 'em comin' along.'

'What's in your cap, Kay?' repeated the devourer of 'toke'.

'Them other two slices,' said Kay; generously adding, 'There, share 'em amongst yer, and somebody give us a whiff of 'bacca.'

Kay showed himself a pleasant companion; what in a higher grade of society is called 'quite an acquisition'. He told stories of thieving, and of a certain 'silver cup' he had been 'put up to', and avowed that he meant to nick it afore the end of the week, if he got seven stretch (seven years?) for it. The cup was worth ten quid (pounds?), and he knew where to melt it within ten minutes of nicking it. He made this statement without any moderation of his sweet voice, and the other received it as a serious statement. Nor was there any affectation of secrecy in another gentleman, who announced amid great applause that he had stolen a towel from the bath-room : 'And s'help me! it's as good as new; never been washed more'n once!'

'Tell us a "rummy" story, Kay,' said somebody : and Kay did. He told stories of so 'rummy' a character that the decent men at the farther end of the room (some of whom had their own little boys sleeping with them) must have lain in a sweat of horror as they listened. Indeed, when Kay broke into a 'rummy' song with a roaring chorus, one of the decent men rose in his bed and swore that he would smash Kay's head if he didn't desist. But Kay sang on till he and his admirers were tired of the entertainment.

'Now,' said he, 'let's have a swearing club! You'll all be in it?'

The principle of this game seemed to rest on the impossibility of either of the young gentlemen making half a dozen observations without introducing a blasphemous or obscene word; and either the basis is a very sound one, or for the sake of keeping the 'club' alive the members purposely made slips. The penalty for 'swearing' was a punch on any part of the body, except a few which the club rules protected. The game was highly successful. Warming with the sport, and indifferent to punches, the members vied with each other in audacity, and in a few minutes Bedlam in its prime could scarcely have produced such a spectacle as was to be seen on the beds behind me. One rule of the club was that any word to be found in the Bible might be used with impunity, and if one member 'punched' another for using such a word the error was to be visited upon him with a double punching all round. This naturally led to much argument; for in vindicating the Bible as his authority, a member became sometimes so much heated as to launch into a flood of 'real swearing', which brought the fists of the club upon his naked carcase quick as hail.

These and other pastimes beguiled the time until, to my delight, the church chimes audibly tolled twelve. After this the noise gradually subsided, and it seemed as though every-body was going to sleep at last. I should have mentioned that during the story-telling and song-singing a few 'casuals' had dropped in, but they were not habitués, and cuddled down with their rugs over their heads without a word to any one.

In a little while all was quiet – save for the flapping of the canvas curtain in the night breeze, the snoring, and the horrible, indescribable sound of impatient hands scratching skins that itched. There was another sound of very frequent occurrence, and that was the clanking of the tin pannikin against the water pail. Whether it is in the nature of workhouse bread or skilley to provoke thirst is more than my limited experience entitles me to say, but it may be truthfully asserted that once at least in the course of five minutes might be heard a rustling of straw, a pattering of foot, and then the noise of water-dipping; and then was to be seen at the pail the figure of a man (sometimes stark naked), gulping down the icy water as he stood upon the icy stones.

And here I may remark that I can furnish no solution to this mystery of the shirt. I only know that some of my com-rades were provided with a shirt, and that to some the luxury was denied. I may say this, however, that *none* of the little boys were allowed one.

Nearly one o'clock. Still quiet, and no fresh arrival for an hour or more. Then suddenly a loud noise of hobnailed boots kicking at a wooden gate, and soon after a tramping of feet and a rapping at Daddy's door, which, it will be remembered, was only separated from our bedroom by an open paved court.

'Hallo!' cried Daddy.

'Here's some more of 'em for you – ten of 'em!' answered the porter, whose voice I recognized at once.

'They'll have to find beds, then,' Daddy grumbled, as he

opened his door. 'I don't believe there are four beds empty. They must sleep double, or something.'

This was terrible news for me. Bad enough, in all conscience, was it to lie as I was lying; but the prospect of sharing my straw with some dirty scoundrel of the Kay breed was altogether unendurable. Perhaps, however, they were *not* dirty scoundrels, but peaceable and decent men, like those in the farther corner.

Alas for my hopes! In the space of five minutes in they came at the rent in the canvas – great hulking ruffians, some with rugs and nothing else, and some with shirts and nothing else, and all madly swearing because, coming in after eleven o'clock, there was no 'toke' for them. As soon as these wrathful men had advanced to the middle of the shed they made the discovery that there was an insufficient number of beds – only three, indeed, for ten competitors.

'Where's the beds? D'ye hear, Daddy! You blessed truth-telling old person, where's the beds?'

'You'll find 'em. Some of 'em is lying on two, or got 'em as pillows. You'll find 'em.'

With a sudden rush our new friends plunged amongst the sleepers, trampling over them, cursing their eyes and limbs, dragging away their rugs; and if by chance they found some poor wretch who had been tempted to take two beds (or bags) instead of one, they coolly hauled him out and took possession. There was no denying them, and no use in remonstrating. They evidently knew that they were at liberty to do just as they liked, and they took full advantage of the privilege.

One of them came up to me, and shouting, 'I want that, you ——,' snatched at my 'birdseye' nightcap and carried it off.

There was a bed close to mine which contained only one occupant, and into this one of the newcomers slipped without a word of warning, driving its lawful owner against the wall to make room. Then he sat up in the bed for a moment, savagely venting his disappointment as to toke, and declaring that never before in his life had he felt the need of it so much. This was opportunity. Slipping my hand under my bed, I withdrew that judiciously hoarded piece of bread and respectfully offered it to him. He snapped at it with thanks.

By the time the churches were chiming two, matters had

once more adjusted themselves, and silence reigned, to be disturbed only by drinkers at the pail, or such as, otherwise prompted, stalked into the open yard. Kay, for one, visited it. I mention this unhappy young wretch particularly, because he went out without a single rag to his back. I looked out at the rent in the canvas, and saw the frosty moon shining on him. When he returned, and crept down between Punch and another, he muttered to himself, 'Warm again! O my G—d! warm again!'

III

Whether there is a rule which closes the casual wards after a certain hour I do not know; but before one o'clock our number was made up, the last comer signalizing his appearance with a grotesque *pas seul*. His rug over his shoulders, he waltzed into the shed, waving his hands, and singing in an affected voice, as he sidled along —

I like to be a swell, a-roaming down Pall Mall,
Or anywhere, — I don't much care, so I can be a swell —

a couplet which had an intensely comical effect. This gentleman had just come from a pantomime where he had learned his song, probably. Too poor to pay for a lodging, he could only muster means for a seat in the gallery of 'the Vic.'; where he was well entertained, judging from the flattering manner in which he spoke of the clown. The columbine was less fortunate in his opinion. 'She's werry dickey! — ain't got what I call "move" about her.' However, the wretched young woman was respited now from the scourge of his criticism; for the critic and his listeners were fast asleep: and yet I doubt whether any one of the company slept very soundly. Every moment some one shifted uneasily; and as the night wore on the silence was more and more irritated by the sound of coughing. This was one of the most distressing things in the whole adventure. The conversation was horrible, the tales that were told more horrible still, and worse than either (though not *by any means* the most infamous things to be heard — I dare not even hint at them) was that song, with its bestial chorus shouted from a dozen throats; but at any rate they kept the blood warm with constant hot flushes of anger; while as for the coughing, to lie on the flagstones in what was nothing better than an open shed, and listen to that, hour after hour, chilled one's very heart with pity. Every variety of cough that ever I heard was to be heard there: the hollow cough; the short cough; the hysterical cough; the bark that comes at regular intervals, like the quarter-chime of a clock, as if to mark off the progress of decay; coughing from vast hollow chests, coughing from little narrow ones – now one, now another, now two or three together, and then a minute's interval of silence in which to think of it all, and wonder who would begin next. One of the young reprobates above me coughed so grotesquely like the chopping of wood that I named him in my mind the Wood-cutter. Now and then I found myself coughing too, which may have added just a little to the poignant distress these awfully constant and various sounds occasioned me. They were good in one way: they made one forget what wretches they were who, to all appearances, were so rapidly 'chopping' their way to a pauper's graveyard. I did not care about the more matured ruffians so much; but, though the youngest, the boys like Kay, were unquestionably amongst the most infamous of my comrades, to hear what cold and hunger and vice had done for them at fifteen was almost enough to make a man cry; and there were boys there even younger than these.

At half-past two, every one being asleep, or at least lying still, Daddy came in and counted us: one, two, three, four, and so on, in a whisper. Then, finding the pail empty (it was nearly full at half-past nine, when I entered), he considerately went and refilled it, and even took much trouble in searching for the tin pot which served as a drinking cup, and which the last comer had playfully thrown to the farther end of the shed. I ought to have mentioned that the pail stood close to my head; so that I had peculiar opportunities of study as one after another of my comrades came to the fountain to drink: just as the brutes do in those books of African travel. The pail refilled, Daddy returned, and was seen no more till morning.

It still wanted four hours and a half to seven o'clock – the hour of rising – and never before in my life did time appear to creep so slowly. I could hear the chimes of a parish church, and of the Parliament Houses, as well as those of a wretched tinkling Dutch clock somewhere on the premises. The parish church was the first to announce the hour (an act of kindness

I feel bound to acknowledge), Westminster came next, the lazy Dutchman declining his consent to the time o' day till fully sixty second afterwards. And I declare I thought that difference of sixty seconds an injury – if the officers of the house took their time from the Dutchman. It may seem a trifle, but a minute is something when a man is lying on a cold flagstone, and the wind of a winter night is blowing in your hair. Three o'clock, four o'clock struck, and still there was nothing to beguile the time but observation, under the one flaring gaslight, of the little heaps of outcast humanity strewn about the floor; and after a while, I find, one may even become accustomed to the sight of one's fellow-creatures lying around you like covered corpses in a railway shed. For most of the company were now bundled under the rugs in the ghastly way I have already described – though here and there a cropped head appeared, surmounted by a billy-cock like my own, or by a greasy cloth cap. Five o'clock, six o'clock chimed, and then I had news – most welcome – of the world without, and of the real beginning of day. Half a dozen factory bells announced that it was time for working men to go to labour; but my companions were not working men, and so snored on. Out through the gap in the canvas the stars were still to be seen shining on the black sky, but that did not alter the fact that it was six o'clock in the morning. I snapped my fingers at the Dutchman, with his sixty seconds slow, for in another hour I fondly hoped to be relieved from duty. A little while, and doors were heard to open and shut; yet a little while, and the voice of Daddy was audible in conversation with another early bird; and then I distinctly caught the word 'bundles'. Blessed sound! I longed for my bundle – for my pleasing brown coat – for my warm if unsightly 'jersey' – for my corduroys and liberty.

'Clang!' went the workhouse clock. 'Now, then! wake 'em up!' cried Daddy. I was already up – sitting up, that is – being anxious to witness the resurrection of the ghastly figures rolled in their rugs. But nobody but myself rose at the summons. They knew what it meant well enough, and in sleepy voices cursed the bell and wished it in several dreadful places; but they did not move until there came in at the hole in the canvas two of the pauper inhabitants of the house, bearing bundles.

'Thirty-two,' 'twenty-eight!' they bawled, but not *my* number, which was thirty-four. Neither thirty-two nor twenty-eight, however, seemed eager to accept his good fortune in being first called. They were called upon three several times before they would answer; and then they replied with a savage 'Chuck it here, can't you!' 'Not before you chucks over your shirt and ticket,' the bundle-holder answered, whereupon 'thirty-eight' sat up, and, divesting himself of his borrowed shirt, flung it with his wooden ticket; and his bundle was flung back in return.

It was some time before bundle No. 34 turned up, so that I had fair opportunity to observe my neighbours. The decent men slipped into their rags as soon as they got them, but the blackguards were in no hurry. Some indulged in a morning pipe to prepare themselves for the fatigue of dressing, while others, loosening their bundles as they squatted naked, commenced an investigation for certain little animals which shall be nameless.

At last my turn came; and 'chucking over' my shirt and ticket, I quickly attired myself in clothes which, ragged as they were, were cleaner than they looked. In less than two minutes I was out of the shed, and in the yard; where a few of the more decent poor fellows were crowding round a pail of water, and scrambling after something that might pass for a 'wash' – finding their own soap, as far as I could observe, and drying their faces on any bit of rag they might happen to have about them, or upon the canvas curtain of the shed.

By this time it was about half-past seven, and the majority of the casuals were up and dressed. I observed, however, that none of the younger boys were as yet up, and it presently appeared that there existed some rule against their dressing in the shed; for Daddy came out of the bath-room, where the bundles were deposited, and called out, 'Now four boys!' and instantly four poor little wretches, some with their rugs trailing about their shoulders and some quite bare, came shivering over the stones and across the bleak yard, and were admitted to the bath-room to dress. 'Now four more boys!' cried Daddy; and so on.

When all were up and dressed, the boys carried the bed rugs into Daddy's room, and the pauper inmates made a heap of the 'beds', stacking them against the wall. As before mentioned, the shed served the treble purpose of bed-chamber, workroom, and breakfast-room; it was impossible to get fairly at the cranks and set them going until the bedding was stowed away.

Breakfast before work, however; but it was a weary while to some of us before it made its appearance. For my own part, I had little appetite, but about me were a dozen poor wretches who obviously had a very great one; they had come in over-night too late for bread, and perhaps may not have broken fast since the morning of the previous day. The decent ones suffered most. The blackguard majority were quite cheerful – smoking, swearing, and playing their pretty horse play, the prime end of which was pain or discomfiture for somebody else. One casual there was with only one leg. When he came in overnight he wore a black hat, which added a certain look of respectability to a worn suit of black. All together his clothes had been delivered up to him by Daddy, but now he was seen hopping disconsolately about the place on his crutch, for the hat was missing. He was a timid man, with a mild voice; and whenever he asked some ruffian 'whether he had seen such a thing as a black hat', and got his answer, he invariably said 'Thank you,' which was regarded as very amusing. At last one sidled up to him with a grin, and showing about three square inches of some fluffy substance, said, 'Is *this* anything like wot you've lost, guv'ner?'

The cripple inspected it. 'That's the rim of it!' he said. 'What a shame!' and hobbled off with tears in his eyes.

Full three-quarters of an hour of loitering and shivering, and then came the taskmaster: a soldierly looking man over six feet high, with quick grey eyes in which 'No trifling' appeared as distinctly as a notice against trespassing on a wayside board. He came in amongst us, and the grey eyes made out our number in a moment. 'Out into the yard, all of you!' he cried; and we went out in a mob. There we shivered for some twenty minutes longer, and then a baker's man appeared with a great wooden tray piled up with just such slices of bread as we had received overnight. The tray was consigned to an able-bodied casual, who took his place with the taskmaster at the shed door; and then in single file we re-entered the shed, each man and boy receiving a slice as he passed in. Pitying, as I suppose, my unaccustomed look, Mr Taskmaster gave me a slice and a large piece over.

The bread devoured, a clamour for 'skilley' began. The rumour had got abroad that this morning, and on all future mornings, there would be skilley at breakfast, and 'Skilley! skilley!' resounded through the shed. No one had hinted that it was not forthcoming, but skilley seems to be thought an extraordinary concession, and after waiting only a few minutes for it, they attacked the taskmaster in the fiercest manner. They called him thief, sneak, and 'crawler'. Little boys black-guarded him in gutter language, and, looking him in the face, consigned him to hell without flinching. He never uttered a word in reply, or showed a sign of impatience; and whenever he was obliged to speak it was quite without temper.

There was a loud 'hooray!' when the longed-for skilley appeared in two pails, in one of which floated a small tin saucepan, with a stick thrust into its handle, by way of a ladle. Yellow pint basins were provided for our use, and large iron spoons. 'Range round the walls!' the taskmaster shouted. We obeyed with the utmost alacrity; and then what I should judge to be about three-fourths of a pint of gruel was handed to each of us as we stood. I was glad to get mine, because the basin that contained it was warm and my hands were numb with cold. I tasted a spoonful, as in duty bound, and wondered more than ever at the esteem in which it was held by my *confrères*. It was a weak decoction of oatmeal and water, bitter, and without even a pinch of salt to flavour it – that I could discover. But it was hot; and on that account, perhaps, was so highly relished that I had no difficulty in persuading one of the decent men to accept my share.

It was now past eight o'clock, and as I knew that a certain quantity of labour had to be performed by each man before he was allowed to go his way, I was anxious to begin. The labour was to be 'crank' labour. The 'cranks' are a series of iron bars extending across the width of the shed, penetrating through the wall, and working a flour mill on the other side. Turning the 'crank' is like turning a windlass. The task is not a severe one. Four measures of corn (bushels they were called – but that is doubtful) have to be ground every morning by the night's batch of casuals. Close up by the ceiling hangs a bell connected with the machinery; and as each measure is

ground the bell rings, so that the grinders may know how they
are going on. But the grinders are as lazy as obscene. We were
no sooner set to work than the taskmaster left us to our own
sweet will, with nothing to restrain its exercise but an
occasional visit from the miller, a weakly expostulating man.
Once or twice he came in and said mildly, 'Now then, my
men, why *don't* you stick to it?' – and so went out again.

The result of this laxity of overseeing would have disgusted
me at any time, and was intensely disgusting then. At least
one half the gang kept their hands from the crank whenever
the miller was absent, and betook themselves to their private
amusements and pursuits. Some sprawled upon the beds and
smoked; some engaged themselves and their friends in tailoring,
and one turned hair-cutter for the benefit of a gentleman who,
unlike Kay, had *not* just come out of prison. There were three
tailors: two of them on the beds mending their own coats,
and the other operating on a recumbent friend in the rearward
part of his clothing. Where the needles came from I do not
know; but for thread they used a strand of the oakum
(evidently easy to deal with) which the boys were picking in
the corners. Other loungers strolled about with their hands in
their pockets, discussing the topics of the day, and playing
practical jokes on the industrious few: a favourite joke being
to take a bit of rag, anoint it with grease from the crank axles,
and clap it unexpectedly over somebody's eye.

The consequence of all this was that the cranks went round
at a very slow rate and now and then stopped altogether. Then
the miller came in; the loungers rose from their couches, the
tailors ceased stitching, the smokers dropped their pipes, and
every fellow was at his post. The cranks spun round furiously
again, the miller's expostulation being drowned amidst a shout
of 'Slap bang, here we are again!' or this extemporized chorus:

We'll hang up the miller on a sour apple tree,
We'll hang up the miller on a sour apple tree,
We'll hang up the miller on a sour apple tree,
  And then go grinding on.
       Glory, glory, Hallelujah, etc., etc.

By such ditties the ruffians enlivened their short spell of
work. Short indeed! The miller departed, and within a minute

afterwards beds were reoccupied, pipes lit, and tailoring resumed. So the game continued – the honest fellows sweating at the cranks, and anxious to get the work done and go out to look for more profitable labour, and the paupers by profession taking matters quite easy. I am convinced that had the work been properly superintended the four measures of corn might have been ground in the space of an hour and a half. As it was, when the little bell tinkled for the fourth time, and the yard gate was opened and we were free to depart, the clock had struck eleven.

I had seen the show – gladly I escaped into the open streets. The sun shone brightly on my ragged, disreputable figure, and showed its squalor with startling distinctness; but within all was rejoicing. A few yards, and then I was blessed with the sight of that same vehicle – waiting for me in the spot where I had parted from it fourteen weary hours before. Did you observe, Mr Editor, with what alacrity I jumped in? I have a vivid recollection of you, Sir – sitting there with an easy patience, lounging through your *Times*, and oh! so detestably clean to look at! But, though I resented your collar, I was grateful for the sight of a familiar face, and for that draught of sherry which you considerately brought for me – a welcome refreshment after so many weary hours of fasting.

And now I have come to the end I remember many little incidents which escaped me in writing this narrative. I ought to have told you of two quiet elderly gentlemen who, amidst all the blackguardism that went on around, held a discussion upon the merits of the English language – one of the disputants showing an especial admiration for the word 'kindle', 'fine old Saxon word as ever was coined'. Then there were some childish games of 'first and last letters', to vary such entertainments as that of the swearing club. I should also have mentioned that on the dissolution of the swearing club a game at 'dumb motions' was started, which presently led to some talk concerning deaf and dumb people, and their method of conversing with each other by means of finger signs; as well as to a little story that sounded strangely enough coming from the mouth of the most efficient member of the club. A good memory for details enables me to repeat this story almost, if not quite, exactly.

'They are a rummy lot, them deaf and dumb,' said the story-teller. 'I was at the workhouse at Stepney when I was a young un, don't you know; and when I got a holiday I used to go and see my old woman as lived in the Borough. Well, one day a woman as was in the house ses to me, ses she, "Don't you go past the Deaf and Dumb School as you goes home?" So I ses, "Yes." So ses she, "Would you mind callin' there and takin' a message to my little girl as is in there deaf and dumb?" So I ses, "No." Well, I goes, and they lets me in, and I tells the message, and they shows me the kid what it was for. Pooty little gal! So they tells her the message, and then she begins making orts and crosses like on her hands. "What's she a doin' that for?" I ses. "She's a talkin' to you," ses they. "Oh!" I ses, "what's she talkin' about?" "She says you're a good boy for comin' and tellin' her about her mother, and she loves you," Blest if I could help laughin'! So I ses, "There ain't no call for her to say that." Pooty little kid she was! I stayed there a goodish bit, and walked about the garden with her, and what d'yer think? Presently she takes a fancy for some of my jacket buttons – brass uns they was, with the name of the "house" on 'em – and I cuts four on 'em off and gives her. Well, when I give her them blow me if she didn't want one of the brass buckles on my shoes. Well, you mightn't think it, but I gave her that too.'

'Didn't yer get into a row when you got back?' some listener asked.

'Rather! Got kep without dinner and walloped as well, as I wouldn't tell what I'd done with 'em. Then they was goin' to wallop me again, so I thought I'd cheek it out; so I up and told the master all about it.'

'And got it wuss?'

'No, I didn't. The master give me new buttons and a buckle without saying another word, and my dinner along with my supper as well.'

The moral of all this I leave to the world. An irregularity which consigned some *forty men* to such a den on the night when somebody happened to be there to see, is probably a frequent one; and it certainty is infamous. And then as to the other workhouses? The Poor Law Board was in ignorance of what was done at Lambeth in this way, and I selected it for a visit quite at random. Do they know what goes on in other workhouses? If they are inclined to inquire, I may, perhaps, be able to assist the investigation by this hint: my companions had a discussion during the night as to the respective merits of the various workhouses; and the general verdict was that those of Tottenham and Poplar were the worst in London. Is it true, as I heard it stated, that at one of these workhouses the casual sleeps on bare boards, without a bed of any sort?

One word in conclusion. I have avoided the detail of horrors infinitely more revolting than anything that appears in these papers.

A MAN AND DOG FIGHT IN HANLEY

From *Low-Life Deeps*

A home for starving dogs would be almost as much out of place at Hanley as an asylum for indigent bees on a common, where the yellow gorse is in flower. I believe that the town in question would hold itself in lasting disgrace if a starving or even a lean or ill-conditioned cur were seen prowling about its streets. Neglected children may be found in plenty; but there is no lack of fatness or sleekness amongst the dogs. The fact is, the hard-working pitman of these parts is not a child-fancier — he is a dog-fancier. This, to be sure, makes it somewhat hard for the small, two-legged creature; but it is difficult to see how it can be helped. It is a nice question whether it would be justifiable to risk shaking the pitman's faith in the burden of 'Rule Britannia', by endeavouring to control any of his little predilections. At the same time let it be distinctly understood that, while I write in this spirit concerning the Hanley pitmen, I allude exclusively to the 'roughs' of the class, who have not yet succumbed to the indefatigable exertions which are being made by his friends for his conversion. It is only just to state that at the present time in Hanley and elsewhere there are tens of thousands of pit hands who are as sober and industrious and well-behaved as any class of workmen in the three kingdoms.

But, as it happened, it was amongst the inferior kind that

my unguided feet led me, and coming down a bye-street I saw a sight that I could not exactly understand. There was a man black as ink, and evidently a pitman, and two deplorably thin and ragged little girls, who appeared to have been to meet father returning from his work – not, however, because of his loving impatience to behold them as soon as his day's toil was over, but to gladden his eyes with the sight of a female dog, of the retriever breed, and two fine pups. The pups the pitman carried, one under each arm, as tenderly as though they were babies born to him, while their mother, walking sedately by his side, bore in her mouth about two pounds of prime looking and perfectly fresh shin of beef. My first idea was that the man had been drinking, and that it was a tipsy freak of his to insist on the dog carrying home the meat that was for the family supper; and I could not, seeing the shoeless, hungry little girls, but reflect on what a sore disaster it would be if the dog were to take it into its head to run away with the joint. I suppose that the pitman read something of this in my face, for when I got up with them, he remarked good-humouredly :

'Never fear, mun; she wull na' droop it.'

'It would be safer, I think, if one of the little girls carried it,' I ventured.

'Na, she's old enow,' rejoined the pitman; 'it's danged hard if the dawg can't carry home her own meat' – a joke which made the two squalid-looking girls laugh as they caressed the retriever and stroked its silken ears.

'She's a lucky dog, I should say,' said I. 'Does she always live on this kind of food?'

The twinkle at once faded out of the pitman's eyes, and he looked serious. 'Mun,' said he, 'she dew. I canna' help it, but she dew. I've a family iv 'em – ' here he jerked his thumb resentfully in the direction of the hungry-looking mites of girls – 'and eightpence the pound is the best I can afford for her!' and, his hands being both engaged, he paused a moment to administer a kind caress with the toe of his boot to the retriever's back.

It was not a difficult task to lead him on to talk about dogs and their habits and customs; nor did it require any tremendous effort to induce him, when he reached his home, to adjourn to the nearest alehouse, where he might at his leisure continue his narrative of the last dog-fight he had been witness to.

At the alehouse we met with doggy company, and the conversation turned on the lamentable decline of that particular British sport in which two of the canine tribe are the chief actors. It was, I was assured, as difficult in these degenerate times to 'pull off a dog-fight all right and regler, and without any hole-and-corner business and fear of the police', as it was to bring about a man-fight under the same open conditions.

'Ah! it was a pretty sport,' remarked my friend, with a sigh; 'and the more lively-like, because, in fighting young dogs, you could never be sure, however tip-top their breeding, that when they were brought to the scratch, they would not "turn felon".'

'Very much depends, perhaps,' I remarked, in quest of further information concerning the 'pretty sport', 'on the way in which a young dog is trained.' At which he laughed, and said there could not be any mistake about that, as there was only one way, and at once he good-naturedly proceeded to explain which way that was.

I was given to understand that the first practice a fighting pup had was with 'a good old gummer' – that is to say, with a dog which had been a good one in his day, but now was old, and toothless and incapable of doing more than 'mumble' the juvenile antagonist that was set against him, the one great advantage being that the young dog gained practical experience in the making of 'points'. The next stage, as I was informed, in training the young aspirant for pit honours, was to treat him to a 'real mouthful', or, in other words, 'to let him taste dog'.

It is a villanous process, and I never felt so grateful to the laws of my country, which have decreed that dog-fighting is an offence punishable with severe imprisonment, as when my informant enlightened me thereon.

'You look about,' said he, 'for a likely-looking street cur of fit size, and if with a bit of blood in it why all the better, and you take it home and tie it up and spice it up with good grub. Then, just before it's wanted, you clip off its hair at those points that you know your young 'un will want to get at, and you lather and shave 'em down to the skin. Then you put your young 'un and the cur in a pit together. Most likely the cur, not knowing his customer, will show fight at once, and there'll be quite a lively set-to between 'em for a few minutes; but breed will tell presently, and then the cur knocks under, and your young 'un has it all his own way, and, being now warm to his work, he doesn't shirk it. If he is slow you set him on. You set him on to the shaved parts, which are the vital parts behind the shoulders and that, and you worry him into letting the cur have it hot. There'll be a awful row, of course, for the cur, now he finds his master, will do nothing but slink and crawl along the floor and into the corners, and kick up such a catawaulin' as may be heard half a mile off. But your young 'un, if he's got the right stuff in him, won't mind that; it'll give him an appetite, and he'll go at the cur, and make a regler meal of him.'

I have not given a quarter of the sickening details that attended the operation of giving the 'young 'un' a 'mouthful' with which the knowing Old Hand favoured me, mistaking for apt attention what was in reality on my part the fascination of horror. Had the individual in question confided to me that he was a descendant of a celebrated ogre family who devoured babies, I don't think I should have experienced such a sense of fear and shrinking towards him as I did. As for the dirty white bull-dog he had with him, who during the recital was engaged in chewing one of his master's boot-laces, as though it were a quid of tobacco, all the while blinking and winking with his red-rimmed eyes as though he perfectly well understood every word that was said, and highly enjoyed it as recalling to his memory one of the happy episodes of his puppyhood, it would have afforded me much satisfaction to have administered to him a dose of strychnine on the spot. Observing what the dog was at, he jerked the hanging boot-lace out of its mouth, and gave it a sounding kick in the ribs.

'Ah, that's right!' remarked another miner, approvingly, 'he'll take all the edge off his teeth, biting that thing. You're a old hand, and know he'll want all the teeth he's got, I'll wager.'

The Old Hand gave him a quick, reproachful look, but it was too late.

'He's in training, I suppose,' said I, with as much indifference as I could assume.

'No, he ain't,' replied the Old Hand; 'don't I tell you that there ain't no dog-fighting done now in these parts? You get under there – ' this to the bull-dog, its master at the same time expediting its retreat under the seat with the heel of his boot. But at that moment the door swung open and a man's head appeared – a head with the nose almost flat to the face, and squinting eyes, and an enormously wide mouth. It was fortunate that the bull-dog's chain was made fast to the leg of the seat, for no sooner did the ugly face appear than the dog made a spring out, its bloodshot eyes starting with fury, its teeth exposed, and straining madly against its tether in its frantic desire to reach its enemy.

'Ha, my beauty! you're there then?' spoke the head, with a grin which if possible increased its ugliness.

The Old Hand was almost as furious as his dog. With a terrible string of oaths, and addressing the owner of the ugly head as 'Brummy', he bade him be off, and tauntingly demanded to know why, if Brummy funked on the match he had made, he did not cry off like a man, instead of coming there to aggravate the dog in the hope that he might have a fit and break a blood-vessel. 'You'll have enough of him quite soon enough, and I'll put another sovereign on it if you like, exclaimed the exasperated Old Hand, whose ire, however, cooled when the grinning head vanished.

By the time a half-pint brandy measure had been filled at my expense, and emptied by the Old Hand and his friend, his good temper was quite restored, and – may Sir Wilfrid forgive me – a little drop more made him quite kind and confidential. With a friendly slap on the shoulder he swore that I was the right sort, and that if I liked to meet him tomorrow night, although he couldn't promise me 'all a dog-fight', I should be treated to a bit of sport it would do any man's heart good to see.

'And that chap who looked in at the door, will he be there?' I asked.

'Well, there won't be no fight if he ain't,' replied the friendly Old Hand with a laugh, and so, with my promise to meet him next night, we parted.

'You had better not meet us at the alehouse,' whispered the Old Hand, as we parted on the previous night; 'after what has happened somebody might smell a rat, and be on the watch.

Stand at the corner of Mill Lane, and when you see us, follow without taking notice.'

The Old Hand and his friend, the owner of the brown retriever, were as faithful to the appointment as I myself, and, when they strolled up Mill Lane, innocently smoking their pipes, a figure whose appearance was somewhat questionable, I fear, in point of attire, happened to be going in the same direction, and kept in their wake, up one street and down another, until the chase began to grow somewhat wearisome. At last, however, a halt was called near a dirty row of houses, at the door of one of which stood a man in miner garb, who, as soon as he perceived us, knocked the ashes out of his pipe against the doorpost, and this evidently was a preconcerted sign that nothing was amiss, for my companions made straight for the house in question without further delay, and speedily the outer door was bolted from within, and further secured with a stout chain. It was quite dark inside, and a woman came out of a back room to us with a candle to light the way down to the cellar or kitchen, whichever it might be called.

Whatever the nature of the coming performance, the company who were privileged to witness it were already assembled. The scene was a place about sixteen feet square, with bare walls and a brick floor, and at the four sides a rope was already extended, leaving a space of about a yard between it and the wall, and here, railed off from the centre, three deep, were the sightseers. Pit-lads most of them, some black as when they came up out of the pit, with a sprinkling of individuals of the 'rough' and costermonger order, the most prominent of the gathering being half a dozen 'swells' of the country 'fancy', with snuff-coloured trousers and cutaway coats, and waistcoats and caps of sealskin.

A paraffin lamp hung from the ceiling, and as the window was quite covered with a shutter, and the only means of ventilation was afforded by the chimney, while the 'swells' had their cigars alight, and the commonalty their short pipes, no wonder that the place was evil-smelling, hot, and stifling. There was, happily, a wide chimney-place, and the stove had been removed. A bit of board based on brick-bats made out of this quite a commodious and airy recess, and I was glad to share it with two promising young pit-lads, who, with a view to thoroughly enjoying the festivities of the evening, had brought a bottle of rum with them.

But the personage who chiefly attracted my attention was a dwarf – a man of at least middle age, judging from his grizzled grey hair, and the enormous size of his head and ears, but certainly not more than four feet and a half in height, yet with tremendous hands and feet and bandy legs. This was 'Brummy', the person whose head and face I had once before seen under circumstances which the reader may possibly remember. Brummy was evidently a person of consideration. He was honoured with much notice on the part of the sporting 'swells', who shook hands with him, ill-looking and repulsive as he appeared to be, even favouring him with their whispered confidence. The grizzled dwarf critically examined the saw-dusted space in the centre of the kitchen, especially at one particular part; there he went down on his knees and felt the bricks all over with the flat of his hand, and, discovering an inequality in them, called for a hammer and remedied the defect.

'He's a careful old codger,' remarked one of my fellow-occupants of the chimney; 'he knows what a slip and a tumble might cost him – it was that wot lost him the match last time.'

'What rot!' growled his companion; 'he didn't make no slip at all; and it's all lies to say he did. He was licked on his merits, like he will be this time, I hope, and win me my quid. What do you say, chap?'

This last query was addressed to me, and it seemed like an opportunity for gaining the enlightenment I was longing for almost as much as for fresh air.

'He'll win, I suppose, if he's better than the other one,' I ventured; at which both the young pitmen laughed as at a good joke.

'T'other one, indeed!' remarked the elder of them; '—— his old carcase – he's as artful as a two-legger, anyhow.'

And then they began to talk about something else. It was still uncertainty with me, though I had an uncomfortable idea of the truth. Whose was the 'old carcase' against which Brummy, the dwarf, was about to exercise himself? It would never do to inquire. Being there, I was, of course, supposed to know all about it.

Then one of the sporting 'gents' took out his timekeeper, and called 'five minutes to time', whereon there was a clapping of hands, and the bandy-legged Dwarf proceeded further to mystify me. He divested himself of his coat and his waistcoat, his blue-checked shirt, and his boots, leaving himself with nothing on but his trousers and a dirty under-flannel, cut off high at the shoulders. Stripped, he appeared an extraordinarily muscular fellow, and his arms, which were nearly covered with hair, were scarred, each of them from the wrists to the elbows, as though at some time or other he had been badly burnt. The creature likewise had a scar, ugly and jagged, within an inch of his collar-bone, and another — now one came to examine him for wounds — at the right side of his chin, which looked like a piece bitten out of a dirty apple and put back again. He now produced a strap, to which was attached a bright iron ring, and this he proceeded to buckle round his waist, at the same time dispensing with his braces. Then he took from a pocket of his coat a phial filled with what looked like oil, which he handed to the sporting 'gent' with the watch, who took out the cork and smelt at it. After which all the sporting 'gents' smelt at it in succession, and pronouncing it 'all right', gave it back to Brummy, who, amidst almost breathless silence, commenced to anoint his arms and fists with it, rubbing it well in.

'Dan'l won't bring in Physic till the last minnit,' remarked one of the young pitmen.

I still managed to refrain at that moment from demanding of my companions in the chimney who was Dan'l, who the physic was for, and what it all meant, but it is to this hour a wonder to me how I resisted.

Yet it would have been a pity if I had shown rash ignorance, for within a minute my curiosity was only too well satisfied.

'All ready?' asked the sporting swell with the watch.

'Ay, mun, bring him as sune as ye like,' grinned the dwarf; and then there was heard the pattering of a four-footed animal, and an anxious whining, and, the kitchen door opening, in came Dan'l, with Physic. It was my friend the elderly miner of the evening before, and Physic was the hideous-jowled dirty white bull-dog. For a few moments the scene of last night at the alehouse was repeated. The instant that Physic caught sight of 'Brummy' he gave a furious gasp, as though he had not for a moment ceased to brood over the insult he had been subjected to when last they met, and though it might cost him his life, was now determined to bring the quarrel to an issue. But Dan'l had him fast by the great leather collar, and, with both hands, hauled him to the wall, where another man hitched a stout chain to a holdfast, while one performed the same office for the dwarf, except that in his case it was a substantial strap which was used. Like the dog, however, he had his measured length of tether, one end of which was attached to the ring at the back of his waist strap and the other to a staple in the wall opposite. I dislike rum, and especially is it to me unpalatable to gulp it out of a bottle; yet, on account of the sudden sensation of sickness which at this moment overcame me, I felt positively grateful when the sociable young pitman by my side pressed a 'nip' on my acceptance. There could no longer be any misunderstanding as to the horrible encounter which was about to happen. This dreadful dwarf had backed himself, or had been backed by his friends, to engage in combat with Dan'l's bull-dog. 'It's their third go in,' said my friendly young pitman as he drank 'T'ord's you' out of the rum bottle; 'it's one and one with 'em as yet; this time it's who shall.'

Perhaps at this juncture I should have escaped, if I could, from the hideous lists; but flight was out of the question, and it was necessary to appear interested. As well as I could make out from the arrangements, and the wrangling and disagreement respecting them, the terms of the fight were that both dog and man were to be allowed length of rope enough, as it was called, to get at each other, but there was not so much of it that either could fail to get out of the other's reach should he deem it prudent to do so. The biped brute was to kneel down or go on all-fours, which he pleased, and was to use no other weapons than his clenched fists. He was by no means to take hold of the quadruped's collar, or to attempt to grapple with the dog unless it 'made fast' to him, when he would be at liberty to use his hands in order to extricate himself. In case the bull-dog should be lucky enough to 'pin' his enemy, the man had only to cry out 'I'm done,' and means would be promptly taken to compel the victor to loosen his grip. On

'Brummy's' part, to win the fight, he was to knock the bull-
dog 'out of time' – in other words, either to stun it or so punish
it that, despite all its master's urging, it would refuse to face
the dwarf again after a full minute's notice. Dan'l set out a
bowl with vinegar and water, and a sponge on his side, while
the dog's antagonist received from the hands of a kind patron
a pint flask of brandy, at which he took a pull, and then stood
'convenient' in a corner, together with a towel. Then he tucked
down his flannel shirt at the neck, spat in his enormous hands,
made them into fists, each almost as big as a stonemason's
mallet, and knelt, smiling. Meanwhile Dan'l was giving the
finishing touches to Physic's fighting toilette, and man and dog
were ready at almost the same moment. There was no need
to encourage the red-eyed Physic; he was too eager for the
fray. He did not bark, but he was frenzied with passion to
that degree that tears trickled down his blunt nose, and his
gaspings became each moment more shrill and hysterical. He
needed no urging on for the first 'round', at all events. As soon
as the umpire called 'Let go,' the dirty, glaring, furious brute
sprang forward with an impetuosity that caused the last link
of its chain to click with a ringing sound against the staple
which held it.

The dwarf, however, was not to be stormed and defeated all
in a moment. Once the ghastly fight began, there was a dire
fascination in it; and I now noted closely the combat. The man
was on all fours when the words 'Let go' were uttered, and,
making accurate allowance for the length of the dog's chain,
he arched his back, cat wise, so as just to escape its fangs,
and fetched it a blow on the crown of its head that brought
it almost to its knees. The dog's recovery, however, was
instantaneous; and before the dwarf could draw back, Physic
made a second dart forward, and this time its teeth grazed the
biped's arm, causing a slight red trickling. He grinned scorn-
fully, and sucked the place; but there was tremendous excitement among the bull-dog's backers, who clapped their hands
with delight, rejoicing in the honour of first blood. The hairy
dwarf was still smiling, however, and while Dan'l held his dog,
preparatory to letting it go for 'Round 2', he was actually
provoking it as much as he could, 'hissing' at it, and presenting
towards it the bleeding arm. The animal, flushed possibly with

his first success, made for its opponent in a sudden leap, but
the dwarf leapt forward too, and smote the bull-dog such a
tremendous blow under the ear as to roll it completely over,
evidently bewildering it for a moment, and causing it to bleed
freely, to the frantic joy of the friends of the man-beast. But
they, in turn, were made to look serious, for, with astonishing
energy, Physic turned about, and, with a dash, was again at
the dwarf, and this time contrived to fix its teeth in one of his
hairy arms, a terrible gash appearing as the man snatched
the limb out of his ravenous jaws. The bull-dog was licking
his lips, and had fewer tears in his eyes as his master drew
him back. As for the dwarf, he retired to his corner for a whet
of brandy and a moment's comforting with the towel. He was
ready and smiling again, however, for 'Round 3', and this time
it was a fight in earnest – the dog worrying the man, and the
man dealing it terrific blows on the ribs and on the head with
those sledge-hammer fists, till in the end both the man's arms
were bleeding, and a horribly cheerful business was going on
behind the ropes at 2 to 1 on Physic. But let me make short
work of the ensuing seven 'rounds', which in some of their
details were so shocking that more than once I would have left
the place if I could. The company generally, however, were
made of far less sensitive stuff. The more furious the ghastly
fight, the keener was their relish for it; and in their excitement
they leant over each other's shoulders, and over the rope, and
mouthed and snarled, and uttered guttural noises when a good
hit or snap was made, just as the dog and the dwarf were
doing. By the time Round 10 was concluded the bull-dog's
head was swelled much beyond its accustomed size; it had lost
two teeth, and one of its eyes was entirely shut up; while
as for the dwarf, his fists, as well as his arms, were reeking,
and his hideous face was ghastly pale with rage and despair
of victory. Fate was kind to him, however. In Round 11 the
bull-dog came on fresh and foaming, with awful persistence of
fury, but, with desperate strength, the dwarf dealt him a
tremendous blow under the chin, and with such effect that the
dog was dashed against the wall, where, despite all its master
could do to revive it, it continued to lie, and being unable to
respond when 'time' was called, Brummy was declared to be
victorious.

George R. Sims

The family background of George Sims (1847–1922) is an interesting blend of two Victorian traditions. His father was a wealthy and respectable London businessman who would have liked Sims to follow his example. In one sense he did so, by becoming an enormously successful writer, but combined with this was a radical streak that descended from his mother, who was an active early feminist, and her father, John Dinmore Stevenson, a Chartist. Sims began work in his father's office, but was determined to become a writer, and achieved success with a weekly column in the *Referee* called 'Mustard and Cress', a once-famous melodrama *The Lights o' London* (1881) and with his 'Dagonet' ballads, which included 'Billy's Rose' and 'In the Workhouse: Christmas Day'. He was also a prolific writer of novels and short stories. *How the Poor Live* was first published serially in *The Pictorial World* with illustrations by Frederick Burnard, as a book in the same year, and was reprinted in 1889 together with a later collection of similar sketches as *How the Poor Live and Horrible London*. The extracts here are taken from this edition.

THE DARK SIDE OF LIFE

From *How the Poor Live*

I commence, with the first of these chapters, a book of travel. An author and an artist have gone hand-in-hand into many a far-off region of the earth, and the result has been a volume eagerly studied by the stay-at-home public, anxious to know something of the world in which they live. In these pages I propose to record the result of a journey into a region which lies at our own doors – into a dark continent that is within easy walking distance of the General Post Office. This continent will, I hope, be found as interesting as any of those newly-explored lands which engage the attention of the Royal Geographical Society – the wild races who inhabit it will, I trust, gain public sympathy as easily as those savage tribes for whose benefit the Missionary Societies never cease to appeal for funds.

I have no shipwrecks, no battles, no moving adventures by flood and field, to record. Such perils as I and my fellow-traveller have encountered on our journey are not of the order which lend themselves to stirring narrative. It is unpleasant to be mistaken, in underground cellars where the vilest outcasts hide from the light of day, for detectives in search of their prey – it is dangerous to breathe for some hours at a stretch an atmosphere charged with infection and poisoned with indescribable effluvia – it is hazardous to be hemmed in down a blind alley by a crowd of roughs who have had hereditarily transmitted to them the maxim of John Leech, that half-bricks were specially designed for the benefit of 'strangers'; but these are not adventures of the heroic order, and they will not be dwelt upon lovingly after the manner of travellers who go farther afield.

My task is perhaps too serious a one even for the light tone of these remarks. No man who has seen 'How the Poor Live' can return from the journey with aught but an aching heart. No man who recognises how serious is the social problem which lies before us can approach its consideration in any but the gravest mood. Let me, then, briefly place before the reader the serious purpose of these pages, and then I will ask him to set out with me on the journey and judge for himself whether there is no remedy for much that he will see. He will have to encounter misery that some good people think it best to leave undiscovered. He will be brought face to face with that dark side of life which the wearers of rose-coloured spectacles turn away from on principle. The worship of the beautiful is an excellent thing, but he who digs down deep in the mire to find the soul of goodness in things evil is a better man and a better Christian than he who shudders at the ugly and the unclean, and kicks it from his path, that it may not come between the wind and his nobility.

But let not the reader be alarmed, and imagine that I am

about to take advantage of his good-nature in order to plunge him neck-high into a mud bath. He may be pained before we part company, but he shall not be disgusted. He may occasionally feel a choking in his throat, but he shall smile now and again. Among the poor there is humour as well as pathos, there is food for laughter as well as for tears, and the rays of God's sunshine lose their way now and again, and bring light and gladness into the vilest of the London slums.

His Royal Highness the Prince of Wales, in his speech at the opening of the Royal College of Music some years ago, said: 'The time has come when class can no longer stand aloof from class, and that man does his duty best who works most earnestly in bridging over the gulf between different classes which it is the tendency of increased wealth and increased civilization to widen.' It is to increased wealth and to increased civilization that we owe the wide gulf which today separates well-to-do citizens from the masses. It is the increased wealth of this mighty city which has driven the poor back inch by inch, until we find them today herding together, packed like herrings in a barrel, neglected and despised, and left to endure wrongs and hardships which, if they were related of a far-off savage tribe, would cause Exeter Hall to shudder till its bricks fell down. It is the increased civilization of this marvellous age which has made life a victory only for the strong, the gifted, and the specially blest, and left the weak, the poor, and the ignorant to work out in their proper persons the theory of the survival of the fittest to its bitter end.

There are not wanting signs that the 'one-roomed helot' and his brood are about to receive a little scientific attention. They have become natural curiosities, and to this fact they may owe the honour in store for them, of dividing public attention with the Zenanas, the Aborigines, and the South Sea Islanders. The long-promised era of domestic legislation is said to be at hand, and prophets with powerful telescopes declare they can see the first faint signs of its dawn upon the political horizon. When that era has come within the range of the naked eye, it is probable that the Homes of the Poor will be one of its burning questions, and the strong arm of the law may be extended protectingly, even at the risk of showing the shortness of its sleeve, as far as the humble toilers who at the present moment suffer only its penalties and enjoy none of its advantages.

That there are remedies for the great evil which lies like a cankerworm in the heart of this fair city is certain. What those remedies are you will be better able to judge when you have seen the condition of the disease for which Dr State is to be called in. Dr State, alas! is as slow to put in an appearance as his parish *confrère* when the patient in need of his services is poor and friendless.

Forgive me this little discourse by the way. It has at any rate filled up the time as we walk along to the outskirts of the land through which we are to travel for a few weeks together. And now, turning out of the busy street alive with the roar of commerce, and where the great marts and warehouses tower stories high, and where Dives adds daily to his wealth, we turn up a narrow court, and find ourselves at once in the slum where Lazarus lays his head – even as he did in the sacred story – at the very gates of the mighty millionaire.

We walk along a narrow dirty passage, which would effectually have stopped the Claimant had he come to this neighbourhood in search of witnesses, and at the end we find ourselves in what we should call a back-yard, but which, in the language of the neighbourhood, is a square. The square is full of refuse; heaps of dust and decaying vegetable matter lie about here and there, under the windows and in front of the doors of the squalid tumble-down houses. The windows above and below are broken and patched; the roofs of these two-storied 'eligible residences' look as though Lord Alcester had been having some preliminary practice with his guns here before he set sail for Alexandria. All these places are let out in single rooms at prices varying from 2s 6d to 4s a week. We can see a good deal of the inside through the cracks and crevices and broken panes, but if we knock at the door we shall get a view of the inhabitants.

If you knew more of these Alsatias, you would be rather astonished that there was a door to knock at. Most of the houses are open day and night, and knockers and bells are things unknown. Here, however, the former luxuries exist; so we will not disdain them.

Knock, knock!

Hey, presto! what a change of scene! Sleepy Hollow has come to life. Every door flies open, and there is a cluster of human beings on the threshold. Heads of matted hair and faces that haven't seen soap for months come out of the broken windows above.

Our knock has alarmed the neighbourhood. Who are we? The police? No. Who are we? Now they recognise one of our number – our guide with a growl. He and we with him can pass without let or hindrance where it would be dangerous for a policeman to go. We are supposed to be on business connected with the School Board, and we are armed with a password which the worst of these outcasts have grown at last sulkily to acknowledge.

This is a very respectable place, and we have taken it first to break the ground gently for an artist who has not hitherto studied 'character' on ground where I have had many wanderings.

To the particular door attacked there comes a poor woman, white and thin and sickly-looking; in her arms she carries a girl of eight or nine with a diseased spine; behind her, clutching at her scanty dress, are two or three other children. We put a statistical question, say a kind word to the little ones, and ask to see the room.

What a room! The poor woman apologizes for its condition, but the helpless child, always needing her care, and the other little ones to look after, and times being bad, etc. Poor creature, if she had ten pair of hands instead of one pair always full, she could not keep this room clean. The walls are damp and crumbling, the ceiling is black and peeling off, showing the laths above, the floor is rotten and broken away in places, and the wind and the rain sweep in through gaps that seem everywhere. The woman, her husband and her six children live, eat, and sleep in this one room, and for this they pay three shillings a week. It is quite as much as they can afford. There has been no breakfast yet, and there won't be any till the husband (who has been out to try and get a job) comes in and reports progress. As to complaining of the dilapidated, filthy condition of the room, they know better. If they don't like it they can go. There are dozens of families who will jump at the accommodation, and the landlord is well aware of the fact.

Some landlords do repair their tenants' rooms. Why, cert'nly. Here is a sketch of one and of the repairs we saw the same day. Rent, 4s a week; condition indescribable. But notice the repairs: a bit of a box-lid nailed across a hole in the wall big enough for a man's head to go through, a nail knocked into a window-frame beneath which still comes in a little fresh air, and a strip of new paper on a corner of the wall. You can't see the new paper because it is not up. The lady of the rooms holds it in her hand. The rent collector has just left it for her to put up herself. Its value, at a rough guess, is threepence. This landlord *has* executed repairs. Items: one piece of a broken soap-box, one yard and a half of paper, and one nail. *And for these repairs he has raised the rent of the room threepence a week.*

We are not in the square now, but in a long, dirty street, full of lodging-houses from end to end, a perfect human warren, where every door stands open night and day – a state of things that shall be described and illustrated a little later on when we come to the "appy dossers'. In this street, close to the repaired residence, we select at hazard an open doorway and plunge into it. We pass along a greasy, grimy passage, and turn a corner to ascend the stairs. Round the corner it is dark. There is no staircase light, and we can hardly distinguish in the gloom where we are going. A stumble causes us to strike a light.

That stumble was a lucky one. The staircase we were ascending, and which men and women and little children go up and down day after day and night after night, is a wonderful affair. The handrail is broken away, the stairs themselves are going – a heavy boot has been clean through one of them already, and it would need very little, one would think, for the whole lot to give way and fall with a crash. A sketch, taken at the time, by the light of successive vestas, fails to give the grim horror of that awful staircase. The surroundings, the ruin, the decay, and the dirt, could not be reproduced.

We are anxious to see what kind of people get safely up and down this staircase, and as we ascend we knock accidentally up against something; it is a door and a landing. The door is opened, and as the light is thrown on to where **we** stand we give an involuntary exclamation of horror; the door opens right on to the corner stair. The woman who comes out would, if she stepped incautiously, fall six feet, and nothing could save her. It is a tidy room this, for the neighbourhood. A good hardworking woman has kept her home neat, even in such surroundings. The rent is four and sixpence a week, and the family living in it numbers eight souls; their total earnings are twelve shillings. A hard lot, one would fancy; but in comparison to what we have to encounter presently it certainly is not. Asked about the stairs, the woman says, 'It is a little ockard-like for the young 'uns a-goin' up and down to school now the Board make 'em wear boots; but they don't often hurt themselves.' Minus the boots, the children had got used to the ascent and descent, I suppose, and were as much at home on the crazy staircase as a chamois on a precipice. *Excelsior* is our motto on this staircase. No maiden with blue eyes comes out to mention avalanches, but the woman herself suggests 'it's werry bad higher up'. We are as heedless of the warning as Longfellow's headstrong banner-bearer, for we go on.

It is 'werry bad' higher up, so bad that we begin to light some more matches and look round to see how we are to get down. But as we continue to ascend the darkness grows less and less. We go a step at a time, slowly and circumspectly, up, up to the light, and at last our heads are suddenly above a floor and looking straight into a room.

We have reached the attic, and in that attic we see a picture which will be engraven on our memory for many a month to come.

The attic is almost bare; in a broken fireplace are some smouldering embers; a log of wood lies in front like a fender. There is a broken chair trying to steady itself against a wall black with the dirt of ages. In one corner, on a shelf, is a battered saucepan and a piece of dry bread. On the scrap of mantel still remaining embedded in the wall is a rag; on a bit of cord hung across the room are more rags – garments of some sort, possibly; a broken flower-pot props open a crazy window-frame, possibly to let the smoke out, or in – looking at the chimney-pots below, it is difficult to say which; and at one side of the room is a sack of Heaven knows what – it is a dirty, filthy sack, greasy and black and evil-looking. I could not guess what was in it if I tried, but what was on it was a little child –

a neglected, ragged, grimed, and bare-legged little baby-girl of four. There she sat, in the bare, squalid room, perched on the sack, erect, motionless, expressionless, on duty.

She was 'a little sentinel', left to guard a baby that lay asleep on the bare boards behind her, its head on its arm, the ragged remains of what had been a shawl flung over its legs.

That baby needed a sentinel to guard it, indeed. Had it crawled a foot or two, it would have fallen head-foremost into that unprotected, yawning abyss of blackness below. In case of some such proceeding on its part, the child of four had been left 'on guard'.

The furniture of the attic, whatever it was like, had been seized the week before for rent. The little sentinel's papa – this we unearthed of the 'deputy' of the house later on – was a militiaman, and away; the little sentinel's mamma was gone out on 'a arrand', which, if it was anything like her usual 'arrands', the deputy below informed us, would bring her home about dark, very much the worse for it. Think of that little child keeping guard on that dirty sack for six or eight hours at a stretch – think of her utter loneliness in that bare, desolate room, every childish impulse checked, left with orders 'not to move, or I'll kill yer', and sitting there often till night and darkness came on, hungry, thirsty, and tired herself, but faithful to her trust to the last minute of the drunken mother's absence! 'Bless yer! I've known that young 'un sit there eight 'our at a stretch. I've seen her there of a mornin' when I've come up to see if I could git the rint, and I've seen her there when I've come agin at night,' says the deputy. 'Lor, that ain't nothing – that ain't.'

Nothing! It is one of the saddest pictures I have seen for many a day. Poor little baby-sentinel! – left with a human soul in its sole charge at four – neglected and overlooked: what will its girl-life be, when it grows old enough to think? I should like some of the little ones whose every wish is gratified, who have but to whimper to have, and who live surrounded by loving, smiling faces, and tendered by gentle hands, to see the little child in the bare garret sitting sentinel over the sleeping baby on the floor, and budging never an inch throughout the weary day from the place that her mother had bidden her stay in.

With our minds full of this pathetic picture of child-life in the 'Homes of the Poor', we descend the crazy staircase, and get out into as much light as can find its way down these narrow alleys.

Outside we see a portly gentleman with a big gold chain across his capacious form, and an air of wealth and good living all over him. He is the owner of a whole block of property such as this, and he waxes rich on his rents. Strange as it may seem, these one-roomed outcasts are the best paying tenants in London. They pay so much for so little, and almost fight to get it. That they should be left to be thus exploited is a disgrace to the Legislature, which is never tired of protecting the oppressed of 'all races that on earth do dwell', except those of that particular race who have the honour to be free-born Englishmen.

FURNISHED ROOMS

From *How the Poor Live*

One room in this district is very like the other. The family likeness of the chairs and tables is truly remarkable, especially in the matter of legs. Most chairs are born with four legs, but the chairs one meets with here are a two-legged race – a four-legged chair is a *rara avis*, and when found should be made a note of. The tables, too, are of a type indigenous to the spot. The survival of the fittest does not obtain in these districts in the matter of tables. The most positively unfit are common, very common objects. What has become of the fittest I hesitate to conjecture. Possibly they have run away. I am quite sure that a table with legs would make use of them to escape from such surroundings.

As to the bedsteads, they are wretched, broken-down old things of wood and iron that look as though they had been rescued a little late from a fire, then used for a barricade, afterwards buried in volcanic eruption, and finally dug out of a dust-heap that had concealed them for a century. The bedding, a respectable coal-sack would blush to acknowledge even as a poor relation.

I have enumerated chairs, tables, and beds, not because they are found in every poor home – there are several rented rooms which can boast of nothing but four walls, a ceiling, and a floor – but because these articles placed in one of these dens constitute what are euphemistically called 'furnished apartments', a species of accommodation with which all very poor neighbourhoods abound.

The 'furnished apartments' fetch as much as tenpence a day, and are sometimes occupied by three or four different tenants during a week.

The 'deputy' comes for the money every day, and it is pay or go with the occupants. If the man who has taken one of these furnished rooms for his 'home, sweet home' does not get enough during the day to pay his rent, out he goes into the street with his wife and children, and enter another family forthwith.

The tenants have not, as a rule, much to be flung after them in the shape of goods and chattels. The clothes they stand upright in, a battered kettle, and, perhaps, a bundle, make up the catalogue of their worldly possessions.

This kind of rough-and-ready lodging is the resource of thousands of industrious people earning precarious livelihoods, and they rarely rise above it to the dignity of taking a room by the week. The great struggle is to get over Saturday, and thank God for Sunday. Sunday is a free day, and no deputy comes to disturb its peaceful calm. The Saturday's rent, according to the custom of the country, makes the tenant free of the apartments until Monday.

It is the custom to denounce the poor as thriftless, and that they are so I grant. The temptation to trust to luck and let every day take care of itself is, it must be remembered, great. Life with them is always a toss-up, a daily battle, an hourly struggle. Thousands of them can never hope to be five shillings ahead of the world if they keep honest. The utmost limit of their wage is reached when they have paid their rent, kept themselves and their horribly large families from starvation, and bought the few rags which keep their limbs decently covered. With them the object of life is attained when the night's rent is paid, and they do not have to hesitate between the workhouse or a corner of the staircase in some doorless house.

PIGGING WITH THEIR RELATIONS

From *How the Poor Live*

The room was no better and no worse than hundreds of its class. It was dirty and dilapidated, with the usual bulging blackened ceiling and the usual crumbling greasy walls. Its furniture was a dilapidated four-post bedstead, a chair, and a deal table. On the bed lay a woman, young, and with features that, before hourly anguish contorted them, had been comely. The woman was dying slowly of heart disease. Death was 'writ large' upon her face. At her breast she held her child, a poor little mite of a baby that was drawing the last drain of life from its mother's breast. The day was a bitterly cold one; through the broken casement the wind came ever and anon in icy gusts, blowing the hanging end of the ragged coverlet upon the bed to and fro like a flag in a breeze. The wind roared in the chimney, too, eddying down into the fireless grate with a low howling noise like the moan of a Banshee round a haunted house. To protect the poor woman from the cold her husband had flung on it his tattered great-coat, a garment that the most ancient four-wheel night cabman would have spurned as a knee-protector. 'He was a plumber,' she whispered to us in a weak, hollow voice; 'he had been out of work for a week, and he had gone out to try and look for a job.' One shivered to think of him wearily trudging the streets this bitter day, half clad and wholly starved; what must have been his torture as he failed at place after place, and the day wore on and brought the night when he would have to return to the poor dying wife with the old sad story?

As one realized the full meaning of this little domestic tragedy, and knew that it was only one of many daily enacted in the richest city in the world – the scene of it laid not a mile from the full tide of all the pomps and vanities of fashion, of all the notorious luxury and extravagances which is the outward show of our magnificence and wealth, it was hard to repress a feeling of something akin to shame and anger – shame for the callous indifference which bids one half the world ignore the sufferings of the other – anger that, with all the gold annually borne along on the broad stream of charity, so little of it ever reaches the really deserving and necessitous poor.

The house this poor woman lay dying in was one of a block which would have been a prize to a sanitary inspector anxious to make a sensational report. For the room in question the plumber out of work had to pay four and sixpence, and the broken pane of glass the landlord had refused to replace. The man was told 'he must do it himself, or if he didn't like it as it was he could go'.

Such stories as this are painful, but they should be told. It is good for the rich that now and again they should be brought face to face with misery, or they might doubt its existence. These people – our fellow-citizens – cannot be neglected with impunity. These fever and pestilence-breeding dens that are still allowed to exist, these death-traps out of which vestrymen and capitalists make large annual incomes, are a danger to the whole community.

While I am on this subject, I may as well quote an instance which bears directly upon the interest – the selfish interest – which the better classes have in lending their voices to swell the chorus of complaints which is going up about the present state of things.

Here is an 'interior' to which I would call the special attention of ladies who employ nurse-girls for their children.

This room when we entered it was in a condition beyond description. The lady was washing the baby, and she made that an excuse for the dirt of everything else. Two ragged boys were sitting on the filthy floor, a dirty little girl was in a corner pulling a dirty kitten's tail, and the smoke from the untidiest grate I ever saw in my life was making the half-washed baby sneeze its little head nearly off. The family, all told, that slept in this room was seven. There was a bed and there was a sofa – so I concluded the floor must have been the resting-place of some of them. 'The eldest girl – ' materfamilias informed us in answer to our questions – 'was gone out. She slept on the sofa.' We knew somebody had slept there, because some rags were on it, which had evidently done duty as bed-clothes.

Outside this room, which opened on to a back-yard, was a

dust-bin. We didn't want eyesight to know that – it appealed with sufficient power to another sense. Inside was an odour which made the dust-bin rather a relief.

I have described this place a little graphically for the sake of that eldest girl. It is not from any gallantry to the fair sex that I have done this, but because the young woman in question was, I ascertained, a domestic servant. She was a nursemaid just home from a place at Norwood, and in a week she was going to a place at Clapham. I remembered, as I gazed on the scene, a certain vigorous letter from Mr Charles Reade which appeared in the *Daily Telegraph* some years ago about servants 'pigging with their relations at home', and wanting the best bedroom and a feather-bed with damask furniture when in service. I never so thoroughly realized what 'pigging with their relations' meant before.

OPENING THE FLOODGATES
OF KNOWLEDGE
From *How the Poor Live*

The difficulty of getting that element of picturesqueness into these chapters which is so essential to success with a large class of English readers becomes more and more apparent as I and my travelling companion explore region after region where the poor are hidden away to live as best they can. There is a monotony in the surroundings which became painfully apparent to us, and were our purpose less earnest than it is, we might well pause dismayed at the task we have undertaken.

The Mint and the Borough present scenes awful enough in all conscience to be worthy of earnest study; but scene after scene is the same. Rags, dirt, filth, wretchedness, the same figures, the same faces, the same old story of one room unfit for habitation yet inhabited by eight or nine people, the same complaint of a ruinous rent absorbing three-fourths of the toiler's weekly wage, the same shameful neglect by the owner of the property of all sanitary precautions, rotten floors, oozing walls, broken windows, crazy staircases, tileless roofs, and in and around the dwelling-place of hundreds of honest citizens the nameless abominations which could only be set forth were we contributing to the *Lancet* instead of writing a book – these are the things which confront us, whether we turn to the right or to the left, whether we linger in the Mint or seek fresh fields in the slums that lie round Holborn, or wind our adventurous footsteps towards the network of dens that lie within a stone's throw of our great National Theatre, Drury Lane.

The story of one slum is the story of another, and all are unrelieved by the smallest patch of that colour which lends a charm to pictures of our poorest peasantry. God made the country, they say, and man made the town; and wretched as is the lot of the agricultural labourer, the handiwork of Heaven still remains to give some relief to the surroundings of his miserable life. Field and tree and flower, the green of the meadow and the hedge, the gold and white of buttercup and daisy, the bright hues of the wild cottage garden – it is in the midst of these the pigsties of the rustic poor are pitched, and there is scope for the artist's brush. But in the slums he can use but one colour; all is a monotone – a sombre gray deepening into the blackness of night. Even the blue, that in the far-off skies seems to defy the man-made town to be utterly colourless, is obscured by the smoke belched forth from a hundred chimneys; and even the sun, which shines with systematic impartiality on the righteous and the unrighteous alike, is foiled in its efforts to get at these outcasts by the cunning builders, who have put house so close to house that even a sunbeam which had trained down to the proportions of Mdlle Sarah Bernhardt, and then been flattened by a steam-roller, could not force its way between the overhanging parapets with any chance of getting to the ground. So what sunshine there is stops on the roofs among the chimney-pots, and is the sole property of the cats of the neighbourhood, who may be seen dozing about in dozens, or indulging in a pastime which they have certainly not learnt of their masters and mistresses, namely, washing their faces.

The cat-life of the slums is peculiar. Dogs are rare, but the cats are as common as blackberries in September. Not over-clean and not over-fat, the cats of the slums yet seem perfectly contented, and rarely leave the district in which they have been reared. They ascend to the roof early in the day, and stay there long after darkness has set in, and in the choice of a local habitation they show their feline sense. The rooms of their respective owners offer neither air nor sunshine, and when 'the family' are all at home it is possibly the inability of finding even a vacant corner to curl up in that drives Thomas to that part of a house which the people of the East consider the best, but which the people of our East have never sought to utilize.

The cats of the slums are certainly domesticated : they marry and have families, and the kittens are the only really pretty things we have seen since we started on our explorations.

The young of most animals are interesting and picturesque; but a kitten is perhaps the prettiest of all; and a painful contrast is there between the sallow dirty face, the sunken eyes and wizard features of a baby we see sitting on a doorstep nursing one, and the dainty face, blue eyes, and plump, pretty figure of the kitten. The mother of the latter has set an example in the matter of philoprogenitiveness and domestic forethought which the mother of the former would do well to imitate.

There are not wanting those who believe that for the present generation of poor little can be done – I mean, of course, the poor who are sunk in the misery and degradation of slum life. Dirtiness is ingrained in them, and if they had decent habitations provided for them tomorrow, they would no more live in them than a gipsy could settle down under any but a canvas roof.

Thrift they do not understand, and are too old to be taught; and ordinary decency is a thing of which they have about as much conception as they would have of the aestheticism of Mr Oscar Wilde or the philosophy of Mr Herbert Spencer.

I am not of the school which says that the regeneration of the masses is hopeless, but I freely confess that the great chance of bringing about a new and better order of things lies among the children who are to be the mothers and fathers of the future. In the old Biblical times water and fire were the elements which solved the knotty problem of regenerating a seething mass of humanity sunk in the lowest abysses of vice and degradation. The deluge that shall do the work now must come of the opening of the floodgates of knowledge. Already, in tiny rivulets as yet, the waters are trickling into the darkest corners of our great cities. The floor can never rise high enough to cleanse those who have grown up ignorant – at best it can but wet their feet; but the children cannot escape it – the waters will gather force and volume and grow into a broad glorious river, through which the boys and girls of today will wade breast high until they gain the banks of the Promised Land. It is this river of knowledge which the modern wanderers in the wilderness must ford to reach the Canaan which the philanthropist sees waiting for them in his dreams.

The first working of the Education Act was fraught with countless difficulties. It was no light task to catch the children of a shifting race, to schedule street Arabs and the offspring of beggars and thieves and prostitutes. But in the course of a few years almost every difficulty has been conquered, and now there is hardly a child above a certain age – no matter how wretched its conditions may be – that is not brought within the beneficial influence of education.

True that many of them come shoeless, ragged, and starving, to learn the three 'R's', to burthen their scanty brains with sums and tasks while their stomachs are empty and their bodies weakened by disease and neglect; but they have at least their chance. Let us take a school where, perhaps, the poorest children come – a school recruited from such homes as we have familiarized you with in previous chapters – and see the little scholars at their dainty tasks. Here is a child who is but one remove from an idiot. The teacher has a hard task, for the Government inspector expects all the scholars to make the same progress. This poor waif – the offspring of a gentleman whose present address is Holloway Gaol, and a lady who has been charged seventy-three times with being drunk and incapable – must pass a certain standard before she can leave school; in her case, if she lives, she will pass out by age, for statistics show that no system can make this class of intellect retain a lesson. It is sowing seed upon a rock, and there will be no harvest; but the child has just sufficient intelligence to escape the asylum, and between the asylum and the school there is no half-way house.

Some benefit, at least, she derives from the discipline, the care, and the motherly sympathy of a kind head-mistress, who

takes a strong personal interest in her little charges. For so
many hours a day at least the child escapes the ghastly
surroundings of the den which is her 'home'.

Side by side with her sits a pretty, intelligent little girl
of nine. This child's eyes are bright with intelligence, the
features are pleasing and regular. As she is called forward, she
rises and smilingly comes towards us. There is none of that
stolid indifference, that mechanical obedience to a command
which distinguishes too many of the little ones who are here
in obedience to the laws. This girl learns quickly, and has had
all the better qualities brought out. She is neat, and takes a
pride in her personal appearance. She has learnt to be ashamed
of dirt, and she is ambitious to be high up in her class.
Ambition is the one quality which will help above all others
to lift the poor out of degradation. The older race have it not;
hence they are content with their present positions, only seeking to gratify their daily appetites, and caring not a fig for the
morrow. This child will do well, whatever she undertakes; and
it is such as she who will survive in the battle of life, and
become the mothers of a better and more useful class.

Yet hers is a sad enough story. Her father was a boatman,
and in a drunken rage struck his wife down with a boat-hook.
Hers was the common offence of asking for money. The
blow injured the woman's brain, and from that day to this
she had been in a lunatic asylum. The father disappeared after
the crime, and the child's grandmother took the orphan with
living parents in, and out of her scanty earnings kept her.
One day this year the old lady passed some men carrying a
body found in the river to the dead-house. Curiosity induced
her to go in with the crowd, and the face of the dead man was
that of her son.

A back-street tragedy – common enough, with a varied plot
and incidents in these parts, but, as it stands, the life-story of
this child.

'And your granny keeps you now?' says the teacher, as
she concludes the little history, and turns to the girl.

'Yes, teacher; and when I grow up I'm going to keep granny.'
So may it be!

There are some hundred girls in the room. Some of them
come from decent homes, and some from cellars; many of

their histories are romances; but they are romances which mostly tend one way – to show the misery, the guilt, and the poverty in which they have been reared; and to recount them would be but to dwell upon a note which perhaps I have touched too often already.

There are brighter stories, too, to be told of their parents, but none so bright as they will be able to tell of themselves when, after years of discipline and culture, they go forth to lead lives which with their fathers and mothers were impossible.

Close to the school where the elder girls are educated, and in the same building, is the department for infants. Here the children under seven are prepared to pass into the upper department.

Directly we enter we are struck with the appearance of these children. Bad faces there are among them – bruises and scars, and bandages and rags – but the bulk of these younger children have a generally *better* appearance than their little neighbours.

There is a theory in the school, and it is borne out to a certain extent by fact, that some of the youngest and best-looking are the children of girls who just got the benefit of the Education Act before they were too old, and who in their young married life have reaped the benefit of those principles of cleanliness and thrift which the Board School inculcates. The young mothers are already a race far ahead of the older ones in this district, and the children naturally benefit by it. It must be borne in mind that the girls of this class marry or take a mate at a very early age. Many of them have three or four children by the time they are twenty, so that they would have been brought under the influence of the present Education Act. These young women, too, live in a better way; their room is tidier and cleaner, there is a little coquetry in them, and they have a sense of shame which renders them excellent service. They are anxious about their children's education, they recognise the advantage the discipline and instruction have been to them, and the general tone of their lives is every way a distinct advance on the old order of things.

I quote these facts because they so fully bear out the theory that Education must be the prime instrument in changing the condition of the poor for the better, whatever results it may have later on upon the condition of the labour market, and the political and social questions of the future. The many theories which are put forward about the result of educating the masses, it is not my province here to discuss; nor need I consider those doctrines which are closely akin to Socialism, and which are the favourite arguments of a school of advanced thinkers when discussing the future condition of the masses.

I have only to confine myself to the facts before me, and I think this great improvement in the children of the young mothers a most important one.

The best examples are in a room which is a kind of *crèche*. Here the babies can be left by the mothers who have to go out to work, and the tiny mites are looked after with motherly care by a kind-hearted creature whose lot I do not envy. Fancy forty infants, some of them little over two years old, to take care of for eight hours a day! Mothers will appreciate the situation better than I can describe it.

Look at the babies at dinner. They have brought their bread and butter with them, and they sit at the little low table enjoying it thoroughly. In the winter, when work is scarce, alas! baby's bread and butter is not always so thick as it is today. Sometimes baby has only a dry crust. But there is a lot of the best sort of Christian character knocking about in the Great City, and an excellent society, which provides dinners for poor Board School children, has done much to alleviate this painful state of things. A starving body, a famished child; there is no fear of imposture here; and if anyone who reads these chapters wishes to support a truly admirable movement, where there is no fear of abuse, he or she may imitate Captain Cuttle, and, having found a good thing, make a note of it.

In addition to the dining and play-table there is a long bed in the room. There the tired babies sleep eight or ten in a row sometimes, and forget their baby troubles. The *crèche* is a boon and a blessing to the poor woman who going out to work has a choice of keeping an elder girl at home to nurse the baby and be summoned for it, or locking the said baby up alone in a room all day with the risk to its life and its limbs inevitable to such a course, not to mention the danger of fire and matches and fits.

It is therefore with grief I hear that there are to be no more built in Board Schools, and that the cost of maintaining those existing must in future be defrayed by voluntary contributions. The Government objects to the *crèche* department on economical grounds.

The lady who manages the infants old enough to learn has no easy task, but the order is perfect, and the children drill like little soldiers. Here, too, the stories of many of them reveal a depth of misery not often sounded except in the police-courts.

Here I see a bright, pretty, golden-haired girl of five who rather upsets my pet theory. She ought to be ugly and dull, if there is anything in breed. Her mamma is seldom out of prison for more than a week. Mamma, not having learned Latin, does not know the difference between *meum* and *tuum*, and is an incorrigible shoplifter and thief. When she is enjoying her liberty, too, she has a habit of tumbling about which is not conducive to health. She has fallen out of a window and damaged the pavement below, and once with a baby in her arms she fell down the stairs of this very school.

When they picked her up the baby's collar-bone was broken, but she was sound enough to exclaim, 'If it hadn't ha' been for that blessed baby I'd a broken my neck, I would.'

It isn't every mother who is philosopher enough to recognise the use of a baby in breaking her fall downstairs.

The father of this little girl is a respectable man; but he has to go a long way for work, and when papa is in the country and mamma is in gaol, some good Sisters of Charity have taken the child and found it a home.

We have made our notes, and the children file out of school to dinner and to play.

One sturdy little chap takes his sister's hand and leads her out like a little father. He has over half a mile to take her home. We are told it is a beautiful sight to see him piloting her across the great thoroughfares when the traffic sweeps wildly up and down, and never leaving go the little hand that is placed so trustingly in his till home is reached and the dangers of the streets are over. They are a pretty pair as they toddle out hand in hand, and they form a pleasant picture in this brief sketch of the little scholars who come daily from the garrets and cellars of the slums to get that 'little learning' which in their cases is surely the reverse of a 'dangerous thing'.

LEGISLATION WANTED,
NOT ALMSGIVING

From *How the Poor Live*

I have necessarily left untrodden whole acres of ground over which a traveller, in search of startling revelations, might with advantage have journeyed. But startling revelations were not the object I had in view when I undertook these sketches. My object was to skim the surface lightly, but sufficiently to awaken in the general mind an interest in one of the great social problems of the day. A few of the evils of the present system of overcrowding and neglected sanitation, I have the courage to believe, have been brought home for the first time to a world of readers outside the hitherto narrow circle of philanthropists who take an active interest in the social condition of the masses.

One word with regard to the many letters which have appeared in the newspapers, and which have reached me privately. There seems a very general and a very earnest desire among the writers to do something for the people on whose behalf I have appealed to their sympathy.

While fully appreciating the kind-heartedness and the generous feelings evoked I cannot help regretting that in too many instances the idea prevails that charity can ameliorate the evils complained of. I have been grievously misunderstood if anything I have said has led to the belief that all Englishmen have to do to help the denizens of the slums and alleys is to put their hands in and pull out a sovereign or a shilling.

It is legislation that is wanted, not almsgiving. It is not a temporary relief, but a permanent one, that can alone affect, in any appreciable manner, the condition of the one-roomed portion of the population of great cities.

Charity is to be honoured wherever it is found, but charity, unless accompanied by something else, may do more evil than good. There are in London scores and scores of men and women who live by getting up bogus charities and sham schemes for the relief of the poor. Hundreds of thousands of pounds pass annually through the hands of men whose antecedents, were they known, would make a careful householder nervous about asking them into his hall if there were any coats and umbrellas about.

I am not a thick and thin supporter of the COS. At various times I have been bitterly opposed both to its theories and its practices; but it certainly has done an immense deal of good in exposing some of the scoundrels who appeal to the best sympathies of human nature under absolutely false pretences.

It is not so long ago that a man who had been convicted of fraud was found to be the flourishing proprietor of a mission to the poor, or something of the sort – whose annual income for two years past had been over a couple of thousand pounds, against an expenditure in tracts, rent, and blankets of one hundred and thirty-six pounds.

In another instance, the promoter of a charity, which had been in a flourishing condition for years, actually had his villa at St John's Wood, and kept his brougham – his total source of income being the charity itself.

If I quote these cases here it is not to hinder the flow of the broad, pure stream of charity by one single obstacle, but to show such of my readers as may need the hint how dangerous and delusive it is to think that careless almsgiving is in any shape or form a real assistance to the poor and suffering.

People who wish to do good must give their time as well as their money. They must personally investigate all those cases they wish to relieve, and they must set about seeing how the causes which lead to misery and suffering can be removed.

How are the evils of overcrowding – how are the present miseries of the poor to be removed? In what way can the social status of the labouring classes be permanently raised? Not by collecting-cards or funds, not by tracts or missions, but by remedial legislation – by State help and State protection, and by the general recognition of those rights of citizenship, which should be as carefully guarded for the lowest class as for the highest.

We live in a country which practically protects the poor and oppressed of every land under the sun at the expense of its own. We organize great military expeditions, we pour out blood and money *ad libitum* in order to raise the social conditions of black men and brown; the woes of an Egyptian, or a Bulgarian, or a Zulu send a thrill of indignation through honest John Bull's veins; and yet at his very door there is a race so oppressed, so hampered, and so utterly neglected, that its condition has become a national scandal.

Is it not time that the long-promised era of domestic legislation gave some faint streaks of dawn in the parliamentary sky? Are we to wait for a revolution before we rescue the poor from the clutches of their oppressors? Are we to wait for the cholera or the plague before we remedy a condition of things which sanitarily is without parallel in civilized countries?

There is a penalty for packing cattle too closely together; why should there be none for improperly packing men and women and children? The law says that no child shall grow up without reading, writing, and arithmetic; but the law does nothing that children may have air, and light, and shelter.

No one urges that the State should be a grandmother to the citizens, but it should certainly exercise ordinary parental care over its family.

To quote an instance of the gross neglect of the interests of the poor by the State, take the working of the Artisans' Dwellings Act. Space after space has been cleared under the provisions of this Act, thousands upon thousands of families have been rendered homeless by the demolition of whole acres of the slums where they hid their heads, and in scores of instances the work of improvement has stopped with the pulling down. To this day the cleared spaces stand empty — a cemetery for cats, a last resting-place for worn-out boots and tea-kettles. The consequence of this is, that the hardships of the displaced families have been increased a hundredfold. So limited is now the accommodation for the class whose wage-earning power is of the smallest, that in the few quarters left open to them rents have gone up 100 per cent in five years — a room which once let for 2s a week is now 4s. Worse even than this — the limited accommodation has left the renters helpless victims of any extortion or neglect the landlords of these places may choose to practise.

The tenants cannot now ask for repairs, for a decent water-supply, or for the slightest boon in the way of improvement. They must put up with dirt, and filth, and putrefaction; with dripping walls and broken windows; with all the nameless abominations of an unsanitary hovel, because if they complain the landlord can turn them out at once, and find dozens of people eager to take their places, who will be less fastidious. It is Hobson's choice – that shelter or none – and it is small wonder that few families are stoical enough to move from a death-trap to a ditch or a doorstep for the sake of a little fresh air. The law which allows them the death-trap denies them the doorstep – that is a property which must not be overcrowded.

Now, is it too much to ask that in the intervals of civilizing the Zulu and improving the condition of the Egyptian fellah the Government should turn its attention to the poor of London, and see if in its wisdom it cannot devise a scheme to remedy this terrible state of things?

The social, moral, and physical improvement of the labouring classes is surely a question as important, say, as the condition of the traffic at Hyde Park Corner, or the disfigurement of the Thames Embankment. If one-tenth of the indignation which burst forth when a ventilator ventured to emit a puff of smoke on the great riverside promenade to the injury of the geraniums in Temple Gardens could only be aroused over the wholesale stifling and poisoning of the poor which now goes on all over London, the first step towards a better state of things would have been taken.

Why does that indignation find no stronger outlet than an occasional whisper, a nod of the head, a stray leading article, or a casual question in the House sandwiched between an inquiry concerning the Duke of Wellington's statue, and one about the cost of cabbage-seed for the kitchen-garden at Buckingham Palace?

The answer probably will be, that up to a recent date the magnitude of the evil has not been brought home to the general public or the members of the Legislature. MPs do not drive through the Mint or Whitechapel, nor do they take their constitutional in the back slums of Westminster and Drury Lane. What the eye does not see the heart does not grieve after, and the conservative spirit born and bred in Englishmen makes them loth to start a crusade against any system of wrong until its victims have begun to start a crusade of their own – to demonstrate in Trafalgar Square, and to hold meetings in Hyde Park. There is a disposition in this country not to know that a dog is hungry till it growls, and it is only when it goes from growling to snarling, and from snarling to sniffing viciously in the vicinity of somebody's leg, that the somebody thinks it time to send out a flag of truce in the shape of a bone. We don't want to wait until the dog shows its teeth to know that he has such things. We want the bone to be offered now – a good marrowy bone, with plenty of legislative meat upon it. He has been a good, patient, long-suffering dog, chained to a filthy kennel for years, and denied even a drink of clean water, let alone a bone, so that the tardy offering is at least deserved.

It would be easy to show how the amelioration of the condition of the lower classes would be beneficial to the entire community, but it is scarcely worth while to put the question on such low grounds. The boon craved should come as an act of justice, not as a concession wrung from unwilling hands by fear, or granted with interested motives.

Briefly, and narrowing the question down to its smallest dimensions, what is wanted is this: The immediate erection on cleared spaces of tenements suitable to the classes dislodged. A system of inspection which would not only cause the demolition of unhealthy houses, but prevent unhealthy houses being erected. A certain space should be insisted on for every human being inhabiting a room – say 300 cubic feet for each person, and this regulation should be enforced by inspection of labouring-class dwellings, the enforcement of proper sanitary regulations, and a higher penalty for any breach of them; the providing of increased bath and washing accommodation in every crowded district; the erection of proper mortuaries in every parish; and the preservation in every district of certain open spaces to act as lungs to the neighbourhood – all these should be items in any remedial scheme. Beyond this, the poor should be encouraged in every possible way to decentralize. They must at present all crowd round the big centres of employment, because the means of travelling to and fro are beyond the reach of their slender purses. But if a system of cheap conveyance by tram or rail for the working classes could be developed, they would scatter themselves more and more about the suburbs, and by their own action reduce the exorbitant rents they are now called upon to pay.

Again, there should be in all new blocks of tenements built for this class accommodation for the hawkers and others who have barrows which they must put somewhere, and who are compelled at times to house the vegetable and animal matter in which they deal. A man who sells cabbages in the streets cannot leave his unsold stock to take care of itself at night, so he takes it home with him. At present he and his family generally sleep on it in their one room, but lock-up sheds and stabling for donkeys and ponies would obviate all the evils of the present system. The men are quite willing to pay for a little extra accommodation, and the removal of the mischief which comes of whole areas polluted with decaying vegetable matter is at least worth an experiment.

The density of the population in certain districts, and the sanitary defects of the tenements, are, at present, absolute dangers to the Public Health. On this ground alone it is desirable to agitate for reform; but there is a broader ground still – humanity. It is on that broad ground I venture to ask those who by these scant sketches of a great evil have become in some slight way acquainted with it, to raise their voices and give strength to the cry which is going up at last for a rigid and searching inquiry into the conditions under which the Poor of this vast city live.

To leave the world a little better than he found it is the best aim a man can have in life, and no labour earns so sweet and so lasting a reward as that which has for its object the happiness of others.

Public opinion boldly expressed never fails to compel the obedience of those who guide the destinies of States. Public opinion is a chorus of voices, and the strength of that chorus depends upon the manner in which each individual member of it exerts his vocal power. How long the scandal which disgraces the age shall continue depends greatly, therefore, good reader, upon your individual exertions. If aught that has been written here, then, has enlisted your sympathy, pass from a recruit to a good soldier of the cause, and help with all your will and all your strength to make so sad a story as this impossible when in future years abler pens than mine shall perhaps once again attempt to tell you How the Poor Live.

Andrew Mearns

The Bitter Cry of Outcast London, An Enquiry into the Condition of the Abject Poor was published anonymously as a penny pamphlet in 1883 and caused an immediate sensation. It was given wide publicity by W. T. Stead in the *Pall Mall Gazette*, provoked the writing of similar pamphlets and articles describing the 'Bitter Cry' of cities throughout Britain, and has been credited as a major influence on the setting up of the Royal Commission on the Housing of the Working Classes, 1884–5, and on subsequent legislation. The authorship of *The Bitter Cry* has long been a controversial issue. It is now generally acknowledged that Andrew Mearns, Secretary of the London Congregational Union, was the main author, though he was helped, as he willingly admitted, by James Munro in the investigation of housing conditions, and by W. C. Preston in the writing of the pamphlet. Mearns claimed : 'The inception was entirely mine, the investigation was carried out under my direction, and the pamphlet was prepared according to my instructions and subject to my revision.' Full details of this controversy are given by Anthony S. Wohl in his edition of *The Bitter Cry* (Leicester 1970). The present text is of the first pamphlet edition.

'THE BITTER CRY OF OUTCAST LONDON'

There is no more hopeful sign in the Christian Church of today than the increased attention which is being given by it to the poor and outcast classes of society. Of these it has never been wholly neglectful; if it had it would have ceased to be Christian. But it has, as yet, only imperfectly realised and fulfilled its mission to the poor. Until recently it has contented itself with sustaining some outside organisations, which have charged themselves with this special function, or, what is worse, has left the matter to individuals or to little bands of Christians having no organisation. For the rest it has been satisfied with a superficial and inadequate district visitation, with the more or less indiscriminate distribution of material charities, and with opening a few rooms here and there into which the poorer people have been gathered, and by which a few have been rescued. All this is good in its way and has done good; but by all only the merest edge of the great dark region of poverty, misery, squalor and immorality has been touched. We are not losing sight of the London City Mission, whose agents are everywhere, and whose noble work our investigations have led us to value more than ever, but after all has been done the churches are making the discovery that seething in the very centre of our great cities, concealed by the thinnest crust of civilization and decency, is a vast mass of moral corruption, of heart-breaking misery and absolute godlessness, and that scarcely anything has been done to take into this awful slough the only influences that can purify or remove it.

Whilst we have been building our churches and solacing ourselves with our religion and dreaming that the millennium was coming, the poor have been growing poorer, the wretched more miserable, and the immoral more corrupt; the gulf has been daily widening which separates the lowest classes of the community from our churches and chapels, and from all decency and civilization. It is easy to bring an array of facts which seem to point to the opposite conclusion – to speak of the noble army of men and women who penetrate the vilest haunts, carrying with them the blessings of the gospel; of the encouraging reports published by Missions, Reformatories, Refuges, Temperance Societies; of Theatre Services, Midnight Meetings and Special Missions. But what does it all amount to? We are simply living in a fool's paradise if we suppose that all these agencies combined are doing a thousandth part of what needs to be done, a hundredth part of what *could* be done by the Church of Christ. We must face the facts; and these compel the conviction that THIS TERRIBLE FLOOD OF SIN AND MISERY IS GAINING UPON US. It is rising every day. This statement is made as the result of a long, patient and sober inquiry, undertaken for the purpose of discovering the actual state of the case and the remedial action most likely to be effective. Convinced that it is high time some combined and organised effort was made by all denominations of Christians, though not for denominational purposes, the London Congregational Union have determined to open in several of the lowest and most needy districts of the metropolis, suitable Mission Halls, as a base of operations for evangelistic work. They have accordingly made this diligent search, and some of the results are set forth in the following pages, in the hope that all who have the power may be stimulated to help the Union in the great and difficult enterprise which they have undertaken.

Two cautions it is important to bear in mind. First, the information given *does not refer to selected cases*. It simply reveals a state of things which is found in house after house, court after court, street after street. Secondly, there *has been absolutely no exaggeration*. It is a plain recital of plain facts. Indeed, no respectable printer would print, and certainly no decent family would admit, even the driest statement of the horrors and infamies discovered in one brief visitation from house to house. *So far from making the worst of our facts for the purpose of appealing to emotion, we have been compelled to tone down everything, and wholly to omit what most needs to be known, or the ears and eyes of our readers would have been insufferably outraged.* Yet even this qualified narration must be to every Christian heart a loud and bitter cry, appealing for the help which it is the supreme mission of the Church to supply. It should be further stated that our investigations were made in the summer. The condition of the poor during the winter months must be very much worse.

NON-ATTENDANCE AT WORSHIP

It is perhaps scarcely necessary to say of the hundreds of thousands who compose the class referred to, that very few attend any place of worship. It is a very tame thing to say, and a very little thing compared with what must follow, but it is needful to a proper statement of our case. Before going to the lower depths, where our investigations were principally carried on, we find in the neighbourhood of Old Ford, in 147 consecutive houses, inhabited for the most part by the respectable working class, 212 families, 118 of which never, under any circumstances, attend a place of worship. Out of 2290 persons living in consecutive houses at Bow Common, only 88 adults and 47 children ever attend, and as 64 of these are connected with one Mission Hall, only 24 out of the entire number worship elsewhere. One street off Leicester Square contains 246 families, and only 12 of these are ever represented at the house of God. In another street in Pentonville, out of 100 families only 12 persons attend any sanctuary, whilst the number of attendants in one district of St George's-in-the-East is 39 persons out of 4235. Often the numbers given of those who do attend include such as only go once or twice a year, at some charity distribution, so that our figures are more favourable than the actual facts. Constantly we come across persons who have never been to church or chapel for 20 years, 28 years, more than 30 years; and some persons as old as 64 never remember having been in a place of worship at all. Indeed, with the exception of a very small proportion, the idea of going has never dawned upon these people. And who can wonder? Think of

THE CONDITION IN WHICH THEY LIVE

We do not say the condition of their homes, for how can those places be called homes, compared with which the lair of a wild beast would be a comfortable and healthy spot? Few who will read these pages have any conception of what these pestilential human rookeries are, where tens of thousands are crowded together amidst horrors which call to mind what we have heard of the middle passage of the slave ship. To get into them you have to penetrate courts reeking with poisonous and malodorous gases arising from accumulations of sewage and refuse scattered in all directions and often flowing beneath your feet; courts, many of them which the sun never penetrates, which are never visited by a breath of fresh air, and which rarely know the virtues of a drop of cleansing water. You have to ascend rotten staircases, which threaten to give way beneath every step, and which, in some places, have already broken down, leaving gaps that imperil the limbs and lives of the unwary. You have to grope your way along dark and filthy passages swarming with vermin. Then, if you are not driven back by the intolerable stench, you may gain admittance to the dens in which these thousands of beings who belong, as much as you, to the race for whom Christ died, herd together. Have you pitied the poor creatures who sleep under railway arches, in carts or casks, or under any shelter which they can find in the open air? You will see that they are to be envied in comparison with those whose lot it is to seek refuge here. Eight feet square – that is about the average size of very many of these rooms. Walls and ceiling are black with the accretions of filth which have gathered upon them through long years of neglect. It is exuding through cracks in the boards overhead; it is running down the walls; it is every-where. What goes by the name of a window is half of it stuffed with rags or covered by boards to keep out wind and rain; the rest is so begrimed and obscured that scarcely can light enter or anything be seen outside. Should you have ascended to the attic, where at least some approach to fresh air might be expected to enter from open or broken window, you look out upon the roofs and ledges of lower tenements, and discover that the sickly air which finds its way into the room has to pass over the putrefying carcases of dead cats or birds, or viler abominations still. The buildings are in such miserable repair as to suggest the thought that if the wind could only reach them they would soon be toppling about the heads of their occupants. As to furniture – you may perchance discover a broken chair, the tottering relics of an old bed-stead, or the mere fragment of a table; but more commonly you will find rude substitutes for these things in the shape of rough boards resting upon bricks, an old hamper or box turned upside down, or, more frequently still, nothing but rubbish and rags.

Every room in these rotten and reeking tenements houses a family, often two. In one cellar a sanitary inspector reports finding a father, mother, three children, and four pigs! In another room a missionary found a man ill with small-pox, his wife just recovering from her eighth confinement, and the children running about half naked and covered with dirt. Here are seven people living in one underground kitchen and a little dead child lying in the same room. Elsewhere is a poor widow, her three children, and a child who had been dead thirteen days. Her husband, who was a cabman, had shortly before committed suicide. Here lives a widow and her six children, including one daughter of 29, another of 21, and a son of 27. Another apartment contains father, mother and six children, two of whom are ill with scarlet fever. In another nine brothers and sisters, from 29 years of age downwards, live, eat and sleep together. Here is a mother who turns her children into the street in the early evening because she lets her room for immoral purposes until long after midnight, when the poor little wretches creep back again if they have not found some miserable shelter elsewhere. Where there are beds they are simply heaps of dirty rags, shavings or straw, but for the most part these miserable beings find rest only upon the filthy boards. The tenant of this room is a widow who herself occupies the only bed, and lets the floor to a married couple for 2s 6d per week. In many cases matters are made worse by the unhealthy occupations followed by those who dwell in these habitations. Here you are choked as you enter by the air laden with particles of the superfluous fur pulled from the skins of rabbits, rats, dogs and other animals in their preparation for the furrier. Here the smell of paste and of drying match-boxes, mingling with other sickly odours, overpowers you; or it may be the fragrance of stale fish or vegetables, not sold on the previous day, and kept in the room overnight. Even when it is possible to do so the people seldom open their windows, but if they did it is questionable whether much would be gained, for the external air is scarcely less heavily charged with poison than the atmosphere within.

Wretched as these rooms are they are beyond the means of many who wander about all day, picking up a living as they can, and then take refuge at night in one of the common lodging-houses that abound. These are often the resorts of thieves and vagabonds of the lowest type, and some are kept by receivers of stolen goods. In the kitchen men and women may be seen cooking their food, washing their clothes, or lolling about smoking and gambling. In the sleeping room are long rows of beds on each side, sometimes 60 or 80 in one room. In many cases both sexes are allowed to herd together without any attempt to preserve the commonest decency. But there is a lower depth still. Hundreds cannot even scrape together the two pence required to secure them the privilege of resting in those sweltering common sleeping rooms, and so they huddle together upon the stairs and landings, where it is no uncommon thing to find six or eight in the early morning.

That people condemned to exist under such conditions take to drink and fall into sin is surely a matter for little surprise. We may rather say, as does one recent and reliable explorer, that they are 'entitled to credit for not being twenty times more depraved than they are'. One of the saddest results of this over-crowding is the inevitable association of honest people with criminals. Often is the family of an honest working man compelled to take refuge in a thieves' kitchen; in the houses where they live their rooms are frequently side by side, and continual contact with the very worst of those who have come out of our gaols is a matter of necessity. There can be no question that numbers of habitual criminals would never have become such, had they not by force of circumstances been packed together in these slums with those who were hardened in crime. Who can wonder that every evil flourishes in such hotbeds of vice and disease? Who can wonder that little children taken from these hovels to the hospital cry, when they are well, through dread of being sent back to their former misery? Who can wonder that young girls wander off into a life of immorality, which promises release from such conditions? Who can wonder that the public-house is 'the Elysian field of the tired toiler'?

IMMORALITY

is but the natural outcome of conditions like these. 'Marriage,' it has been said, 'as an institution, is not fashionable in these districts.' And this is only the bare truth. Ask if the men and women living together in these rookeries are married, and your simplicity will cause a smile. Nobody knows. Nobody cares. Nobody expects that they are. In exceptional cases only could your question be answered in the affirmative. Incest is common; and no form of vice and sensuality causes surprise or attracts attention. Those who appear to be married are often separated by a mere quarrel, and they do not hesitate to form similar companionships immediately. One man was pointed out who for some years had lived with a woman, the mother of his

three children. She had died and in less than a week he had
taken another woman in her place. A man was living with a
woman in the low district called 'The Mint'. He went out one
morning with another man for the purpose of committing a
burglary and by that other man was murdered. The murderer
returned saying that his companion had been caught and taken
away to prison; and the same night he took the place of the
murdered man. The only check upon communism in this
regard is jealousy and not virtue. The vilest practices are
looked upon with the most matter-of-fact indifference. The
low parts of London are the sink into which the filthy and
abominable from all parts of the country seem to flow. Entire
courts are filled with thieves, prostitutes and liberated convicts.
In one street are 35 houses, 32 of which are known to be
brothels. In another district are 43 of these houses, and 428
fallen women and girls, many of them not more than 12 years
of age. A neighbourhood whose population is returned at
10,100 contains 400 who follow this immoral traffic, their ages
varying from 13 to 50; and of the moral degradation of the
people, some idea may be formed from an incident which was
brought to our notice. An East End missionary rescued a young
girl from an immoral life, and obtained for her a situation
with people who were going abroad. He saw her to Southamp-
ton, and on his return was violently abused by the girl's
grandmother, who had the sympathy of her neighbours, for
having taken away from a poor old woman her means of
subsistence.

The misery and sin caused by drink in these districts have
often been told, but these horrors can never be set forth
either by pen or artist's pencil. In the district of Euston Road
is one public-house to every 100 people, counting men, women
and children. Immediately around our chapel in Orange Street,
Leicester Square, are 100 gin-palaces, most of them very large;
and these districts are but samples of what exists in all the
localities which we have investigated. Look into one of these
glittering saloons, with its motley, miserable crowd, and you
may be horrified as you think of the evil that is nightly
wrought there; but contrast it with any of the abodes which
you find in the fetid courts behind them, and you will wonder
no longer that it is crowded. With its brightness, its excitement,

and its temporary forgetfulness of misery, it is a comparative heaven to tens of thousands. How can they be expected to resist its temptations? They could not live if they did not drink, even though they know that by drinking they do worse than die. All kinds of depravity have here their schools. Children who can scarcely walk are taught to steal, and mercilessly beaten if they come back from their daily expeditions without money or money's worth. Many of them are taken by the hand or carried in the arms to the gin-palace, and not seldom may you see mothers urging and compelling their tender infants to drink the fiery liquid. Lounging at the doors and lolling out of windows and prowling about street corners were pointed out several well-known members of the notorious band of 'Forty Thieves', who, often in conspiracy with abandoned women, go out after dark to rob people in Oxford Street, Regent Street, and other thoroughfares. Here you pass a coffee-house, there a wardrobe shop, there a tobacconist's, and there a grocer's, carrying on a legitimate trade no doubt, but a far different and more remunerative one as well, especially after evening sets in – all traps to catch the unwary. These particulars indicate but faintly the moral influences from which the dwellers in these squalid regions have no escape, and by which is bred 'infancy that knows no innocence, youth without modesty or shame, maturity that is mature in nothing but suffering and guilt, blasted old age that is a scandal on the name we bear'.

Another difficulty with which we have to contend, and one in large measure the cause of what we have described, is the

POVERTY

of these miserable outcasts. The poverty, we mean, of those who try to live honestly; for notwithstanding the sickening revelations of immorality which have been disclosed to us, those who endeavour to earn their bread by honest work far outnumber the dishonest. And it is to their infinite credit that it should be so, considering that they are daily face to face with the contrast between their wretched earnings and those which are the produce of sin. A child seven years old is known easily to make 10s 6d a week by thieving, but what can he earn by such work as match-box making, for which $2\frac{1}{4}d$ a gross is paid, the maker having to find his own fire for drying the boxes, and his own paste and string? Before he can gain as much as the young thief he must make 56 gross of matchboxes a week, or 1296 a day. It is needless to say that this is impossible, for even adults can rarely make more than an average of half that number. How long then must the little hands toil before they can earn the price of the scantiest meal! Women, for the work of trousers finishing (i.e. sewing in linings, making button-holes and stitching on the buttons) receive 2½d a pair, and have to find their own thread. We ask a woman who is making tweed trousers how much she can earn in a day, and are told one shilling. But what does a day mean to this poor soul? *Seventeen hours!* From five in the morning to ten at night – no pause for meals. She eats her crust and drinks a little tea as she works, making in very truth, with her needle and thread, not her living only, but her shroud. For making men's shirts these women are paid 10d a dozen; lawn tennis aprons, 3d a dozen; and babies' hoods, from 1s 6d to 2s 6d a dozen. In St George's-in-the-East large numbers of women and children, some of the latter only seven years old, are employed in sack-making, for which they get a farthing each. In one house was found a widow and her half-idiot daughter making palliasses at 1¾d each. Here is a woman who has a sick husband and a little child to look after. She is employed at shirt finishing at 3d a dozen, and by the utmost effort can only earn 6d a day, out of which she has to find her own thread. Another, with a crippled hand, maintains herself and a blind husband by match-box making, for which she is remunerated on the liberal scale mentioned above; and out of her 2¼d a gross she has to pay a girl a penny a gross to help her. Others obtain at Covent Garden in the season 1d or 2d a peck for shelling peas, or 6d a basket for walnuts; and they do well if their labour brings them 10d or a shilling a day. With men it is comparatively speaking no better. 'My master,' says one man visited by a recent writer in the *Fortnightly Review*, 'gets a pound for what he gives me 3s for making.' And this it is easy to believe, when we know that for a pair of fishing boots which will be sold at three guineas, the poor workman receives 5s 3d if they are made to order, or 4s 6d if made for stock. An old tailor and his wife are employed in making policeman's overcoats. They have to make, finish, hot-press, put on the buttons, and find their own thread, and for all this they receive 2s 10d for each coat. This old couple work from half-past six in the morning until ten at night, and between them can just manage to make a coat in two days. Here is a mother who has taken away whatever articles of clothing she can strip from her four little children without leaving them absolutely naked. She has pawned them, not for drink, but for coals and food. A shilling is all she can procure, and with this she has bought seven pounds of coals and a loaf of bread. We might fill page after page with these dreary details, but they would become sadly monotonous, for it is the same everywhere. And then it should not be forgotten how hardly upon poverty like this must press the exorbitant demand for rent. Even the rack-renting of Ireland, which so stirred our indignation a little while ago, was merciful by comparison. If by any chance a reluctant landlord can be induced to execute or pay for some long-needed repairs, they become the occasion for new exactions. Going through these rooms we come to one in which a hole, as big as a man's head, has been roughly covered, and how? A piece of board, from an old soap box, has been fixed over the opening by one nail, and to the tenant has been given a yard and a half of paper with which to cover it; and for this expenditure – perhaps 4d at the outside – *threepence a week has been put upon the rent*. If this is enough to arouse our indignation, what must be thought of the following? The two old people just mentioned have lived in one room for 14 years, during which time it has only once been partially cleansed. The landlord has undertaken that it shall be done shortly, and for the past three months has been taking 6d a week extra for rent for what he is thus *going to do*. This is what the helpless have to submit to; they are charged for these pestilential dens a rent which consumes half the earnings of a family, and leaves them no more than from 4d to 6d a day for food, clothing and fire; a grinding of the faces of the poor which could scarcely be paralleled in lands of slavery and of notorious oppression. This, however, is not all; for even these depths of poverty and degradation are reached by the Education Act, and however beneficent its purpose, it bears with cruel weight upon the class we have described, to whom twopence or a penny a week for the school fees of each of three or four children, means so much lack of bread.

Amidst such poverty and squalor it is inevitable that one should be constantly confronted with scenes of

HEART-BREAKING MISERY—

misery so pitiful that men whose daily duty it has been for years to go in and out amongst these outcasts, and to be intimately acquainted with their sufferings, and who might, therefore, be supposed to regard with comparatively little feeling that which would overwhelm an unaccustomed spectator, sometimes come away from their visits so oppressed in spirit and absorbed in painful thought, that they know not whither they are going. How these devoted labourers can pursue their work at all is a marvel, especially when it is remembered that the misery they actually see suggests to them the certain existence of so much more which no human eye discovers. Who can even imagine the suffering which lies behind a case like the following? A poor woman in an advanced stage of consumption, reduced almost to a skeleton, lives in a single room with a drunken husband and five children. When visited she was eating a few green peas. The children were gone to gather some sticks wherewith a fire might be made to boil four potatoes which were lying on the table, and which would constitute the family dinner for the day. Or, take another case, related by Rev. Archibald Brown, who, with his missionaries, is doing a noble work amongst the poor in the East of London. People had doubted the accuracy of reports presented by the missionaries, and he accordingly devoted a considerable time to personal visitation and inquiry. He found case after case proving that but little of the wretchedness had been told, and here is a *fair specimen*. At the top of an otherwise empty house lived a family; the husband had gone to try and find some work. The mother, 29 years of age, was sitting on the only chair in the place, in front of a grate destitute of any fire. She was nursing a baby six weeks old, that had never had anything but one old rag around it. The mother had nothing but a gown on, and that dropping to pieces; it was all she had night or day. There were six children under 13 years of age. They were barefooted, and the few rags on them scarcely covered their nakedness. In this room, where was an unclothed infant, the ceiling was in holes. An old bedstead was in the place, and seven sleep in it at night, the eldest girl being on the floor.

This is bad, but it is not the worst. In a room in Wych Street, on the third floor, over a marine store dealer's, there was, a short time ago, an inquest as to the death of a little baby. A man, his wife and three children were living in that room. The infant was the second child who had died, poisoned by the foul atmosphere; and this dead baby was cut open in the one room where its parents and brothers and sisters lived, ate and slept, *because the parish had no mortuary and no room in which post-mortems could be performed!* No wonder that the jurymen who went to view the body sickened at the frightful exhalations. This case was given by Mr G. R. Sims, in his papers on 'How the Poor live'; but all the particulars are found in the dry newspaper reports of the inquest. In another miserable room are eight destitute children. Their father died a short time ago, and 'on going into the house today', says the missionary, 'the mother was lying in her coffin'. Here is a filthy attic, containing only a broken chair, a battered saucepan and a few rags. On a dirty sack in the centre of the room sits a neglected, ragged, bare-legged little baby girl of four. Her father is a militiaman, and is away. Her mother is out all day and comes home late at night more or less drunk, and this child is left in charge of the infant that we see crawling about the floor; left for six or eight hours at a stretch – hungry, thirsty, tired, but never daring to move from her post. And this is the kind of sight which may be seen in a Christian land where it is criminal to ill-treat a horse or an ass.

The child-misery that one beholds is the most heart-rending and appalling element in these discoveries; and of this not the least is the misery inherited from the vice of drunken and dissolute parents, and manifest in the stunted, misshapen, and often loathsome objects that we constantly meet in these localities. From the beginning of their lives they are utterly neglected; their bodies and rags are alive with vermin; they are subjected to the most cruel treatment; many of them have never seen a green field, and do not know what it is to go beyond the streets immediately around them, and they often pass the whole day without a morsel of food. Here is one of three years old picking up some dirty pieces of bread and eating them. We go in at the doorway where it is standing and find a little girl twelve years old. 'Where is your mother?' 'In the madhouse.' 'How long has she been there?' 'Fifteen months.' 'Who looks after you?' The child, who is sitting at an old table making match-boxes, replied, 'I look after my little brothers and sisters as well as I can.' 'Where is your father? Is he in work?' 'He has been out of work three weeks, but he has gone to a job of two days this morning.' Another house visited contains nine motherless children. The mother's death was caused by witnessing one of her children being run over. The eldest is only fourteen years old. All live in one small room, and there is one bed for five. Here is a poor woman deserted by her husband and left with three little children. One met with an accident a few days ago, and broke his arm. He is lying on a shake-down in one corner of the room, with an old sack round him. And here, in a cellar kitchen, are nine little ones. You can scarcely see across the room for smoke and dirt. They are without food and have scarcely any clothing.

It is heart crushing to think of the misery suggested by such revelations as these; and there is something unspeakably pathetic in the brave patience with which the poor not seldom endure their sufferings, and the tender sympathy which they show toward each other. Where, amongst the well conditioned, can anything braver and kinder be found than this? A mother, whose children are the cleanest and tidiest in the Board School which they attend, was visited. It was found that, though she had children of her own, she had taken in a little girl, whose father had gone off tramping in search of work. She was propped up in a chair, looking terribly ill, but in front of her, in another chair, was the wash-tub, and the poor woman was making a feeble effort to wash and wring out some of the children's things. She was dying from dropsy, scarcely able to breathe and enduring untold agony, but to the very last striving to keep her little ones clean and tidy. A more touching sight it would be difficult to present; we might, however, unveil many more painful ones, but must content ourselves with saying that the evidence we have gathered from personal observation more than justifies the words of the writer before referred to, that 'there are (i.e. in addition to those who find their way to our hospitals) men and women who lie and die day by day in their wretched single rooms, sharing all the family trouble, enduring the hunger and the cold, and waiting without hope, without a single ray of comfort, until God curtains their staring eyes with the merciful film of death'.

WHAT IT IS PROPOSED TO DO

That something needs to be done for this pitiable outcast population must be evident to all who have read these particulars as to their condition – at least, to all who believe them. We are quite prepared for incredulity. Even what we have indicated seems all too terrible to be true. But we have sketched only in faintest outline. Far more vivid must be our colours, deeper and darker far the shades, if we are to present a truth picture of 'Outcast London'; and so far as we have been able to go we are prepared with evidence, not only to prove every statement, but to show that these statements represent the general condition of thousands upon thousands in this metropolis. Incredulity is not the only difficulty in the way of stirring up Christian people to help. Despair of success in any such undertaking may paralyse many. We shall be pointed to the fact that without State interference nothing effectual can be accomplished upon any large scale. And *it is* a fact. These wretched people must live somewhere. They must live near the centres where their work lies. They cannot afford to go out by train or tram into the suburbs; and how, with their poor emaciated, starved bodies, can they be expected – in addition to working twelve hours or more, for a shilling, or less – to walk three or four miles each way to take and fetch? It is notorious that the Artizans' Dwellings Act has, in some respects, made matters worse for them. Large spaces have been cleared of fever-breeding rookeries to make way for the building of decent habitations, but the rents of these are far beyond the means of the abject poor. They are driven to crowd more closely together in the few stifling places still left to them; and so Dives makes a richer harvest out of their misery, buying up property condemned as unfit for habitation, and turning it into a goldmine because the poor must have shelter somewhere, even though it be the shelter of a living tomb.

The State must make short work of this iniquitous traffic, and secure for the poorest the rights of citizenship; the right to live in something better than fever dens; the right to live as something better than the uncleanest of brute beasts. This must be done before the Christian missionary can have much chance with them. But because we cannot do all we wish, are we to do nothing? Even as things are something can be accomplished. Is no lifeboat to put out and no lifebelt be thrown because only half a dozen out of the perishing hundreds can be saved from the wreck? The very records which supply the sad story we have been telling, give also proofs of what can be done by the Gospel and by Christian love and tact and devotion. Gladly do many of these poor creatures receive the Gospel. Little match-box makers are heard singing at their toil, 'One more day's work for Jesus'. 'If only mother was a Christian we should all be happy,' said one; and on his miserable bed, amidst squalor and want and pain, a poor blind man dies with the prayer upon his lips, 'Jesus, lover of my soul, Let me to thy bosom fly.' Another writes, 'You have filled my heart with joy, and my little room with sunshine.' A second, who now regularly attends a place of worship, says, speaking of the visits of the missionary, 'Before he came to visit me I used to sit and make match-boxes on Sunday, but a word now and then has enabled me to look up to the Lord. I don't feel like the same person.' Another who himself became a missionary to his own class, and exercised great power over them whenever he spoke, was able to say, 'I was as bad as any of you, but the Lord Jesus had mercy upon me, and has made me better and so happy.' This man had been a 'coal-whipper' of notoriously evil life, and was rescued through his casually going into a room in one of the courts of which we have spoken, where a missionary was holding a meeting. Such results should rebuke our faithlessness. Even in these dark and noisome places the lamp of Life may be kindled; even from these miry spots bright gems may be snatched, worth all the labour and all the cost.

It is little creditable to us that all our wealth and effort should be devoted to providing for the spiritual needs of those who are comfortably conditioned, and none of it expended upon the abject poor. It is true that we have not half done our duty to any class, but this fact is no justification of our having wholly neglected this rescue work. To shut up our compassion against those who need it most, because we have not yet done our duty to those who need it less, is a course that we should find it hard to justify to our Master and Lord. His tones were ever those of pitying love even to the most sinful outcast, but would they not gather sternness as He met us with the rebuke: 'This ought ye to have done, and not to have left the other undone'? An 'exceeding bitter cry' is this which goes up to heaven from the misery of London against the apathy of the Church. It is time that Christians opened their ears to it and let it sink down into their hearts. Many pressing needs are taxing the resources of the London Congregational Union, but the Committee feel that this work amongst the poor must no longer be neglected, and that they must do all they can to arouse the Churches of their order to undertake their share of responsibility. They have determined to take immediate action. Having selected three of the very worst districts in London, from which many of the foregoing facts have been gathered, they have resolved at once to begin operations in the very heart of them. No denominational purpose will sway them, except that they will try to awaken their own denomination to a sense of its duty; there will be no attempt to make Congregationalists or to present Congregationalism. Deeper, broader and simpler must this work be than any which can be carried on upon denominational lines. In such a forlorn hope there is no room for sectarianism. The Gospel of the love of Christ must be presented in its simplest form, and the one aim in everything must be to rescue and not to proselytise. Help will be thankfully welcomed from whatever quarter it may come, and help will be freely given to other workers in the same field, if only by any means some may be saved. It is impossible here, and yet, to give details as to the methods which it is proposed to pursue; suffice it to say that in each district a Mission Hall will be erected, or some existing building transformed into a Hall having appliances and conveniences requisite for the successful prosecution of the Mission. Services and meetings of all kinds will be arranged, and, as far as possible, an agency for house to house visitation organised. An attempt must be made to relieve in some wise and practical, though very limited way, the abounding misery, whilst care is taken to prevent the abuse of charity. In this matter the injudicious and inexperienced may easily do more harm than good, pauperising the people whom they wish to help, and making hypocrites instead of Christians. To indicate what we mean we may mention one case pointed out to us of a woman who attended three different places of worship on the Sunday and some others during the week, because she obtained charitable help from all. But we cannot on this account refuse to try some means of mitigating the suffering with which we come into contact. Therefore this must be attempted along with whatever other means the Committee, in conference with those who have had long experience of this work, may think likely to answer the end they have before them. Their hope is that at least some, even of the lowest and worst, may be gathered in; and their aim will be to make as many of these as they can missionaries to the others; for manifestly those who have been accustomed to speak to and work amongst a somewhat better section of the community will not be so likely to labour successfully amongst these outcasts as will those who have themselves been of their number. The three districts already fixed upon are, as it will be understood, intended only to afford a field for the immediate commencement of this beneficent work. Other districts will be occupied as funds come in and the resources of the Committee are enlarged; but even the comparatively limited operations already undertaken will necessitate so great an expenditure and require so much aid from those who are qualified for the work, that they cannot wisely attempt more at present. For not only will the cost and furnishing of Halls and of carrying on the work be very large, but a relief fund will be needed as indicated above. The Committee, therefore, can only hope to carry forward with any success the project to which they have already put their hands, by the really devoted help of the churches which they represent.

DESCRIPTION OF THE DISTRICTS

The district known as Collier's Rents is one of the three to which attention will first be given, and the old chapel, long disused, is now in the builders' hands and will soon be ready for opening, not as a chapel, but as a bright, comfortable, and in every way suitable Hall. It would be impossible to find a building better situated for working among the very poor and degraded than this. It stands in a short street, leading out of Long Lane, Bermondsey, the locality in which were recently found the bodies of nine infants, which had been deposited in a large box at the foot of some stairs in an undertaker's shop. There are around the Hall some 650 families, or 3250 people, living in 123 houses. The houses are largely occupied by costermongers, bird catchers, street singers, liberated convicts, thieves, and prostitutes. There are many low lodging-houses in the neighbourhood of the worst type. Some of them are tenanted chiefly by thieves, and one was pointed out which is kept by a receiver of stolen goods. In some cases two of the houses are united by means of a passage, which affords a ready method of escape in case of police interference.

Turning out of one of these streets you enter a narrow passage, about ten yards long and three feet wide. This leads into a court eighteen yards long and nine yards wide. Here are twelve houses of three rooms each, and containing altogether 36 families. The sanitary condition of the place is indescribable. A large dust-bin charged with all manner of filth and putrid matter stands at one end of the court, and four water-closets at the other. In this confined area all the washing of these 36 families is done, and the smell of the place is intolerable. Entering a doorway you go up six or seven steps into a long passage, so dark that you have to grope your way by the clammy, dirt-encrusted wall, and then you find a wooden stair, some of the steps of which are broken through. Ascending as best you can, you gain admission to one of the rooms. You find that although the front and back of the house are of brick, the rooms are separated only by partitions of boards, some of which are an inch apart. There are no locks on the doors, and it would seem that they can only be fastened on the outside by padlock. In this room to which we have come an old bed, on which are some evil-smelling rags, is, with the exception of a broken chair, the only article of furniture. Its sole occupant just now is a repulsive, half-drunken Irishwoman. She is looking at some old ragged garments in hope of being able to raise something upon them at the pawnshop, and being asked if she is doing this because she is poor, she gets into a rage and cries, 'Call me poor? I have got half a loaf of bread in the house, and a little milk'; and then from a heap of rubbish in one corner she pulls out a putrid turkey, utterly unfit for human food, which she tells us she is going to cook for dinner. This woman has just 'done seven days' for an assault upon a police officer. We find that she has a husband, but he spends almost all his money at the public-house. Rooms such as this are let furnished (!) at 3s 6d and 4s a week, or 8d a night, and we are told that the owner is getting from 50 to 60 per cent upon his money.

And this is a specimen of the neighbourhood. Reeking courts, crowded public-houses, low lodging-houses, and numerous brothels are to be found all around. Even the cellars are tenanted. Poverty, rags, and dirt everywhere. The air is laden with disease-breeding gases. The missionaries who labour here are constantly being attacked by some malady or other resulting from blood poisoning, and their tact and courage are subjected to the severest tests. In going about these alleys and courts no stranger is safe if alone. Not long ago a doctor on his rounds was waylaid by a number of women, who would not let him pass to see his patient until he had given them money; and a Bible-woman, visiting 'Kent Street', was robbed of most of her clothing. Even the police seldom venture into some parts of the district except in company. Yet bad as it is there are elements of hopefulness which encourage us to believe that our work will not be in vain. Many of its denizens would gladly break away from the dismal, degrading life they are leading, if only a way were made for them to do so; as it is they are hemmed in and chained down by their surroundings in hopeless and helpless misery.

Such is Collier's Rents. To describe the other two localities where our work is to be commenced, in Ratcliff and Shadwell, would, in the main, be but to repeat the same heart-sickening story. Heart-sickening but soul-stirring. We have opened but a little way the door that leads into this plague-house of sin and misery and corruption, where men and women and little children starve and suffer and perish, body and soul. But even the glance we have got is a sight to make one weep. We shall not wonder if some, shuddering at the revolting spectacle, try to persuade themselves that such things cannot be in Christian England, and that what they have looked upon is some dark vision conjured by a morbid pity and a responding faith. To such we can only say, Will you venture to come with us and see for yourselves the ghastly reality? Others, looking on, will believe, and pity, and despair. But another vision will be seen by many, and in this lies our hope – a vision of Him who had 'compassion upon the multitude because they were as sheep having no shepherd', looking with Divine pity in His eyes, over this outcast London, and then turning to the consecrated host of His Church with the appeal, 'Whom shall we send and who will go for us?'

Charles Booth

Charles Booth (1840–1916) was born in Liverpool. His father was a successful corn merchant, and both parents were Unitarians. His own career shows the influence of both business and nonconformist traditions, and also reflects his early interest in the work of Auguste Comte. At the age of twenty-two he formed a steamship company with his brother Alfred, and was chairman of it for the greater part of his life, and from an early age he was passionately involved in the discussion of social reforms and public affairs. In 1873, following an illness caused by overwork, he spent some time travelling and then moved to London where he later devoted himself to the study of poverty. The first volume of *Life and Labour of the People in London*, dealing solely with the East End, was published in 1889, and the second, which covered poverty in London as a whole, in 1891. These two volumes were expanded to nine in 1897, and seventeen in 1902–3. Booth always realized that the true importance of his work lay in the methods he was developing as much as any conclusions he should reach, and he was hesitant about advocating specific remedies. Although far from radical in his political views, and firmly committed to the objectivity of scientific analysis, Booth's writing is never cold or impersonal. He found much to admire in working-class life and tried to convey this, recognizing that while statistical evidence was essential if social problems were to be understood and solved, human factors were also of crucial importance. The following extracts are taken from volumes 1 and 2 of *Life and Labour*.

EAST LONDON: THE EIGHT CLASSES

From *Life and Labour of the People in London*

The area dealt with . . . contains in all about 900,000 inhabitants . . . The eight classes into which I have divided these people are:
A. The lowest class of occasional labourers, loafers, and semi-criminals.
B. Casual earnings – 'very poor'.
C. Intermittent earnings } together the 'poor'.
D. Small regular earnings }
E. Regular standard earnings – above the line of poverty.
F. Higher class labour.
G. Lower middle class.
H. Upper middle class.

The divisions indicated here by 'poor' and 'very poor' are necessarily arbitrary. By the word 'poor' I mean to describe those who have a sufficiently regular though bare income, such as 18s to 21s per week for a moderate family, and by 'very poor' those who from any cause fall much below this standard. The 'poor' are those whose means may be sufficient, but are barely sufficient, for decent independent life; the 'very poor' those whose means are insufficient for this according to the usual standard of life in this country. My 'poor' may be described as living under a struggle to obtain the necessaries of life and make both ends meet; while the 'very poor' live in a state of chronic want. It may be their own fault that this is so; that is another question; my first business is simply with the numbers who, from whatever cause, do live under conditions of poverty or destitution . . .

A. The lowest class, which consists of some occasional labourers, street-sellers, loafers, criminals and semi-criminals, I put at 11,000, or 1¼ per cent of the population, but this is no more than a very rough estimate, as these people are beyond enumeration, and only a small proportion of them are on the School Board visitors' books. If I had been content to build up the total of this class from those of them who are parents of children at school in the same proportions as has been done with the other classes, the number indicated would not have greatly exceeded 3000, but there is little regular family life among them, and the numbers given in my tables are obtained by adding in an estimated number from the inmates of common lodging houses, and from the lowest class of streets. With these ought to be counted the homeless outcasts who on any given night take shelter where they can, and so may be supposed to be in part outside of any census. Those I have attempted to count consist mostly of casual labourers of low character, and their families, together with those in a similar way of life who pick up a living without labour of any kind. Their life is the life of savages, with vicissitudes of extreme hardship and occasional excess. Their food is of the coarsest description, and their only luxury is drink. It is not easy to say how they live; the living is picked up, and what is got is frequently shared; when they cannot find 3d for their night's lodging, unless favourably known to the deputy, they are turned out at night into the street, to return to the common kitchen in the morning. From these come the battered figures who slouch through the streets, and play the beggar or the bully, or help to foul the record of the unemployed; these are the worst class of corner men who hang round the doors of public-houses, the young men who spring forward on any chance to earn a copper, the ready materials for disorder when occasion serves. They render no useful service, they create no wealth: more often they destroy it. They degrade whatever they touch, and as individuals are perhaps incapable of improvement; they may be to some extent a necessary evil in every large city, but their numbers will be affected by the economical condition of the classes above them, and the discretion of 'the charitable world'; their way of life by the pressure of police supervision.

It is much to be desired and hoped that this class may become less hereditary in its character. There appears to be no doubt that it is now hereditary to a very considerable extent. The children are the street arabs, and are to be found separated from the parents in pauper or industrial schools, and in such homes as Dr Barnardo's. Some are in the Board schools, and more in ragged schools, and the remainder, who cannot be counted, and may still be numerous, are every year confined within narrowing bounds by the persistent pressure of the School Board and other agencies.

While the number of children left in charge of this class is proportionately small, the number of young persons belonging to it is not so – young men who take naturally to loafing; girls who take almost as naturally to the streets; some drift back from the pauper and industrial schools, and others drift down from the classes of casual and irregular labour. I have attempted to describe the prevailing type amongst these people, but I do not mean to say that there are not individuals of every sort to be found in the mass. Those who are able to wash the mud may find some gems in it. There are, at any rate, many very piteous cases. Whatever doubt there may be as to the exact numbers of this class, it is certain that they bear a very small proportion to the rest of the population, or even to class B with which they are mixed up, and from which it is at times difficult to separate them. The hordes of barbarians of whom we have heard, who, issuing from their slums, will one day overwhelm modern civilization, do not exist. There are barbarians, but they are a handful, a small and decreasing percentage; a disgrace but not a danger.

This class is recruited with adult men from all the others. All such recruits have been in some way unfortunate, and most, if not all, have lost their characters. Women, too, drop down, sometimes with the men, more often from the streets. A considerable number of discharged soldiers are to be found in classes A and B.

Class B – Casual earnings – very poor – add up almost exactly to 100,000, or 11¼ per cent of the whole population. This number is made up of men, women and children in about the following proportions:

Married men	17,000
Their wives	17,000
Unmarried men	7,000
Widows	6,500
Unmarried women	5,000
Young persons, 15–20	9,500
Children	38,000
	100,000

Widows or deserted women and their families bring a large contingent to this class, but its men are mostly [casual labourers] . . . This classification cannot be made exact. These sections not only melt into each other by insensible degrees, but the only divisions which can be made are rather divisions of sentiment than of positive fact: the line between [loafers and casual labourers] is of this character, difficult to test, and not otherwise to be established; and the boundaries . . . are constantly fluctuating; for the casual labourer, besides being pressed on from below, when times are hard is also flooded from above; every class, even artisans and clerks, furnishing those who, failing to find a living in their own trade, compete at the dock gates for work . . .

In East London the largest field for casual labour is at the Docks; indeed, there is no other important field, for although a large number of men, in the aggregate, look out for work from day to day at the wharves and canals, or seek employment as porters in connection with the markets, there seems to be more regularity about the work, and perhaps less competition, or less chance of competition, between outsiders and those who, being always on the spot, are personally known to the employers and their foremen . . . The number of those who are casually employed at the Docks does not seem large compared to the very great public concern which has been aroused, but as a test of the condition of other classes, the ebb and flow of this little sea is really important; it provides a test of the condition of trade generally, as well as of certain trades in particular – a sort of 'distress meter' – and connects itself very naturally with the question of the unemployed.

The labourers of class B do not, on the average, get as much as three days' work a week, but it is doubtful if many of them could or would work full time for long together if they had the opportunity. From whatever section Class B is drawn, except the sections of poor women, there will be found many of them who from shiftlessness, helplessness, idleness, or drink, are inevitably poor. The ideal of such persons is to work when they like and play when they like; these it is who are rightly called the 'leisure class' amongst the poor – leisure bounded very closely by the pressure of want, but habitual to the extent of second nature. They cannot stand the regularity and dulness of civilized existence, and find the excitement they need in the life of the streets, or at home as spectators of or participators in some highly coloured domestic scene. There is drunkenness amongst them, especially amongst the women; but drink is not their special luxury, as with the lowest class, nor is it their passion, as with a portion of those with higher wages and irregular but severe work. The earnings of the men vary with the state of trade, and drop to a few shillings a week or nothing at all in bad times; they are never high, nor does this class make the hauls which come at times in the more hazardous lives of the class below them; when, for instance, a sensational newspaper sells by thousands in the streets for 2d to 6d a copy. The wives in this class mostly do some work, and those who are sober, perhaps, work more steadily than the men; but their work is mostly of a rough kind, or is done for others almost as poor as themselves. It is in all cases wretchedly paid, so that if they earn the rent they do very well.

Both boys and girls get employment without much difficulty the girls earn enough to pay their mothers 4s or 5s a week if they stay at home; and if the boys do not bring in enough, they are likely to be turned adrift, being in that case apt to sink into Class A; on the other hand, the more industrious or capable boys no doubt rise into Classes C, D or E.

Class B, and especially the 'labour' part of it, is not one in which men are born and live and die, so much as a deposit of those who from mental, moral, and physical reasons are incapable of better work.

Class C – Intermittent earnings – numbering nearly 75,000, or about 8 per cent of the population, are more than any others the victims of competition, and on them falls with particular severity the weight of recurrent depressions of trade . . . Here may perhaps be found the most proper field for systematic charitable assistance; provided always some evidence of thrift is made the pre-condition or consequence of assistance.

. . . Class C consists of men who usually work by the job, or who are in or out of work according to the seas n or the nature of their employment.* This irregularity of employment

* In considering the status as to employment and means, a whole year has, so far as possible, been taken as the unit of time.

may show itself in the week or in the year: stevedores and waterside porters may secure only one or two days' work in a week, whereas labourers in the building trades may get only eight or nine months in the year . . . The great body of the labouring class (as distinguished from the skilled workmen) have a regular steady income, such as it is.

Some of the irregularly employed men earn very high wages, fully as high as those of the artisan class. These are men of great physical strength, working on coal or grain, or combining aptitude and practice with strength, as in handling timber. It is amongst such men, especially those carrying grain and coal, that the passion for drink is most developed. A man will very quickly earn 15s or 20s, but at the cost of great exhaustion, and many of them eat largely and drink freely till the money is gone, taking very little of it home. Others of this class earn wages approaching to artisan rates when, as in the case of stevedores, their work requires special skill, and is protected by trade organization . . . While trade is dull the absorption of surplus labour by other employment is extremely slow. There are also in this section a large number of wharf and warehouse hands, who depend on the handling of certain crops for the London market. They have full work and good work when the wool or tea sales are on, and at other times may be very slack. These classes of irregular labour depend on the shipping trades . . .

Besides those whose living depends on the handling of merchandise, there are in this section all the builders' labourers, and some others whose work is regulated by the seasons. With regard to these employments the periods of good and bad work are various, one trade being on while another is off; more goods to be handled, for instance, on the whole, in winter than in summer, against the stoppage of building in cold weather. I do not think, however, that one employment is dovetailed with another to any great extent; it would not be easy to arrange it, and most of the men make no effort of the kind. They take things as they come; work when they can get work in their own line, and otherwise go without, or, if actually hard up, try, almost hopelessly, for casual work. The more enterprising ones who fill up their time in some way which ekes out their bare earnings are the exceptions . . . The pressure is also very severe where there are many young children; a man and his wife by themselves can get along, improvident or not, doing on very little when work fails; the children who have left school, if they live at home, readily keep themselves, and sometimes do even more. It is in the years when the elder children have not yet left school, while the younger ones are still a care to the mother at home, that the pressure of family life is most felt . . .

I fear that the bulk of those whose earnings are irregular are wanting in ordinary prudence. Provident thrift, which lays by for tomorrow is not a very hardy plant in England, and needs the regular payment of weekly wages to take root freely. It seems strange that a quality so much needed, and so highly rewarded, should not be developed more than seems to be the case. There may, however, be more of such thrift among the irregularly employed than is generally supposed, for it is those who do not have it who come most under observation. I understand that death clubs with a weekly subscription of $\frac{1}{2}d$ to $2d$ per head are very commonly subscribed to, and there are instances of a system by which tradesmen are paid small sums all through the summer against the winter expenditure at their shop, receiving the money on a deposit card, and acting in fact as a sort of savings bank. But such cases are exceptional; the reverse would be the rule, credit being given in winter against repayment in summer. Most benefit societies, death clubs, goose clubs, etc., are held at public-houses, and the encouragement to thrift is doubtful. The publican is left too much in possession of the field as friend of the working man, and his friendship does not practically pay the latter, who is apt to spend more than he saves.

There will be many of the irregularly employed who could not keep a permanent job if they had it, and who must break out from time to time. [They are for the most part a] hard-working struggling people, not worse morally than any other class, though shiftless and improvident, but out of whom the most capable are either selected for permanent work, or equally lifted out of the section by obtaining preferential employment in irregular work. They are thus a somewhat helpless class, not belonging usually to any trade society, and for the most part without natural leaders or organization . . .

Class D – Small regular earnings, poor – are about 129,000, or nearly 14½ per cent of the population. It must not be understood that the whole of these have quite regular work; but only that the earnings are constant enough to be treated as a regular income, which is not the case with the earnings of class C. Of D and C together we have 203,000, and if this number is equally divided to represent those whose earnings are regular and irregular, which would be to place the standard of regularity a little higher than has been done in this inquiry, the result would be equal numbers of each grade of poverty – 100,000 of B or casual, 100,000 of C or intermittent, and 100,000 of D or regular earnings, out of a total population of 900,000, or one-ninth of each grade . . .

The men . . . are the better end of the casual dock and water-side labour, those having directly or indirectly a preference for employment. It includes also a number of labourers in the gas works whose employment falls short in summer but never entirely ceases. The rest of this section are the men who are in regular work all the year round at a wage not exceeding 21s a week. These are drawn from various sources, including in their numbers factory, dock, and warehouse labourers, carmen, messengers, porters, etc.; a few of each class. Some of these are recently married men, who will, after a longer period of service, rise into the next class; some are old and superannuated, semi-pensioners; but others are heads of families, and instances are to be met with (particularly among carmen) in which men have remained fifteen or twenty years at a stationary wage of 21s or even less, being in a comparatively comfortable position at the start, but getting poorer and poorer as their family increased, and improving again as their children became able to add their quota to the family income. In such cases the loss of elder children by marriage is sometimes looked upon with jealous disfavour.

Of the whole section none can be said to rise above poverty, unless by the earnings of the children, nor are many to be classed as very poor. What they have comes in regularly, and except in times of sickness in the family, actual want rarely presses, unless the wife drinks. As a general rule these men have a hard struggle to make ends meet, but they are, as a body, decent steady men, paying their way and bringing up their children respectably. The work they do demands little skill or intelligence.

In the whole class with which this section is identified the women work a good deal to eke out the man's earnings, and the children begin to make more than they cost when free from school: the sons go as van boys, errand boys, etc., and the daughters into daily service, or into factories, or help the mother with whatever she has in hand.

The comfort of their homes depends, even more than in other classes, on a good wife. Thrift of the 'make-the-most-of-everything' kind is what is needed, and in very many cases must be present, or it would be impossible to keep up so respectable an appearance as is done on so small an income.

E. Regular Standard Earnings . . . A large proportion of the artisans and most other regular wage earners. I also include here, as having equal means, the best class of street sellers and general dealers, a large proportion of the small shopkeepers, the best off amongst the home manufacturers, and some of the small employers. This is by far the largest class of the population under review, adding up to 377,000, or over 42 per cent.

[It] contains all, not artisans or otherwise scheduled, who earn from 22s to 30s a week for regular work. There are some of them who, when wages are near the lower figure, or the families are large, are not lifted above the line of poverty; but few of them are *very poor*, and the bulk of this large section can, and do, lead independent lives, and possess fairly comfortable homes.

As a rule the wives do not work, but the children all do: the boys commonly following the father (as is everywhere the case above the lowest classes), the girls taking to local trades, or going out to service.

The men in this section are connected with almost every form of industry, and include in particular carmen, porters and messengers, warehousemen, permanent dock labourers, stevedores, and many others. Of these some, such as the market porters and stevedores, do not earn regular wages, but both classes usually make a fair average result for the week's work . . .

It may be noted that Classes D and E together form the actual middle class in this district, the numbers above and below them being very fairly balanced.

The wage earners of Class E take readily any gratuities which fall in their way, and all those who constitute it will mutually give or receive friendly help without sense of patronage or degradation; but against anything which could be called charity their pride rises stiffly. This class is the recognized field of all forms of co-operation and combination, and I believe, and am glad to believe, that it holds its future in its own hands. No body of men deserves more consideration; it does not constitute a majority of the population in the East of London, nor, probably, in the whole of London, but it perhaps may do so taking England as a whole. It should be said that only in a very general way of speaking do these people form one class, and beneath this generality lie wide divergences of character, interests, and ways of life. This class owns a good deal of property in the aggregate.

Class F consists of higher class labour . . . and the best paid of the artisans, together with others of equal means and position from other sections, and amounts to 121,000, or about 13½ per cent of the population . . . Besides foremen are included City warehousemen of the better class, and first-hand lightermen; they are usually paid for responsibility, and are men of very good character and much intelligence.

This . . . is not a large section of the people, but it is a distinct and very honourable one. These men are the non-commissioned officers of the industrial army. No doubt there are others as good in the ranks, and vacant places are readily filled with men no less honest and trustworthy; all the men so employed have been selected out of many. The part they play in industry is peculiar. They have nothing to do with the planning or direction (properly so called) of business operations; their work is confined to superintendence. They supply no initiative, and having no responsibility of this kind they do not share in profits; but their services are very valuable, and their pay enables them to live reasonably comfortable lives, and provide adequately for old age. No large business could be conducted without such men as its pillars of support, and their loyalty and devotion to those whom they serve is very noteworthy. Most employers would admit this as to their own foremen, but the relation is so peculiar and personal in its character that most employers also believe no other foremen to be equal to their own.

Their sons take places as clerks, and their daughters get employment in first-class shops or places of business; if the wives work at all, they either keep a shop, or employ girls at laundry work or at dressmaking.

There is a great difference between these men and the artisans who are counted with them as part of Class F: the foreman of ordinary labour generally sees things from the employer's point of view, while the skilled artisan sees them from the point of view of the employed. Connected with this fact it is to be observed that the foremen are a more contented set of men than the most prosperous artisans . . .

Following the . . . artisans in my schedules come other wage earners, such as railway servants, policemen, and seamen, and the classification by industry then passes from wage earners – who, to give value to their work, have to please the wage payers – to profit earners, who, in order to be paid, have to please the public – a marked difference. The commonest labourer and the most skilful highly-paid mechanic are alike in that whatever they do their labour will be wasted if mis-applied, and that as to its application they have no respon-sibility: they are paid their wages equally whether they have or have not produced the value in consumption that is to be hoped for out of their work; but the master manufacturer, like the poor flower-girl, or the common street acrobat, must please his public to earn anything. The distinction is no question of wealth; with the artisans, as with ordinary labour, we have seen under one denomination very varied conditions of life; and among the profit earners also we shall again find all classes . . .

G. Lower Middle Class – Shopkeepers and small employers, clerks, etc., and subordinate professional men. A hard-working, sober, energetic class, which I will not more fully describe here, as they no doubt will be comparatively more numerous in other districts of London. Here they number 34,000, or nearly 4 per cent. It is to be noted that Class G, which in the whole district compares with the class above it as 34 to 45, for East London proper compares as 32 to 12. The exaggeration of Class H, as compared to Class G, is entirely due to Hackney.

H. Upper Middle Class – All above G are here lumped together, and may be shortly defined as the servant-keeping class. They count up to about 45,000, or 5 per cent of the population. Of these more than two-thirds are to be found in Hackney, where one-fifth of the population live in houses which, owing to their high rental, are not scheduled by the School Board visitors. In the other districts scattered houses are to be found above the value at which the School Board usually draws the line; but the visitors generally know something of the inmates. In Hackney, however, there are many streets as to which the visitors have not even the names in their books. The estimated number of residents in these unscheduled houses I have placed in Class H, to which they undoubtedly belong, excepting that the servants (also an estimated number) appear under Class E, from which they are mostly drawn.

It is to be remembered that the dividing lines between all these classes are indistinct; each has, so to speak, a fringe of those who might be placed with the next division above or below; nor are the classes, as given, homogeneous by any means. Room may be found in each for many grades of social rank . . .

PERSONAL EXPERIENCES

From *Life and Labour of the People in London*

It is not easy for any outsider to gain a sufficient insight into the lives of these people. The descriptions of them in the books we read are for the most part as unlike the truth as are descriptions of aristocratic life in the books they read. Those who know, think it a matter without interest, so that again and again in my inquiries, when some touch of colour has been given illuminating the ways of life among the people who are above the need for help, it has been cut short by a semi-apology : 'But that is not what you want to know about.' Something may be gleaned from a few books, such for instance as 'Demos'; something perhaps may be learnt from the accounts of household expenditure in the preceding chapter. Of personal knowledge I have not much. I have no doubt that many other men possess twenty or a hundred times as much experience of East End people and their lives. Yet such as it is, what I have witnessed has been enough to throw a strong light on the materials I have used, and, for me, has made the dry bones live. For three separate periods I have taken up quarters, each time for several weeks, where I was not known, and as a lodger have shared the lives of people who would figure in my schedules as belonging to classes C, D and E. Being more or less boarded, as well as lodged, I became intimately acquainted with some of those I met, and the lives and habits of many others came naturally under observation. My object, which I trust was a fair one, was never suspected, my position never questioned. The people with whom I lived became, and are still, my friends. I may have been exceptionally fortunate, and three families are not many, but I can only speak as I have found: wholesome, pleasant family life, very simple food, very regular habits, healthy bodies and healthy minds; affectionate relations of husbands and wives, mothers and sons, of elders with children, of friend with friend – all these things I found, and amongst those with whom I lodged I saw little to mar a very agreeable picture, fairly representative of class E, and applicable to some at least of classes C and D. Of others, belonging to the lower of these classes, who came under my observation, I cannot give so good an account. In the room above mine at one of the houses, a room about nine feet square, lived a carman and his wife and their two children, girls of seven and thirteen. The man, though a heavy drinker, was not a bad fellow, and steady enough over his work. It was the wife who was bad. She also drank, and as to work, 'never did a thing'. Late to bed and late to rise was her rule. The father went out early and returned to breakfast, which was prepared for him by the child of thirteen, who made the tea and toast and cooked the herring at a fire in the wash-house, which, the weather being warm, served for the cookery of the entire household. She also made ready her own and her sister's breakfast, left the tea for her mother (who was too lazy to make it even for herself), and then proceeded with her sister to school. The little sister was the pretty one and the pet of her parents; the elder one was the drudge, and twice this child had run away and stayed out all night before or after a beating. What chance of respectable life had she? This is an example of class D, with bad wife and bad mother. No less disreputable was a woman of the same class or lower, who with her daughter lived in another room of the same house. She had a small allowance from her husband, which went mainly in drink. He lived elsewhere. The daughter earned a trifle and tried vainly to keep her mother sober.

I do not mean to suggest that such specimens predominate in class D, or that they are never to be found in E or F, with which we are more particularly dealing. There is no gulf set between adjoining classes; E passes imperceptibly into either the irregular position of C or the bare remuneration of D, but from each of these there is another step as wide to reach the wretched casual character of class B. I watched with much interest the relations existing between classes E and D in the persons of my landlady and her other tenants. *Mutatis mutandis*, they were not very different from those which exist in the country between hall and village. There was the present of a dress altered to suit the hard-worked, ill-dressed child (it was forthwith pawned, the poor girl never wore it); the rebuke, dignified, well timed, and, as it appeared, efficacious, of the father's drunken ways; amounting in the end to 'amend your ways or go'; and the word in season to the little girl whose 'tongue was too long and must have a bit cut off' (she having told some tale about her sister); the women met over their washing in the yard, and the children were allowed to play together – play at house, or plant a garden with cut flowers stuck in the earth, or swing, or dress their dolls, but if there were sweets to be eaten it was my landlady's little girl who paid for them. In short, there was evinced a keen sense of social responsibility, not unaccompanied by a sense of social superiority.

The children in class E, and still more in class D, have when young less chance of surviving than those of the rich, but I certainly think their lives are happier, free from the paraphernalia of servants, nurses and governesses, always provided they have decent parents. They are more likely to suffer from spoiling than from harshness, for they are made much of, being commonly the pride of their mother, who will sacrifice much to see them prettily dressed, and the delight of their father's heart. This makes the home, and the happiness of the parents; but it is not this, it is the constant occupation, which makes the children's lives so happy. They have their regular school hours, and when at home, as soon as they are old enough, there is 'mother' to help, and they have numbers of little friends. In class E they have for playground the back yard, in class D the even greater delights of the street. With really bad parents the story would be different, but men and women may be very bad, and yet love their children and make them happy. In the summer holidays, when my carman had a load to carry for some building in the country, he would take two of the children with him. Supplied with bread and butter and 2d to buy fruit, they would start off early and come home in the evening happy, tired, and dirty, to tell of all the sights they had seen.

I perhaps build too much on my slight experience, but I see nothing improbable in the general view that the simple natural lives of working-class people tend to their own and their children's happiness more than the artificial complicated existence of the rich. Let it not be supposed, however, that on this I propose to base any argument against the desire of this class to better its position. Very far from it. Their class ambition as well as their efforts to raise themselves as individuals deserve the greatest sympathy. They might possess and spend a good deal more than they now do without seriously endangering the simplicity of their lives or their chances of happiness, and it would be well if their lot included the expenditure of a larger proportion of our surplus wealth than is now the case. Moreover, the uncertainty of their lot, whether or not felt as an anxiety, is ever present as a danger. The position of the class may be secure – some set of men and their families must hold it – but that of the individual is precarious. For the wife and family it will depend on the health, or habits, or character of the man. He drinks or he falls ill; he loses his job; some other man takes his place. His employment becomes irregular and he and they fall into class C, happy if they stop there and do not drop as low as B. Or it may be the woman who drags her family down. Marriage is a lottery, and child-bearing often leads to drink. What chance for a man to maintain respectability and hold up his head among his neighbours if he has a drunken wife at home, who sells the furniture and pawns his clothes? What possibility of being beforehand and prepared to meet the waves of fortune? Or it may be that trade shrinks, so that for a while one man in ten or perhaps one in seven is not wanted. Some must be thrown out of work. The lot falls partly according to merit and partly according to chance, but whatever the merit or the lack of it, the same number will be thrown out of work. Thus we see that the 'common lot of humanity', even though not much amiss in itself, is cursed by insecurity against which it is not easy for any prudence to guard.

PUBS AND COCOA ROOMS

From *Life and Labour of the People in London*

Public-houses play a larger part in the lives of the people than clubs or friendly societies, churches or missions, or perhaps than all put together, and bad it would be if their action and influence were altogether evil. This is not so, though the bad side is very palpable and continually enforced upon our minds.

A most horrible and true picture may be drawn of the trade in drink, of the wickedness and misery that goes with it. So horrible that one cannot wonder that some eyes are blinded to all else, and there is a cry of away with this accursed abomination. There is, however, much more to be said. Anyone who frequents public-houses knows that actual drunkenness is very much the exception. At the worst houses in the worst neighbourhoods many, or perhaps most, of those who stand at the bars, whether men or women, are stamped with the effects of drink, and, if orderly at the moment, are perhaps at other times mad or incapable under its influence; but at the hundreds of respectable public-houses, scattered plentifully all through the district, this is not the case. It could not be. They live by supplying the wants of the bulk of the people, and it is not possible that they should be much worse than the people they serve. Go into any of these houses – the ordinary public-house at the corner of any ordinary East End street – there, standing at the counter, or seated on the benches against wall or partition, will be perhaps half-a-dozen people, men and women, chatting together over their beer – more often beer than spirits – or you may see a few men come in with no time to lose, briskly drink their glass and go. Behind the bar will be a decent middle-aged woman, something above her customers in class, very neatly dressed, respecting herself and respected by them. The whole scene comfortable, quiet, and orderly. To these houses those who live near send their children with a jug as readily as they would send them to any other shop.

I do not want to press this more cheerful point of view further than is necessary to relieve the darker shades of the picture. I would rather admit the evils and try to show how they may be lessened and what the tendencies are that make for improvement.

It is evident that publicans, like all the rest of us, are feeling the stress of competition. Walk through the streets and everywhere it may be seen that the public-houses are put to it to please their customers. Placards announcing change of management frequently meet the eye, while almost every house vigorously announces its reduced prices. 'So much the worse,' some will say. But no! It is a good thing that they should be considering how to make themselves more attractive. Undermined by the increasing temperance of the people, and subject to direct attack from the cocoa rooms on the one side and the clubs on the other, the licensed victuallers begin to see that they cannot live by drink alone. Look more closely at the signs in their windows. There is hardly a window that does not show the necessity felt to cater for other wants besides drink. All sell tobacco, not a few sell tea. 'Bovril' (a well-advertised novelty) is to be had everywhere. Hot luncheons are offered, or a mid-day joint; or 'sausages and mashed' are suggested to the hungry passer-by; at all events there will be sandwiches, biscuits, and bread and cheese. Early coffee is frequently provided, and temperance drinks too have now a recognized place. Ginger beer is sold everywhere, and not infrequently kept on draught.* These things are new, and

* It is then called 'Brewed Ginger Beer' – a sort of sheep in wolf's clothing.

though trifles in themselves, they serve as straws to show the way of the wind. The public-houses also connect themselves with benefit clubs, charitable concerts, and 'friendly draws'. No doubt in all these things there is an eye to the ultimate sale of drink, but every accessory attraction or departure from the simple glare of the gin palace is an improvement. In order to succeed, each public-house now finds itself impelled to become more of a music hall, more of a restaurant, or more of a club, or it must ally itself with thrift. The publican must consider other desires besides that for strong drink. Those that do not, will be beaten in the race.

In all these efforts there is bad as well as good, and a monstrous ingenuity may be exerted in tempting men to drink – gambling and other vices being used to draw people together and open their purses. As public servants, the licensed victuallers are on their trial. The field is still in their possession, but let them be warned; for if they would keep their place they must adapt themselves to the requirements of the times. If they should neglect the larger wants of the great mass of the people, content to find their principal customers amongst the depraved, they would deserve the ruin that would inevitably fall on them.

In such a situation it would be a fatal mistake to decrease the number of the houses in the cause of temperance. To encourage the decent and respectable publican by making existence difficult to the disreputable is the better policy, but let us on no account interfere with a natural development, which, if I am right, is making it every day more difficult to make a livelihood by the simple sale of drink.

Cocoa Rooms, and especially Lockhart's cocoa rooms, have become an important factor in the life of the people. At first cocoa rooms, or 'coffee palaces' as they were then called, were the result of philanthropic or religious effort. They were to pay their way; but they did not do it. They were to provide good refreshments; but tea, coffee, cocoa and cakes were alike bad. It was not till the work was taken up as a business that any good was done with it. Now it strides forward, and though Lockhart's are the best and the most numerous, others are following and are bound to come up to, or excel, the standard so established. Very soon we shall have no length of principal street without such a place, and we shall wonder how we ever got on without them. In their rules they are wisely liberal: those who drink the cocoa may sit at the tables to eat the dinner or breakfast they have brought from home, or bringing the bread and butter from home they can add the sausage or whatever completes the meal.

STREET MARKETS

From *Life and Labour of the People in London*

Each district has its character – its peculiar flavour. One seems to be conscious of it in the streets. It may be in the faces of the people, or in what they carry – perhaps a reflection is thrown in this way from the prevailing trades or it may lie in the sounds one hears, or in the character of the buildings . . .

The neighbourhood of old Petticoat Lane on Sunday is one of the wonders of London, a medley of strange sights, strange sounds, and strange smells. Streets crowded so as to be thoroughfares no longer, and lined with a double or treble row of hand-barrows, set fast with empty cases, so as to assume the guise of market stalls. Here and there a cart may have been drawn in, but the horse has gone and the tilt is used as a rostrum whence the salesmen with stentorian voices cry their wares, vying with each other in introducing to the surrounding crowd their cheap garments, smart braces, sham jewellery, or patent medicines. Those who have something showy, noisily push their trade, while the modest merit of the utterly cheap makes its silent appeal from the lower stalls, on which are to be found a heterogeneous collection of such things as cotton sheeting, American cloth for furniture covers, old clothes, worn-out boots, damaged lamps, chipped china shepherdesses, rusty locks, and rubbish indescribable. Many, perhaps most, things of the 'silent cheap' sort are bought in the way of business; old clothes to renovate, old boots to translate, hinges and door-handles to be furbished up again. Such things cannot *look* too bad, for the buyer may then persuade himself that he has a bargain unsuspected by the seller. Other stalls supply daily wants – fish is sold in large quantities – vegetables and fruit – queer cakes and outlandish bread. In nearly all cases the Jew is the seller, and the Gentile the buyer; Petticoat Lane is the exchange of the Jew, but the lounge of the Christian.

Nor is this great market the only scene of the sort in the neighbourhood on Sunday morning. Where Sclater Street crosses Brick Lane, near the Great Eastern Station, is the market of the 'fancy'. Here the streets are blocked with those coming to buy, or sell, pigeons, canaries, rabbits, fowls, parrots, or guinea pigs, and with them or separately all the appurtenances of bird or pet keeping. Through this crowd the seller of shell-fish pushes his barrow; on the outskirts of it are moveable shooting galleries, and patent Aunt Sallies, while some man standing up in a dog-cart will dispose of racing tips in sealed envelopes to the East End sportsman.

Brick Lane should itself be seen on Saturday night, though it is in almost all its length a gay and crowded scene every evening of the week, unless persistent rain drives both buyers and sellers to seek shelter. But this sight – the 'market street' – is not confined to Brick Lane, nor peculiar to Whitechapel, nor even to the East End. In every poor quarter of London it is to be met with – the flaring lights, the piles of cheap comestibles, and the urgent cries of the sellers. Everywhere, too, there is the same absolute indifference on the part of the buyer to these cries. They seem to be accepted on both sides as necessary, though entirely useless. Not infrequently the goods are sold by a sort of Dutch auction – then the prices named are usually double what the seller, and every bystander, knows to be the market price of the street and day, 'Eightpence?' 'Sevenpence?' 'Sixpence?' 'Fivepence?' – Say 'Fourpence?' – well, then, 'Threepence halfpenny?' A bystander, probably a woman, nods imperceptibly; the fish or whatever it is passes from the right hand of the seller on which it has been raised to view, on to the square of newspaper, resting in his left hand, is bundled up and quick as thought takes its place in the buyer's basket in exchange for the $3\frac{1}{2}d$, which finds its place in the seller's apron or on the board beside the fish – and then begins again the same routine, 'Eightpence?' 'Sevenpence?' 'Sixpence' etc.

THE STATISTICS OF POVERTY

From *Life and Labour of the People in London*

The inhabitants of every street, and court, and block of buildings in the whole of London, have been estimated in proportion to the numbers of the children, and arranged in classes according to the known position and condition of the parents of these children. The streets have been grouped together according to the School Board sub-divisions or 'blocks', and for each of these blocks full particulars are given in the tables of the Appendix. The numbers included in each block vary from less than 2000 to more than 30,000, and to make a more satisfactory unit of comparison I have arranged them in contiguous groups, two, three or four together, so as to make areas having each about 30,000 inhabitants, these areas adding up into the large divisions of the School Board administration. The population is then classified by Registration districts, which are likewise grouped into School Board divisions, each method finally leading up to the total for all London.

The classes into which the population of each of these blocks and districts is divided are the same as were used in describing East London, only somewhat simplified. They may be stated thus:

A. The lowest class – occasional labourers, loafers and semi-criminals.

B. The very poor – casual labour, hand-to-mouth existence, chronic want.

C and D. The poor – including alike those whose earnings are small, because of irregularity of employment, and those whose work, though regular, is ill-paid.

E and F. The regularly employed and fairly-paid working class of all grades.

G and H. Lower and upper middle class and all above this level.

The Classes C and D, whose poverty is similar in degree but different in kind, can only be properly separated by information as to employment which was obtained for East London, but which, as already explained, the present inquiry does not yield. It is the same with E and F, which cover the various grades of working-class comfort. G and H are given together for convenience.

Outside of, and to be counted in addition to, these classes, are the inmates of institutions whose numbers are specially reported in every census, and finally there are a few who, having no shelter, or no recognized shelter, for the night, elude official enumeration and are not counted at all.

The proportions of the different classes shown for all London are as follows:

A (lowest)	37,610 or	·9 per cent.	In poverty, 30·7 per cent.
B (very poor)	316,834 "	7·5 per cent.	
C and D (poor)	938,293 "	22·3 per cent.	
E and F (working class, comfortable)	2,166,503 "	51·5 per cent.	In comfort, 69·3 per cent.
G and H (middle class and above)	749,930 "	17·8 per cent.	
	4,209,170	100 per cent.	
Inmates of Institutions	99,830		
	4,309,000		

Graphically, the proportions may be shown thus:

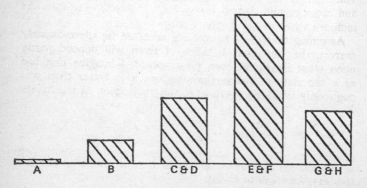

A   B   C & D   E & F   G & H

The description of these classes given already as to East London, may be taken as applying with equal force to the whole population. Much might be added to make the description more complete, but nothing need be taken away. The numbers of the lowest class (A), it is admitted, are given at a very rough estimate; they are hardly to be counted by families and so partly escape the meshes of our School Board net. They are to be found in the common lodging-houses and in the lowest streets, and a very full description of their lives and habits is given in the special chapters which treat of these subjects. Class B is fairly counted, and of what it consists, many examples are given in the description of specimen streets, but neither it nor any of the working classes, C, D, E or F, can be dealt with properly apart from their trades or employments, as the conditions under which these people live, depend mainly upon the conditions under which they work or fail to find work. An account of the life of each of the several classes that are grouped under the letters G and H would be very interesting, but is beyond the scope of this book. I am, however, able to make a division in the figures which answers pretty closely, though not quite exactly, to that between upper and lower middle class. This division is provided by the line of rental value, beyond which the School Board do not go in making their schedules. Out of the 750,000 people included in Classes G and H, as nearly as possible 250,000 live in scheduled and 500,000 in unscheduled houses. These figures may be counted as representing roughly the lower and upper middle classes respectively. The wealthy classes are included with the upper middle class.*

Assuming that these figures are accepted as approximately correct, the view that is taken of them will depend partly upon what may have been pre-supposed. I imagine that bad as is the state of things they disclose it is better than was commonly imagined previous to the publication of the figures

* The unscheduled population has been estimated in proportion to the number of houses in some cases, and assumed by way of remainder in other cases, and in every instance the assumed number of servants has been added to Classes E, F, to which by position they may be taken to belong.

obtained for East London. On the other hand they are probably worse, especially in regard to the numbers of Classes C and D, than may have been anticipated by those who have studied and accepted the East End figures.

That is to say, the poverty of the rest of London as compared to East London is perhaps greater than most people have supposed. For myself it was so. In 1888 I made an estimate based on the facts as to East London, and the comparative density of population in other parts, on the theory that density would probably coincide with the degree of poverty. The result was to show a probable 25 per cent of poor for all London, or nearly 6 per cent less than we now get. South London and the district about Holborn are mainly responsible for the difference.

THE ARITHMETIC OF WOE

From *Life and Labour of the People in London*

There are two ways of looking even at mere figures by which very different impressions may be produced by the same facts. It may with some show of reason be regarded as not so very bad that a tenth of the population should be reckoned as very poor, in a district so confessedly poverty-stricken as East London; but when we count up the 100,000 individuals, the 20,000 families, who lead so pinched a life among the population described, and remember that there are in addition double that number who, if not actually pressed by want, yet have nothing to spare, we shrink aghast from the picture. The divergence between these two points of view, between relative and absolute, is in itself enough to cause the whole difference between pessimism and optimism. To judge rightly we need to bear both in mind, never to forget the numbers when thinking of the percentages, nor the percentages when thinking of the numbers. This last is difficult to those whose daily experience or whose imagination brings vividly before them the trials and sorrows of individual lives. They refuse to set off and balance the happy hours of the same class, or even of the same people, against these miseries; much less can they consent to bring the lot of other classes into the account, add up the opposing figures, and contentedly carry forward a credit balance. In the arithmetic of woe they can only add or multiply, they cannot subtract or divide. In intensity of feeling such as this, and not in statistics, lies the power to move the world. But by statistics must this power be guided if it would move the world aright.

RAISING THE CURTAIN

From *Life and Labour of the People in London*

East London lay hidden from view behind a curtain on which were painted terrible pictures: Starving children, suffering women, overworked men; horrors of drunkenness and vice; monsters and demons of inhumanity; giants of disease and despair. Did these pictures truly represent what lay behind, or did they bear to the facts a relation similar to that which the pictures outside a booth at some country fair bear to the performance or show within? The writers of this book have each of them at different points, tried to lift this curtain and to see for themselves the world it hid. Agreeing in a common object, they have also agreed to a remarkable extent in the conclusions reached. With very slight variations all tell the same story. No one of them is responsible for what any other has written, but it is scarcely necessary to insist on this. For my own part such a declaration is indeed an empty form, so little do I find in any one of the contributed chapters to which I should not have been perfectly ready to sign my name.

It will be observed that our attempt has in the main been confined to showing how things are. Little is said as to how they come to be as they are, or whither they are tending. The line of inquiry which we have neglected is perhaps more interesting than that which we have taken up, and is certainly more commonly adopted. An inquiry as to tendency appeals controversially, and therefore attractively, to two opposite schools of thought. One of these holds that the condition of the people is becoming year by year more deplorable and its problems more pressing, and casts a backward glance upon some Golden Age of the past; while the other finds on all sides proof of marked improvement, preaches patience as to the evils which still remain, and will say, when pushed, that 'if Golden Age there be, it is today'.

It is manifest that this alternative has an important bearing whether considered simply as a difference of opinion, and so concerning only the on-looker, or positively as a difference of fact. Seen from without, the same habits of life, amount of income, method of expenditure, difficulties, occupations, amusements, will strike the mind of the on-looker with an entirely different meaning according as they are viewed as part of a progress towards a better and higher life, or a descent towards a more miserable and debased existence. Felt from within, a position will be acceptable and even happy on the upward road, which on the downward path may be hardly endurable. The contrast with that to which men have been accustomed is doubtless the principal factor in sensations of well or ill being, content or discontent; but we have also to take account of the relation of the present life, whatever it may be, to the ideal or expectation. It may happen that on the upward path, where, on our hypothesis, contentment ought to reign, the ideal so far outstrips the advance as to produce discontent and even discomfort. Or the opposite may happen, and a slipping downwards be accompanied by a feeling of greater ease, a sense of relief. In all this what is true of the individual is no less true of the class. To interpret aright the life of either we need to lay open its memories and understand its hopes.

Nor have we yet exhausted the complicated relativities which are crowded into the phrase 'point of view'; for we have to take into account the condition of the on-looker's mind and of public sentiment generally, and the changes of feeling that occur, in this or that direction, by which it becomes more sensitive or more callous. On these three points – (1) the relation to past experience; (2) the relation to expectation; (3) the degree of sensitiveness of the public mind – we have room for great gulfs of difference in considering the same facts.

These points apply with varying force to the condition of each class or industry, and to the terms of each problem involved. In a general way, I find that with few exceptions, those who have had a lengthened experience of East London, agree that its state was much worse when they first knew the district than it is now. Beyond this, such glimpses as we can obtain of a remoter past seem to tell a similar story of improvement, and however we test the question the same answer is given; so that I am inclined to think that if an inquiry, such as the present, had been made at any previous time in the history of London, it would have shown a greater proportion of depravity and misery than now exists, and a lower general standard of life . . .

Whatever the miseries of Class A, they are not the result of a too exalted ideal, nor due to any consciousness of degradation. This savage semi-criminal class of people had its golden age in the days when whole districts of London were in their undisputed possession. They mainly desire to be let alone, to be allowed to make an Alsatia of their own. Improvement in our eyes is destruction in theirs. Their discontent is the measure of our success. On the other hand, the impression of horror that the condition of this class makes upon the public mind today is out of all proportion to that made when its actual condition was far worse, and consequently the need to deal with the evils involved becomes more pressing. This, moreover, is no mere question of sentiment, but (if we admit a general all-round improvement) an imperative need of the rising standard of life. What might be an admissible state of things in days past is admissible no longer. It drags us back, and how to put an end to it has become a question of the first importance. The outcasts themselves are sufficiently conscious of this, and opposing, dumbly, the efforts of philanthropy or order, their instinct of self-preservation seeks some undisturbed sanctuary where they can still herd together, and, secured by the mutual protection of each other's character for evil, keep respectability at bay. This it is that must be prevented. No sooner do they make a street their own than it is ripe for destruction and should be destroyed. Destruction of such property involves no general loss. The houses in which they live have, in truth, a negative value, and merely to destroy them is an improvement. The owners may perhaps lose, but there can be no reasonable vested interest in a public nuisance, and the penalty of destruction paid once, might have a wide-spread effect in a clearer recognition of the responsibilities of ownership. A glance at the map will show the extent of the 'black' streets. It does not follow that all of these need to be destroyed, but, even if they were, the total destruction would not be a very serious matter. The numbers of this class are not large. I think the 11,000 (or 1¼ per cent) given in my schedules an ample estimate . . . Persistent dispersion is the policy to be pursued by the State in its contest with them, for to scatter them is necessarily to place them under better influences. The chances for their children, especially, would be better; the hereditary taint less inevitable. Beyond this much would be gained if we could heighten the distinction between them and the lowest industrial class, and put an end to the interchange and give and take which now makes it difficult to draw the line between Classes A and B.

Class A must not be confounded with the criminal classes. Every social grade has its criminals, if not by conviction, at least by character. Of these the lowest grade mix freely with Class A, and are not to be distinguished from it. But there are many of Class A who are not criminals, as well as plenty of criminals who have nothing to do with Class A. It would be interesting to study the sources of crime by analysing the criminal classes, but this would have to be done for the whole of London. It is not particularly an East End subject.

William Booth

William Booth (1829–1919), the founder of the Salvation Army, was born in Nottingham where his father was a speculative builder. At the age of thirteen, on the failure of his father's business, he was apprenticed to a pawnbroker. He became a Methodist in 1844 and moved to London where he once again worked for a pawnbroker, but in 1861, with his wife Catherine, he began the revivalist movement that was to develop into the Salvation Army. In the early stages of the Army emphasis was placed almost entirely on the saving of souls through personal conversion, but experience led Booth to believe that his religious campaign could never be entirely successful unless combined with attempts to alleviate poverty. *In Darkest England and the Way Out* (1890) outlines the way this is to be achieved. The heightened style of the book comes from W. T. Stead, the crusading editor of the *Pall Mall Gazette*, who helped Booth to write it. In this as in the other social issues publicized by Stead, which included the notorious 'Maiden Tribute' campaign and *The Bitter Cry of Outcast London*, the social explorer tradition is combined with the techniques and methods of modern journalism. The greater part of *Darkest England* is concerned with Booth's plans to solve the problem of poverty by work colonies; the extracts included here are taken from the more general introductory chapters.

WHY DARKEST ENGLAND?

From In Darkest England and the Way Out

This summer the attention of the civilised world has been arrested by the story which Mr Stanley has told of 'Darkest Africa' and his journeyings across the heart of the Lost

Continent. In all that spirited narrative of heroic endeavour, nothing has so much impressed the imagination as his description of the immense forest, which offered an almost impenetrable barrier to his advance. The intrepid explorer, in his own phrase, 'marched, tore, ploughed, and cut his way for one hundred and sixty days through this inner womb of the true tropical forest'. The mind of man with difficulty endeavours to realise this immensity of wooded wilderness, covering a territory half as large again as the whole of France, where the rays of the sun never penetrate, where in the dark, dank air, filled with the steam of the heated morass, human beings dwarfed into pygmies and brutalised into cannibals lurk and live and die. Mr Stanley vainly endeavours to bring home to us the full horror of that awful gloom. He says:

Take a thick Scottish copse dripping with rain; imagine this to be a mere undergrowth nourished under the impenetrable shade of ancient trees ranging from 100 to 180 feet high; briars and thorns abundant; lazy creeks meandering through the depths of the jungle, and sometimes a deep affluent of a great river. Imagine this forest and jungle in all stages of decay and growth, rain pattering on you every other day of the year; an impure atmosphere with its dread consequences, fever and dysentery; gloom throughout the day and darkness almost palpable throughout the night; and then if you can imagine such a forest extending the entire distance from Plymouth to Peterhead, you will have a fair idea of some of the inconveniences endured by us in the Congo forest.

The denizens of this region are filled with a conviction that the forest is endless – interminable. In vain did Mr Stanley and his companions endeavour to convince them that outside the dreary wood were to be found sunlight, pasturage and peaceful meadows.

They replied in a manner that seemed to imply that we must be strange creatures to suppose that it would be possible for any world to exist save their illimitable forest. 'No,' they replied, shaking their heads compassionately, and pitying our absurd questions, 'all like this,' and they moved their hands sweepingly to illustrate that the world was all alike, nothing but trees, trees and trees – great trees rising as high as an arrow shot to the sky, lifting their crowns, intertwining their branches, pressing and crowding one against the other, until neither the sunbeam nor shaft of light can penetrate it.

'We entered the forest,' says Mr Stanley, 'with confidence; forty pioneers in front with axes and bill-hooks to clear a path through the obstructions, praying that God and good fortune would lead us.' But before the conviction of the forest dwellers that the forest was without end, hope faded out of the hearts of the natives of Stanley's company. The men became sodden with despair, preaching was useless to move their brooding sullenness, their morbid gloom.

The little religion they knew was nothing more than legendary lore, and in their memories there dimly floated a story of a land which grew darker and darker as one travelled towards the end of the earth and drew nearer to the place where a great serpent lay supine and coiled round the whole world. Ah! then the ancients must have referred to this, where the light is so ghastly, and the woods are endless, and are so still and solemn and grey; to this oppressive loneliness, amid so much life, which is so chilling to the poor distressed heart; and the horror grew darker with their fancies; the cold of early morning, the comfortless grey of dawn, the dead white mist, the ever-dripping tears of the dew, the deluging rains, the appalling thunder bursts and the echoes, and the wonderful play of the dazzling lightning. And when the night comes with its thick palpable darkness, and they lie huddled in their damp little huts, and they hear the tempest overhead, and the howling of the wild winds, the grinding and groaning of the storm-tost trees, and the dread sounds of the falling giants, and the shock of the trembling earth which sends their hearts with fitful leaps to their throats, and the roaring and a rushing as of a mad overwhelming sea – oh, then the horror is intensified! When the march has begun once again, and the files are slowly moving through the woods, they renew their morbid broodings, and ask themselves: How long is this to last? Is the joy of life to end thus? Must we jog on day after day in this cheerless gloom and this joyless duskiness, until we stagger and fall and rot among the toads? Then they disappear into the woods by twos, and threes, and sixes; and after the caravan has passed they return by the trail, some to reach Yambuya and upset the young officers with their tales of woe and war; some to fall sobbing under a spear-thrust; some to wander and stray in the dark mazes of the woods, hopelessly lost; and some to be carved for the cannibal feast. And those who remain compelled to it by fears of greater danger, mechanically march on, a prey to dread and weakness.

That is the forest. But what of its denizens? They are comparatively few; only some hundreds of thousands living in small tribes from ten to thirty miles apart, scattered over an area on which ten thousand million trees put out the sun from a region four times as wide as Great Britain. Of these pygmies there are two kinds: one a very degraded specimen with ferretlike eyes, close-set nose, more nearly approaching the baboon than was supposed to be possible, but very human; the other very handsome, with frank, open, innocent features, very prepossessing. They are quick and intelligent, capable of deep affection and gratitude, showing remarkable industry and patience. A pygmy boy of eighteen worked with consuming zeal; time with him was too precious to waste in talk. His mind seemed ever concentrated on work. Mr Stanley said:

'When I once stopped him to ask him his name, his face seemed to say, "Please don't stop me. I must finish my task."

'All alike, the baboon variety and the handsome innocents, are cannibals. They are possessed with a perfect mania for meat. We were obliged to bury our dead in the river, lest the bodies be exhumed and eaten, even when they had died from smallpox.'

Upon the pygmies and all the dwellers of the forest has descended a devastating visitation in the shape of the ivory raiders of civilisation. The race that wrote the Arabian Nights, built Bagdad and Granada, and invented Algebra, sends forth men with the hunger for gold in their hearts, and Enfield muskets in their hands, to plunder and to slay. They exploit the domestic affections of the forest dwellers in order to strip them of all they possess in the world. That has been going on for years. It is going on today. It has come to be regarded as the natural and normal law of existence. Of the religion of these hunted pygmies Mr Stanley tells us nothing, perhaps because there is nothing to tell. But an earlier traveller, Dr Kraff, says that one of these tribes, by name Doko, had some notion of a Supreme Being, to whom, under the name of Yer, they sometimes addressed prayers in moments of sadness or terror. In these prayers they say : 'Oh Yer, if Thou dost really exist why dost Thou let us be slaves? We ask not for food or clothing, for we live on snakes, ants, and mice. Thou hast made us, wherefore dost Thou let us be trodden down?'

It is a terrible picture, and one that has engraved itself deep on the heart of civilisation. But while brooding over the awful presentation of life as it exists in the vast African forest, it seemed to me only too vivid a picture of many parts of our own land. As there is a darkest Africa is there not also a darkest England? Civilisation, which can breed its own barbarians, does it not also breed its own pygmies? May we not find a parallel at our own doors, and discover within a stone's throw of our cathedrals and palaces similar horrors to those which Stanley has found existing in the great Equatorial forest?

The more the mind dwells upon the subject, the closer the analogy appears. The ivory raiders who brutally traffic in the unfortunate denizens of the forest glades, what are they but the publicans who flourish on the weakness of our poor? The two tribes of savages, the human baboon and the handsome dwarf, who will not speak lest it impede him in his task, may be accepted as the two varieties who are continually present with us – the vicious, lazy lout, and the toiling slave. They, too, have lost all faith of life being other than it is and has been. As in Africa, it is all trees, trees, trees with no other world conceivable; so is it here – it is all vice and poverty and crime. To many the world is all slum, with the Workhouse as an intermediate purgatory before the grave. And just as Mr Stanley's Zanzibaris lost faith, and could only be induced to plod on in brooding sullenness of dull despair, so the most of our social reformers, no matter how cheerily they may have started off, with forty pioneers swinging blithely their axes as they force their way into the wood, soon become depressed and despairing. Who can battle against the ten thousand million trees? Who can hope to make headway against the innumerable adverse conditions which doom the dweller in Darkest England to eternal and immutable misery? What wonder is it that many of the warmest hearts and enthusiastic workers feel disposed to repeat the lament of the old English chronicler, who, speaking of the evil days which fell upon our forefathers in the reign of Stephen, said, 'It seemed to them as if God and his Saints were dead.'

An analogy is as good as a suggestion; it becomes wearisome when it is pressed too far. But before leaving it, think for a moment how close the parellel is, and how strange it is that so much interest should be excited by a narrative of human squalor and human heroism in a distant continent, while greater squalor and heroism not less magnificent may be observed at our very doors.

The Equatorial Forest traversed by Stanley resembles that Darkest England of which I have to speak, alike in its vast extent – both stretch, in Stanley's phrase, 'as far as from Plymouth to Peterhead'; its monotonous darkness, its malaria and its gloom, its dwarfish de-humanized inhabitants, the slavery to which they are subjected, their privations and their misery. That which sickens the stoutest heart, and causes many of our bravest and best to fold their hands in despair, is the apparent impossibility of doing more than merely to peck at the outside of the endless tangle of monotonous undergrowth; to let light into it, to make a road clear through it, that shall not be immediately choked up by the ooze of the morass and the luxuriant parasitical growth of the forest – who dare hope for that? At present, alas, it would seem as though no one dares even to hope! It is the great Slough of Despond of our time.

And what a slough it is no man can gauge who has not waded therein, as some of us have done, up to the very neck for long years. Talk about Dante's Hell, and all the horrors and cruelties of the torture-chamber of the lost! The man who walks with open eyes and with bleeding heart through the shambles of our civilisation needs no such fantastic images of the poet to teach him horror. Often and often, when I have seen the young and the poor and the helpless go down before my eyes into the morass, trampled underfoot by beasts of prey in human shape that haunt these regions, it seemed as if God were no longer in His world, but that in His stead reigned a fiend, merciless as Hell, ruthless as the grave. Hard it is, no doubt, to read in Stanley's pages of the slave-traders coldly arranging for the surprise of a village, the capture of the inhabitants, the massacre of those who resist, and the violation of all the women; but the stony streets of London, if they could but speak, would tell of tragedies as awful, of ruin as complete, of ravishments as horrible, as if we were in Central Africa; only the ghastly devastation is covered, corpselike, with the artificialities and hypocrisies of modern civilisation.

The lot of a Negress in the Equatorial Forest is not, perhaps, a very happy one; but is it so very much worse than that of many a pretty orphan girl in our Christian capital? We talk about the brutalities of the Dark Ages, and we profess to shudder as we read in books of the shameful exaction of the rights of feudal superior. And yet here, beneath our very eyes, in our theatres, in our restaurants, and in many other places, unspeakable though it be but to name it, the same hideous abuse flourishes unchecked. A young penniless girl, if she be pretty, is often hunted from pillar to post by her employers, confronted always by the alternative – Starve or Sin. And when once the poor girl has consented to buy the right to earn her living by the sacrifice of her virtue, then she is treated as a slave and an outcast by the very men who have ruined her. Her word becomes unbelievable, her life an ignominy, and she is swept downward, ever downward, into the bottomless perdition of prostitution. But there, even in the lowest depths, excommunicated by Humanity and outcast from God, she is far nearer the pitying heart of the One true Saviour than all the men who forced her down, aye, and than all the Pharisees and Scribes who stand silently by while these fiendish wrongs are perpetrated before their very eyes.

The blood boils with impotent rage at the sight of these

enormities, callously inflicted, and silently borne by these miserable victims. Nor is it only women who are the victims, although their fate is the most tragic. Those firms which reduce sweating to a fine art, who systematically and deliberately defraud the workman of his pay, who grind the faces of the poor, and who rob the widow and the orphan, and who for a pretence make great professions of public-spirit and philanthropy, these men nowadays are sent to Parliament to make laws for the people. The old prophets sent them to Hell – but we have changed all that. They send their victims to Hell, and are rewarded by all that wealth can do to make their lives comfortable. Read the House of Lords' Report on the Sweating System, and ask if any African slave system, making due allowance for the superior civilisation, and therefore sensitiveness, of the victims, reveals more misery.

Darkest England, like Darkest Africa, reeks with malaria. The foul and fetid breath of our slums is almost as poisonous as that of the African swamp. Fever is almost as chronic there as on the Equator. Every year thousands of children are killed off by what is called defects of our sanitary system. They are in reality starved and poisoned, and all that can be said is that, in many cases, it is better for them that they were taken away from the trouble to come.

Just as in Darkest Africa it is only a part of the evil and misery that comes from the superior race who invade the forest to enslave and massacre its miserable inhabitants, so with us, much of the misery of those whose lot we are considering arises from their own habits. Drunkenness and all manner of uncleanness, moral and physical, abound. Have you ever watched by the bedside of a man in delirium tremens? Multiply the sufferings of that one drunkard by the hundred thousand, and you have some idea of what scenes are being witnessed in all our great cities at this moment. As in Africa streams intersect the forest in every direction, so the gin-shop stands at every corner with its River of the Water of Death flowing seventeen hours out of the twenty-four for the destruction of the people. A population sodden with drink, steeped in vice, eaten up by every social and physical malady, these are the denizens of Darkest England amidst whom my life has been spent, and to whose rescue I would now summon all that is best in the manhood and womanhood of our land.

But this book is no mere lamentation of despair. For Darkest England, as for Darkest Africa, there is a light beyond. I think I see my way out, a way by which these wretched ones may escape from the gloom of their miserable existence into a higher and happier life. Long wandering in the Forest of the Shadow of Death at our doors has familiarised me with its horrors; but while the realisation is a vigorous spur to action it has never been so oppressive as to extinguish hope. Mr Stanley never succumbed to the terrors which oppressed his followers. He had lived in a larger life, and knew that the forest, though long, was not interminable. Every step forward brought him nearer his destined goal, nearer to the light of the sun, the clear sky, and the rolling uplands of the grazing land. Therefore he did not despair. The Equatorial Forest was, after all, a mere corner of one quarter of the world. In the knowledge of the light outside, in the confidence begotten by past experience of successful endeavour, he pressed forward; and when the 160 days' struggle was over, he and his men came out into a pleasant place where the land smiled with peace and plenty, and their hardships and hunger were forgotten in the joy of a great deliverance.

So I venture to believe it will be with us. But the end is not yet. We are still in the depths of the depressing gloom. It is in no spirit of light-heartedness that this book is sent forth into the world. The magnitude of the evils and the difficulty of dealing with them are immense.

If this were the first time that this wail of hopeless misery had sounded on our ears the matter would have been less serious. It is because we have heard it so often that the case is so desperate. The exceeding bitter cry of the disinherited has become to be as familiar in the ears of men as the dull roar of the streets or as the moaning of the wind through the trees. And so it rises unceasing, year in and year out, and we are too busy or too idle, too indifferent or too selfish, to spare it a thought. Only now and then, on rare occasions, when some clear voice is heard giving more articulate utterance to the miseries of the miserable men, do we pause in the

regular routine of our daily duties, and shudder as we realise
for one brief moment what life means to the inmates of the
Slums. But one of the grimmest social problems of our time
should be sternly faced, not with a view to the generation of
profitless emotion, but with a view to its solution.

Is it not time? There is, it is true, an audacity in the mere
suggestion that the problem is not insoluble that is enough
to take away the breath. But can nothing be done? If, after
full and exhaustive consideration, we come to the deliberate
conclusion that nothing can be done, and that it is the inevitable and inexorable destiny of thousands of Englishmen to be
brutalised into worse than beasts by the condition of their
environment, so be it. But if, on the contrary, we are unable
to believe that this 'awful slough', which engulfs the manhood
and womanhood of generation after generation, is incapable
of removal; and if the heart and intellect of mankind alike
revolt against the fatalism of despair, then, indeed, it is time,
and high time, that the question were faced in no mere dilet-
tante spirit, but with a resolute determination to make an end
of the crying scandal of our age.

What a satire it is upon our Christianity and our civilisation,
that the existence of these colonies of heathens and savages
in the heart of our capital should attract so little attention!
It is no better than a ghastly mockery – theologians might use
a stronger word – to call by the name of One who came to
seek and to save that which was lost those Churches which
in the midst of lost multitudes either sleep in apathy or display
a fitful interest in a chasuble. Why all this apparatus of temples
and meeting-houses to save men from perdition in a world
which is to come, while never a helping hand is stretched out
to save them from the inferno of their present life? Is it not
time that, forgetting for a moment their wranglings about the
infinitely little or infinitely obscure, they should concentrate
all their energies on a united effort to break this terrible
perpetuity of perdition, and to rescue some at least of those
for whom they profess to believe their Founder came to die?

Before venturing to define the remedy, I begin by describing
the malady. But even when presenting the dreary picture of
our social ills, and describing the difficulties which confront
us, I speak not in despondency but in hope. 'I know in whom

I have believed.' I know, therefore do I speak. Darker England is but a fractional part of 'Greater England'. There is wealth enough abundantly to minister to its social regeneration so far as wealth can, if there be but heart enough to set about the work in earnest. And I hope and believe that the heart will not be lacking when once the problem is manfully faced, and the method of its solution plainly pointed out.

THE SUBMERGED TENTH

From In Darkest England and the Way Out

In setting forth the difficulties which have to be grappled with, I shall endeavour in all things to understate rather than over-state my case. I do this for two reasons: first, any exaggeration would create a reaction: and secondly, as my object is to demonstrate the practicability of solving the problem, I do not wish to magnify its dimensions. In this and in subsequent chapters I hope to convince those who read them that there is no overstraining in the representation of the facts, and nothing Utopian in the presentation of remedies. I appeal neither to hysterical emotionalists nor headlong enthusiasts; but having tried to approach the examination of this question in a spirit of scientific investigation, I put forth my proposals with the view of securing the support and co-operation of the sober, serious, practical men and women who constitute the saving strength and moral backbone of the country. I fully admit that there is much that is lacking in the diagnosis of the disease, and, no doubt, in this first draft of the prescription there is much room for improvement, which will come when we have the light of fuller experience. But with all its draw-backs and defects, I do not hesitate to submit my proposals to the impartial judgment of all who are interested in the solution of the social question as an immediate and practical mode of dealing with this, the greatest problem of our time.

The first duty of an investigator in approaching the study of any question is to eliminate all that is foreign to the inquiry, and to concentrate his attention upon the subject to be dealt with. Here I may remark that I make no attempt in this book to deal with Society as a whole. I leave to others the formulation of ambitious programmes for the reconstruction of our entire social system; not because I may not desire its reconstruction, but because the elaboration of any plans which are more or less visionary and incapable of realisation for many years would stand in the way of the consideration of this Scheme for dealing with the most urgently pressing aspect of the question, which I hope may be put into operation at once.

In taking this course I am aware that I cut myself off from a wide and attractive field; but as a practical man, dealing with sternly prosaic facts, I must confine my attention to that particular section of the problem which clamours most pressingly for a solution. Only one thing I may say in passing. There is nothing in my scheme which will bring it into collision either with Socialists of the State, or Socialists of the Municipality, with Individualists or Nationalists, or any of the various schools of thought in the great field of social economics – excepting only those anti-Christian economists who hold that it is an offence against the doctrine of the survival of the fittest to try to save the weakest from going to the wall, and who believe that when once a man is down the supreme duty of a self-regarding Society is to jump upon him. Such economists will naturally be disappointed with this book. I venture to believe that all others will find nothing in it to offend their favourite theories, but perhaps something of helpful suggestion which they may utilise hereafter.

What, then, is Darkest England? For whom do we claim that 'urgency' which gives their case priority over that of all other sections of their countrymen and countrywomen?

I claim it for the Lost, for the Outcast, for the Disinherited of the World.

These, it may be said, are but phrases. Who are the Lost? I reply, not in a religious, but in a social sense, the lost are those who have gone under, who have lost their foothold in Society, those to whom the prayer to our Heavenly Father, 'Give us day by day our daily bread', is either unfulfilled, or only fulfilled by the Devil's agency: by the earnings of vice, the proceeds of crime, or the contribution enforced by the threat of the law.

But I will be more precise. The denizens in Darkest England, for whom I appeal, are (1) those who, having no capital or income of their own, would in a month be dead from sheer starvation were they exclusively dependent upon the money earned by their own work; and (2) those who by their utmost exertions are unable to attain the regulation allowance of food which the law prescribes as indispensable even for the worst criminals in our gaols.

I sorrowfully admit that it would be Utopian in our present social arrangements to dream of attaining for every honest Englishman a gaol standard of all the necessaries of life. Some time, perhaps, we may venture to hope that every honest worker on English soil will always be as warmly clad, as healthily housed, and as regularly fed as our criminal convicts — but that is not yet.

Neither is it possible to hope for many years to come that human beings generally will be as well cared for as horses. Mr Carlyle long ago remarked that the four-footed worker has already got all that this two-handed one is clamouring for: 'There are not many horses in England, able and willing to work, which have not due food and lodging and go about sleek coated, satisfied in heart.' You say it is impossible; but, said Carlyle, 'The human brain, looking at these sleek English horses, refused to believe in such impossibility for English men.' Nevertheless, forty years have passed since Carlyle said that, and we seem to be no nearer the attainment of the four-footed standard for the two-handed worker. 'Perhaps it might be nearer realisation,' growls the cynic, 'if we could only produce men according to demand, as we do horses, and promptly send them to the slaughter-house when past their prime' — which, of course, is not to be thought of.

What, then, is the standard towards which we may venture to aim with some prospect of realisation in our time? It is a very humble one, but if realised it would solve the worst problems of modern Society.

It is the standard of the London Cab Horse.

When in the streets of London a Cab Horse, weary or careless or stupid, trips and falls and lies stretched out in the midst of the traffic, there is no question of debating how he came to stumble before we try to get him on his legs again. The

Cab Horse is a very real illustration of poor broken-down humanity; he usually falls down because of overwork and underfeeding. If you put him on his feet without altering his conditions, it would only be to give him another dose of agony; but first of all you'll have to pick him up again. It may have been through overwork or underfeeding, or it may have been all his own fault that he has broken his knees and smashed the shafts, but that does not matter. If not for his own sake, then merely in order to prevent an obstruction of the traffic, all attention is concentrated upon the question of how we are to get him on his legs again. The load is taken off, the harness is unbuckled, or, if need be, cut, and everything is done to help him up. Then he is put in the shafts again and once more restored to his regular round of work. That is the first point. The second is that every Cab Horse in London has three things: a shelter for the night, food for its stomach, and work allotted to it by which it can earn its corn.

These are the two points of the Cab Horse's Charter. When he is down he is helped up, and while he lives he has food, shelter and work. That, although a humble standard, is at present absolutely unattainable by millions – literally by millions – of our fellow-men and women in this country. Can the Cab Horse Charter be gained for human beings? I answer, yes. The Cab Horse standard can be attained on the Cab Horse terms. If you get your fallen fellow on his feet again, Docility and Discipline will enable you to reach the Cab Horse ideal, otherwise it will remain unattainable. But Docility seldom fails where Discipline is intelligently maintained. Intelligence is more frequently lacking to direct, than obedience to follow direction. At any rate it is not for those who possess the intelligence to despair of obedience, until they have done their part. Some, no doubt, like the bucking horse that will never be broken in, will always refuse to submit to any guidance but their own lawless will. They will remain either the Ishmaels or the Sloths of Society. But man is naturally neither an Ishmael nor a Sloth.

The first question, then, which confronts us is, what are the dimensions of the Evil? How many of our fellow-men dwell in this Darkest England? How can we take the census of those who have fallen below the Cab Horse standard to which it is our aim to elevate the most wretched of our countrymen?

The moment you attempt to answer this question, you are confronted by the fact that the Social Problem has scarcely been studied at all scientifically. Go to Mudie's and ask for all the books that have been written on the subject, and you will be surprised to find how few there are. There are probably more scientific books treating of diabetes or of gout than there are dealing with the great social malady which eats out the vitals of such numbers of our people. Of late there has been a change for the better. The Report of the Royal Commission on the Housing of the Poor, and the Report of the Committee of the House of Lords on Sweating, represent an attempt at least to ascertain the facts which bear upon the Condition of the People question. But, after all, more minute, patient, intelligent observation has been devoted to the study of Earthworms than to the evolution, or rather the degradation, of the Sunken Section of our people. Here and there in the immense field individual workers make notes, and occasionally emit a wail of despair, but where is there any attempt even so much as to take the first preliminary step of counting those who have gone under?

One book there is, and so far as I know at present, only one, which even attempts to enumerate the destitute. In his *Life and Labour in the East of London*, Mr Charles Booth attempts to form some kind of an idea as to the numbers of those with whom we have to deal. With a large staff of assistants, and provided with all the facts in possession of the School Board Visitors, Mr Booth took an industrial census of East London. This district, which comprises Tower Hamlets, Shoreditch, Bethnal Green and Hackney, contains a population of 908,000; that is to say, less than one-fourth of the population of London.

How do his statistics work out? If we estimate the number of the poorest class in the rest of London as being twice as numerous as those in the Eastern District, instead of being thrice as numerous, as they would be if they were calculated according to the population in the same proportion, the following is the result:

PAUPERS	East London	Estimate for rest of London	Total
Inmates of Workhouses, Asylums and Hospitals	17,000	34,000	51,000
HOMELESS			
Loafers, Casuals, and some Criminals	11,000	22,000	33,000
STARVING			
Casual earnings between 18s. per week and chronic want	100,000	200,000	300,000
THE VERY POOR.			
Intermittent earnings 18s. to 21s. per week	74,000	148,000	222,000
Small regular earnings 18s. to 21s. per week	129,000	258,000	387,000
	331,000	662,000	993,000
Regular wages, artizans, etc. 22s. to 30s. per week	377,000		
Higher class labour, 30s. to 50s. per week	121,000		
Lower middle class, shopkeepers, clerks, etc	34,000		
Upper middle class (servant keepers)	45,000		
	908,000		

It may be admitted that East London affords an exceptionally bad district from which to generalise for the rest of the country. Wages are higher in London than elsewhere, but so is rent, and the number of the homeless and starving is greater in the human warren at the East End. There are 31 millions of people in Great Britain, exclusive of Ireland. If destitution existed everywhere in East London proportions, there would be 31 times as many homeless and starving people as there are in the district round Bethnal Green.

But let us suppose that the East London rate is double the

average for the rest of the country. That would bring out the
following figures:

HOUSELESS

	East London	United Kingdom
Loafers, Casuals, and some Criminals	11,000	165,500
STARVING		
Casual earnings or chronic want	100,000	1,550,000
Total Houseless and Starving	111,000	1,715,500
In Workhouses, Asylums, &c.	17,000	190,000
	128,000	1,905,500

Of those returned as homeless and starving, 870,000 were
in receipt of outdoor relief.

To these must be added the inmates of our prisons. In 1889,
174,779 persons were received in the prisons, but the average
number in prison at any one time did not exceed 60,000. The
figures, as given in the Prison Returns, are as follows:

In Convict Prisons	11,660
In Local Prisons	20,883
In Reformatories	1,270
In Industrial Schools	21,413
Criminal Lunatics	910
	56,136

Add to this the number of indoor paupers and lunatics
(excluding criminals) 78,966 – and we have an army of nearly
two millions belonging to the submerged classes. To this there
must be added, at the very least, another million, representing
those dependent upon the criminal, lunatic and other classes,
not enumerated here, and the more or less helpless of the class
immediately above the houseless and starving. This brings my
total to three millions, or, to put it roughly to one-tenth of
the population. According to Lord Brabazon and Mr Samuel
Smith, 'between two and three millions of our population
are always pauperised and degraded'. Mr Chamberlain says
there is a 'population equal to that of the metropolis [that is,
between four and five millions] which has remained constantly

in a state of abject destitution and misery'. Mr Giffen is more moderate. The submerged class, according to him, comprises one in five of manual labourers, six in 100 of the population. Mr Giffen does not add the third million which is living on the border line. Between Mr Chamberlain's four millions and a half, and Mr Giffen's 1,800,000, I am content to take three millions as representing the total strength of the destitute army.

Darkest England, then, may be said to have a population about equal to that of Scotland, Three million men, women and children, a vast despairing multitude in a condition nominally free, but really enslaved – these it is whom we have to save.

It is a large order. England emancipated her Negroes sixty years ago, at a cost of £40,000,000, and has never ceased boasting about it since. But at our own doors, from 'Plymouth to Peterhead', stretches this waste Continent of humanity – three million human beings who are enslaved – some of them to taskmasters as merciless as any West Indian overseer, all of them to destitution and despair.

Is anything to be done with them? Can anything be done for them? Or is this million-headed mass to be regarded as offering a problem as insoluble as that of the London sewage, which, feculent and festering, swings heavily up and down the basin of the Thames with the ebb and flow of the tide?

This Submerged Tenth – is it, then, beyond the reach of the nine-tenths in the midst of whom they live, and around whose homes they rot and die? No doubt, in every large mass of human beings there will be some incurably diseased in morals and in body, some for whom nothing can be done, some of whom even the optimist must despair, and for whom he can prescribe nothing but the beneficently stern restraints of an asylum or a gaol.

But is not one in ten a proportion scandalously high? The Israelites of old set apart one tribe in twelve to minister to the Lord in the service of the Temple; but must we doom one in ten of 'God's Englishmen' to the service of the great Twin Devils – Destitution and Despair?

THE HOMELESS

From *In Darkest England and the Way Out*

Darkest England may be described as consisting broadly of three circles, one within the other. The outer and widest circle is inhabited by the starving and the homeless, but honest, Poor. The second by those who live by Vice; and the third and innermost region at the centre is peopled by those who exist by Crime. The whole of the three circles is sodden with Drink. Darkest England has many more public-houses than the Forest of the Aruwimi has rivers, of which Mr Stanley sometimes had to cross three in half-an-hour.

The borders of this great lost land are not sharply defined. They are continually expanding or contracting. Whenever there is a period of depression in trade, they stretch; when prosperity returns, they contract. So far as individuals are concerned, there are none among the hundreds of thousands who live upon the outskirts of the dark forest who can truly say that they or their children are secure from being hopelessly entangled in its labyrinth. The death of the bread-winner, a long illness, a failure in the City, or any one of a thousand other causes which might be named, will bring within the first circle those who at present imagine themselves free from all danger of actual want. The death-rate in Darkest England is high. Death is the great gaol-deliverer of the captives. But the dead are hardly in the grave before their places are taken by others. Some escape, but the majority, their health sapped by their surroundings, become weaker and weaker, until at last they fall by the way, perishing without hope at the very doors of the palatial mansion which, maybe, some of them helped to build.

Some seven years ago a great outcry was made concerning the Housing of the Poor. Much was said, and rightly said – it could not be said too strongly – concerning the disease-breeding, manhood-destroying character of many of the tenements in which the poor herd in our large cities. But there is a depth below that of the dweller in the slums. It is that of the dweller in the street, who has not even a lair in the slums

which he can call his own. The houseless Out-of-Work is in
one respect at least like Him of whom it was said, 'Foxes have
holes, and birds of the air have nests, but the Son of Man
hath not where to lay His head.'

The existence of these unfortunates was somewhat rudely
forced upon the attention of Society in 1887, when Trafalgar
Square became the camping ground of the Homeless Outcasts
of London. Our Shelters have done something, but not enough,
to provide for the outcasts, who this night and every night
are walking about the streets, not knowing where they can
find a spot on which to rest their weary frames.

Here is the return of one of my Officers who was told off
this summer to report upon the actual condition of the Homeless who have no roof to shelter them in all London :

There are still a large number of Londoners and a considerable percentage of wanderers from the country in search of
work, who find themselves at nightfall destitute. These now
betake themselves to the seats under the plane trees on the
Embankment. Formerly they endeavoured to occupy all the
seats, but the lynx-eyed Metropolitan Police declined to allow
any such proceedings, and the dossers, knowing the invariable kindness of the City Police, made tracks for that portion
of the Embankment which, lying east of the Temple, comes
under the control of the Civic Fathers. Here, between the
Temple and Blackfriars, I found the poor wretches by the
score; almost every seat contained its full complement of
six – some men, some women – all reclining in various pos-
tures and nearly all fast asleep. Just as Big Ben strikes two,
the moon, flashing across the Thames and lighting up the
stone work of the Embankment, brings into relief a pitiable
spectacle. Here on the stone abutments, which afford a
slight protection from the biting wind, are scores of men
lying side by side, huddled together for warmth, and of
course, without any other covering than their ordinary
clothing, which is scanty enough at the best. Some have
laid down a few pieces of waste paper, by way of taking
the chill off the stones, but the majority are too tired, even
for that, and the nightly toilet of most consists of first
removing the hat, swathing the head in whatever old rag

may be doing duty as a handkerchief, and then replacing the hat.

The intelligent-looking elderly man, who was just fixing himself up on a seat, informed me that he frequently made that his night's abode. 'You see,' quoth he, 'there's nowhere else so comfortable. I was here last night, and Monday and Tuesday as well, that's four nights this week. I had no money for lodgings, couldn't earn any, try as I might. I've had one bit of bread today, nothing else whatever, and I've earned nothing today or yesterday; I had threepence the day before. Gets my living by carrying parcels, or minding horses, or odd jobs of that sort. You see I haven't got my health, that's where it is. I used to work on the London General Omnibus Company and after that on the Road Car Company, but I had to go to the infirmary with bronchitis and couldn't get work after that. What's the good of a man what's got bronchitis and just left the infirmary? Who'll engage him, I'd like to know? Besides, it makes me short of breath at times, and I can't do much. I'm a widower; wife died long ago. I have one boy, abroad, a sailor, but he's only lately started and can't help me. Yes! it's very fair out here of nights, seat's rather hard, but a bit of waste paper makes it a lot softer. We have women sleep here often, and children, too. They're very well conducted, and there's seldom many rows here, you see, because everybody's tired out. We're too sleepy to make a row.'

Another party, a tall, dull, helpless-looking individual, had walked up from the country; would prefer not to mention the place. He had hoped to have obtained a hospital letter at the Mansion House so as to obtain a truss for a bad rupture, but failing, had tried various other places, also in vain, winding up minus money or food on the Embankment.

In addition to these sleepers, a considerable number walk about the streets up till the early hours of the morning to hunt up some job which will bring a copper into the empty exchequer, and save them from actual starvation. I had some conversation with one such, a stalwart youth lately discharged from the militia, and unable to get work.

'You see,' said he, pitifully, 'I don't know my way about like most of the London fellows. I'm so green, and don't know how to pick up jobs like they do. I've been walking the streets almost day and night these two weeks and can't get work. I've got the strength, though I shan't have it long at this rate. I only want a job. This is the third night running that I've walked the streets all night; the only money I get is by minding blacking-boys' boxes while they go into Lockhart's for their dinner. I got a penny yesterday at it, and twopence for carrying a parcel, and today I've had a penny. Bought a ha'porth of bread and a ha'penny mug of tea.'

Poor lad! probably he would soon get into thieves' company, and sink into the depths, for there is no other means of living for many like him; it is starve or steal, even for the young. There are gangs of lad thieves in the low Whitechapel lodging-houses, varying in age from thirteen to fifteen, who live by thieving eatables and other easily obtained goods from shop fronts.

In addition to the Embankment, *al fresco* lodgings are found in the seats outside Spitalfields Church, and many homeless wanderers have their own little nooks and corners of resort in many sheltered yards, vans, etc., all over London. Two poor women I observed making their home in a shop doorway in Liverpool Street. Thus they manage in the summer; what it's like in winter time is terrible to think of. In many cases it means the pauper's grave, as in the case of a young woman who was wont to sleep in a van in Bedfordbury. Some men who were aware of her practice surprised her by dashing a bucket of water on her. The blow to her weak system caused illness, and the inevitable sequel – a coroner's jury came to the conclusion that the water only hastened her death, which was due, in plain English, to starvation.

The following are some statements taken down by the same Officer from twelve men whom he found sleeping on the Embankment on the nights of June 13th and 14th, 1890:

No. 1. 'I've slept here two nights; I'm a confectioner by trade; I come from Dartford. I got turned off because I'm getting elderly. They can get young men cheaper, and I have the rheumatism so bad. I've earned nothing these two days; I thought I could get a job at Woolwich, so I walked there, but could get nothing. I found a bit of bread in the road wrapped up in a bit of newspaper. That did me for yesterday. I had a bit of bread and butter today. I'm 54 years old. When it's wet we stand about all night under the arches.'

No. 2. 'Been sleeping out three weeks all but one night; do odd jobs, mind horses, and that sort of thing. Earned nothing today, or shouldn't be here. Have had a pen'orth of bread today. That's all. Yesterday had some pieces given to me at a cook-shop. Two days last week had nothing at all from morning till night. By trade I'm a feather-bed dresser, but it's gone out of fashion, and besides that, I've a cataract in one eye, and have lost the sight of it completely. I'm a widower, have one child, a soldier, at Dover. My last regular work was eight months ago, but the firm broke. Been doing odd jobs since.'

No. 3. 'I'm a tailor; have slept here four nights running. Can't get work. Been out of a job three weeks. If I can muster cash I sleep at a lodging-house in Vere Street, Clare Market. It was very wet last night. I left these seats and went to Covent Garden Market and slept under cover. There were about thirty of us. The police moved us on, but we went back as soon as they had gone. I've had a pen'orth of bread and pen'orth of soup during the last two days – often goes without altogether. There are women sleep out here. They are decent people, mostly charwomen and such like who can't get work.'

No. 4. Elderly man; trembles visibly with excitement at mention of work; produces a card carefully wrapped in old newspaper, to the effect that Mr J. R. is a member of the Trade Protection League. He is a waterside labourer; last job at that was a fortnight since. Has earned nothing for five days. Had a bit of bread this morning, but not a scrap since. Had a cup of tea and two slices of bread yesterday, and the same the day before; the deputy at a lodging-house gave it to him. He is fifty years old, and is still damp from sleeping out in the wet last night.

No. 5. Sawyer by trade, machinery cut him out. Had a job, haymaking near Uxbridge. Had been on same job lately for a month; got 2s 6d a day. (Probably spent it in drink, seems a very doubtful worker.) Has been odd jobbing a long time, earned 2d today, bought a pen'orth of tea and ditto of sugar (produces same from pocket) but can't get any place to make the tea; was hoping to get to a lodging-house where he could borrow a teapot, but had no money. Earned nothing yesterday, slept at a casual ward; very poor place, get insufficient food, considering the labour. Six ounces of bread and a pint of skilly for breakfast, one ounce of cheese and six or seven ounces of bread for dinner (bread cut by guess). Tea same as breakfast; no supper. For this you have to break 10 cwt of stones, or pick 4 lb. of oakum.

No. 6. Had slept out four nights running. Was a distiller by trade; been out four months; unwilling to enter into details of leaving, but it was his own fault. (Very likely; a heavy, thick, stubborn, and senseless-looking fellow, six feet high, thick neck, strong limbs, evidently destitute of ability.) Does odd jobs; earned 3d for minding a horse, bought a cup of coffee and pen'orth of bread and butter. Has no money now. Slept under Waterloo Bridge last night.

No. 7. Good-natured-looking man; one who would suffer and say nothing; clothes shining with age, grease, and dirt; they hang on his joints as on pegs; awful rags! I saw him endeavouring to walk. He lifted his feet very slowly and put them down carefully in evident pain. His legs are bad; been in infirmary several times with them. His uncle and grand-father were clergymen; both dead now. He was once in a good position in a money office, and afterwards in the London and County Bank for nine years. Then he went with an auctioneer who broke, and he was left ill, old, and with-out any trade. 'A clerk's place,' says he, 'is never worth having, because there are so many of them, and once out you can only get another place with difficulty. I have a brother-in-law on the Stock Exchange, but he won't own me. Look at my clothes? Is it likely?'

No. 8. Slept here four nights running. Is a builder's labourer by trade, that is, a handy-man. Had a settled job for a few weeks which expired three weeks since. Has earned nothing for nine days. Then helped wash down a shop front and got 2s 6d for it. Does anything he can get. Is

46 years old. Earns about 2*d* or 3*d* a day at horse minding. A cup of tea and a bit of bread yesterday, and same today, is all he has had.

No 9. A plumber's labourer (all these men who are somebody's 'labourers' are poor samples of humanity, evidently lacking in grit, and destitute of ability to do any work which would mean decent wages.) Judging from appearance, they will do nothing well. They are a kind of automaton, with the machinery rusty; slow, dull, and incapable. The man of ordinary intelligence leaves them in the rear. They could doubtless earn more even at odd jobs, but lack the energy. Of course, this means little food, exposure to weather, and increased incapability day by day. ('From him that hath not,' etc.) Out of work through slackness, does odd jobs; slept here three nights running. Is a dock labourer when he *can* get work. Has 6*d* an hour; works so many hours, according as he is wanted. Gets 2*s*, 3*s* or 4*s* 6*d* a day. Has to work very hard for it. Casual ward life is also very hard, he says, for those who are not used to it, and there is not enough to eat. Has had today a pen'orth of bread, for minding a cab. Yesterday he spent 3½*d* on a breakfast, and that lasted him all day. Age 25.

No. 10. Been out of work a month. Carman by trade. Arm withered, and cannot do work properly. Has slept here all the week; got an awful cold through the wet. Lives at odd jobs (they all do). Got sixpence yesterday for minding a cab and carrying a couple of parcels. Earned nothing today, but had one good meal; a lady gave it him. Has been walking about all day looking for work, and is tired out.

No. 11. Youth, aged 16. Sad case; Londoner. Works at odd jobs and matches selling. Has taken 3*d* today, i.e. net profit 1½*d*. Has five boxes still. Has slept here every night for a month. Before that slept in Covent Garden Market or on doorsteps. Been sleeping out six months, since he left Feltham Industrial School. Was sent there for playing truant. Has had one bit of bread today; yesterday had only some gooseberries and cherries, i.e. bad ones that had been thrown away. Mother is alive. She 'chucked him out' when he returned home on leaving Feltham because he couldn't find her money for drink.

No. 12. Old man, age 67. Seems to take rather a humorous view of the position. Kind of Mark Tapley. Says he can't say he does like it, but then he *must* like it! Ha, ha! Is a slater by trade. Been out of work some time; younger men naturally get the work. Gets a bit of bricklaying sometimes; can turn his hand to anything. Goes miles and gets nothing. Earned one and twopence this week at holding horses. Finds it hard, certainly. Used to care once, and get downhearted, but that's no good; don't trouble now. Had a bit of bread and butter and cup of coffee today. Health is awful bad, not half the size he was; exposure and want of food is the cause; got wet last night, and is very stiff in consequence. Has been walking about since it was light, that is 3 a.m. Was so cold and wet and weak, scarcely knew what to do. Walked to Hyde Park, and got a little sleep there on a dry seat as soon as the park opened.

These are fairly typical cases of the men who are now wandering homeless through the streets. That is the way in which the nomads of civilization are constantly being recruited from above.

Such are the stories gathered at random one Midsummer night this year under the shade of the plane trees of the Embankment. A month later, when one of my staff took the census of the sleepers out of doors along the line of the Thames from Blackfriars to Westminster, he found three hundred and sixty-eight persons sleeping in the open air. Of these, two hundred and seventy were on the Embankment proper, and ninety-eight in and about Covent Garden Market, while the recesses of Waterloo and Blackfriars Bridges were full of human misery.

This, be it remembered, was not during a season of bad trade. The revival of business has been attested on all hands, notably by the barometer of strong drink. England is prosperous enough to drink rum in quantities which appall the Chancellor of the Exchequer, but she is not prosperous enough to provide other shelter than the midnight sky for these poor outcasts on the Embankment . . .

ON THE VERGE OF THE ABYSS

From In Darkest England and the Way Out

There is, unfortunately, no need for me to attempt to set out, however imperfectly, any statement of the evil case of the sufferers whom we wish to help. For years past the Press has been filled with echoes of the 'Bitter Cry of Outcast London', with pictures of 'Horrible Glasgow', and the like. We have had several volumes describing 'How the Poor Live', and I may therefore assume that all my readers are more or less cognizant of the main outlines of 'Darkest England'. My slum officers are living in the midst of it; their reports are before me, and one day I may publish some more detailed account of the actual facts of the social condition of the Sunken Millions. But not now. All that must be taken as read. I only glance at the subject in order to bring into clear relief the salient points of our new Enterprise.

I have spoken of the houseless poor. Each of these represents a point in the scale of human suffering below that of those who have still contrived to keep a shelter over their heads. A home is a home, be it ever so low; and the desperate tenacity with which the poor will cling to the last wretched semblance of one is very touching. There are vile dens, fever-haunted and stenchful crowded courts, where the return of summer is dreaded because it means the unloosing of myriads of vermin which render night unbearable, which, nevertheless, are regarded at this moment as havens of rest by their hard-working occupants. They can scarcely be said to be furnished. A chair, a mattress, and a few miserable sticks constitute all the furniture of the single room in which they have to sleep, and breed, and die; but they cling to it as a drowning man to a half-submerged raft. Every week they contrive by pinching and scheming to raise the rent, for with them it is pay or go; and they struggle to meet the collector as the sailor nerves himself to avoid being sucked under by the foaming wave. If at any time work fails or sickness comes they are liable to drop helplessly into the ranks of the homeless. It is bad for a single man to have to confront the struggle for life in the streets and Casual Wards. But how much more terrible must it be for the married man with his wife and children to be turned out into the streets. So long as the family has a lair into which it can creep at night, he keeps his footing; but when he loses that solitary foothold then arrives the time if there be such a thing as Christian compassion, for the helping hand to be held out to save him from the vortex that sucks him downward – ay, downward to the hopeless under-strata of crime and despair.

'The heart knoweth its own bitterness and the stranger inter-meddleth not therewith.' But now and then out of the depths there sounds a bitter wail as of some strong swimmer in his agony as he is drawn under by the current. A short time ago a respectable man, a chemist in Holloway, fifty years of age, driven hard to the wall, tried to end it all by cutting his throat. His wife also cut her throat, and at the same time they gave strychnine to their only child. The effort failed, and they were placed on trial for attempted murder. In the Court a letter was read which the poor wretch had written before attempting his life:

MY DEAREST GEORGE – Twelve months have I now passed of a most miserable and struggling existence, and I really cannot stand it any more. I am completely worn out, and relations who could assist me won't do any more, for such was uncle's last intimation. Never mind; he can't take his money and comfort with him, and in all probability will find himself in the same boat as myself. He never enquires whether I am starving or not. £3 – a mere flea-bite to him – would have put us straight, and with his security and good interest might have obtained me a good situation long ago. I can face poverty and degradation no longer, and would sooner die than go to the workhouse, whatever may be the awful consequences of the steps we have taken. We have, God forgive us, taken our darling Arty with us out of pure love and affection, so that the darling should never be cuffed about, or reminded or taunted with his heartbroken parents' crime. My poor wife has done her best at needle-work, washing, house-minding, etc., in fact, anything and everything that would bring in a shilling; but it would only keep us in semi-starvation. I have now done six weeks' travelling from morning till night, and not received one farthing for it. If that is not enough to drive you mad — wickedly mad — I don't know what is. No bright prospect anywhere; no ray of hope.

May God Almighty forgive us for this heinous sin, and have mercy on our sinful souls, is the prayer of your miserable, broken-hearted, but loving brother, Arthur. We have now done everything that we can possibly think of to avert this wicked proceeding, but can discover no ray of hope. Fervent prayer has availed us nothing; our lot is cast, and we must abide by it. It must be God's will or He would have ordained it differently. Dearest Georgy, I am exceedingly sorry to leave you all, but I am mad — thoroughly mad. You, dear, must try and forget us, and, if possible, forgive us; for I do not consider it our own fault we have not succeeded. If you could get £3 for our bed it will pay our rent, and our scanty furniture may fetch enough to bury us in a cheap way. Don't grieve over us or follow us, for we shall not be worthy of such respect. Our clergyman has never called on us or given us the least consolation, though I called on him a month ago. He is paid to preach, and there he considers his responsibility ends, the rich excepted. We have only yourself and a very few others who care one pin what becomes of us, but you must try and forgive us, is the last fervent prayer of your devotedly fond and affectionate but broken-hearted and persecuted brother.　　　　　(Signed) R.A.O——.

That is an authentic human document — a transcript from the life of one among thousands who go down inarticulate into the depths. They die and make no sign, or, worse still, they continue to exist, carrying about with them, year after year, the bitter ashes of a life from which the furnace of misfortune has burnt away all joy, and hope, and strength. Who is there who has not been confronted by many despairing ones, who come, as Richard O—— went, to the clergyman, crying for help, and how seldom have we been able to give it them? It is unjust, no doubt, for them to blame the clergy and the comfortable well-to-do — for what can they do but preach and offer good advice? To assist all the Richard O——s' by direct financial advance would drag even Rothschild into the gutter. And what else can be done? Yet something else must be done if Christianity is not to be a mockery to perishing men.

Here is another case, a very common case, which illustrates how the Army of Despair is recruited.

Mr T., Margaret Place, Gascoign Place, Bethnal Green, is a bootmaker by trade. Is a good hand, and has earned 3s 6d to 4s 6d a day. He was taken ill last Christmas, and went to the London Hospital; was there three months. A week after he had gone Mrs T. had rheumatic fever, and was taken to Bethnal Green Infirmary, where she remained about three months. Directly after they had been taken ill, their furniture was seized for the three weeks' rent which was owing. Consequently, on becoming convalescent, they were homeless. They came out about the same time. He went out to a lodging-house for a night or two, until she came out. He then had 2d, and she had 6d, which a nurse had given her. They went to a lodging-house together, but the society there was dreadful. Next day he had a day's work, and got 2s 6d, and on the strength of this they took a furnished room at 10d per day (payable nightly). His work lasted a few weeks, when he was again taken ill, lost his job, and spent all their money. Pawned a shirt and apron for 1s; spent that, too. At last pawned their tools for 3s, which got them a few days' food and lodging. He is now minus tools and cannot work at his own job, and does anything he can. Spent their last twopence on a pen'orth each of tea and sugar. In two days they had a slice of bread and butter each, that's all. They are both very weak through want of food.

'Let things alone', the laws of supply and demand, and all the rest of the excuses by which those who stand on firm ground salve their consciences when they leave their brother to sink, how do they look when we apply them to the actual loss of life at sea? Does 'Let things alone' man the lifeboat? Will the inexorable laws of political economy save the shipwrecked sailor from the boiling surf? They often enough are responsible for his disaster. Coffin ships are a direct result of the wretched policy of non-interference with the legitimate operations of commerce, but no desire to make it pay created the National Lifeboat Institution, no law of supply and demand actuates the volunteers who risk their lives to bring the shipwrecked to shore.

What we have to do is to apply the same principle to society. We want a Social Lifeboat Institution, a Social Lifeboat Brigade, to snatch from the abyss those who, if left to themselves, will perish as miserably as the crew of a ship that founders in mid-ocean.

The moment that we take in hand this work we shall be compelled to turn our attention seriously to the question whether prevention is not better than cure. It is easier and cheaper, and in every way better, to prevent the loss of home than to have to re-create that home. It is better to keep a man out of the mire than to let him fall in first and then risk the chance of plucking him out. Any Scheme, therefore, that attempts to deal with the reclamation of the lost must tend to develop into an endless variety of ameliorative measures of some of which I shall have somewhat to say hereafter. I only mention the subject here in order that no one may say I am blind to the necessity of going further and adopting wider plans of operation than those which I put forward in this book. The renovation of our Social System is a work so vast that no one of us, nor all of us put together, can define all the measures that will have to be taken before we attain even the Cab-Horse Ideal of existence for our children and children's children. All that we can do is to attack, in a serious, practical spirit the worst and most pressing evils, knowing that if we do our duty we obey the voice of God. He is the Captain of our Salvation. If we but follow where He leads we shall not want for marching orders, nor need we imagine that He will narrow the field of operations.

I am labouring under no delusions as to the possibility of inaugurating the Millennium by any social specific. In the struggle of life the weakest will go to the wall, and there are so many weak. The fittest, in tooth and claw, will survive. All that we can do is to soften the lot of the unfit and make their suffering less horrible than it is at present. No amount of assistance will give a jellyfish a backbone. No outside propping will make some men stand erect. All material help from without is useful only in so far as it develops moral strength within. And some men seem to have lost even the very faculty of self-help. There is an immense lack of common sense and of vital energy on the part of multitudes.

It is against Stupidity in every shape and form that we have to wage our eternal battle. But how can we wonder at the want of sense on the part of those who have had no advantages, when we see such plentiful absence of that commodity on the part of those who have had all the advantages?

How can we marvel if, after leaving generation after generation to grow up uneducated and underfed, there should be developed a heredity of incapacity, and that thousands of dull-witted people should be born into the world, disinherited before their birth of their share in the average intelligence of mankind?

Besides those who are thus hereditarily wanting in the qualities necessary to enable them to hold their own, there are the weak, the disabled, the aged, and the unskilled; worse than all, there is the want of character. Those who have the best of reputation, if they lose their foothold on the ladder, find it difficult enough to regain their place. What, then, can men and women who have no character do? When a master has the choice of a hundred honest men, is it reasonable to expect that he will select a poor fellow with tarnished reputation?

All this is true, and it is one of the things that makes the problem almost insoluble. And insoluble it is, I am absolutely convinced, unless is it possible to bring new moral life into the soul of these people. This should be the first object of every social reformer, whose work will only last if it is built on the solid foundation of a new birth, to cry 'You must be born again.'

To get a man soundly saved it is not enough to put on him a pair of new breeches, to give him regular work, or even to give him a University education. These things are all outside a man, and if the inside remains unchanged you have wasted your labour. You must in some way or other graft upon the man's nature a new nature, which has in it the element of the Divine. All that I propose in this book is governed by that principle.

The difference between the method which seeks to regenerate the man by ameliorating his circumstances and that which ameliorates his circumstances in order to get at the regeneration of his heart, is the difference between the method of the gardener who grafts a Ribstone Pippin on a crab-apple tree and one who merely ties apples with string upon the branches of the crab. To change the nature of the individual, to get at the heart, to save his soul is the only real, lasting method of doing him any good. In many modern schemes of social regeneration it is forgotten that 'it takes a soul to move a body, e'en to a cleaner sty', and at the risk of being misunderstood and misrepresented, I must assert in the most unqualified way that it is primarily and mainly for the sake of saving the soul that I seek the salvation of the body.

But what is the use of preaching the Gospel to men whose whole attention is concentrated upon a mad, desperate struggle to keep themselves alive? You might as well give a tract to a shipwrecked sailor who is battling with the surf which has drowned his comrades and threatens to drown him. He will not listen to you. Nay, he cannot hear you any more than a man whose head is under water can listen to a sermon. The first thing to do is to get him at least a footing on firm ground, and to give him room to live. Then you may have a chance. At present you have none. And you will have all the better opportunity to find a way to his heart, if he comes to know that it was you who pulled him out of the horrible pit and the miry clay in which he was sinking to perdition.

Robert Sherard

Robert Sherard (1861–1943) was born in Melton Mowbray, the son of the Rev. Bennet Sherard Kennedy and a great-grandson of William Wordsworth. He was educated at Oxford and Bonn universities, and from 1884 was a professional journalist working as a special correspondent in various parts of the world for English, American and Australian newspapers. He wrote several books on France, where he lived for many years, and the French. Alone among the social explorers in this anthology he had strong connections with the 'yellow' side of late-Victorian England, being a friend and biographer of Oscar Wilde. He founded the Vindex Publishing Company, Calvi, in 1933. *The White Slaves of England* (1897) was published originally as articles in *Pearson's Magazine* in 1896 with the intention of bringing to light, 'the worst paid and most murderous trades of England'. *The Child-Slaves of Britain* (1905) was commissioned by the editor of *The London Magazine* where it was first published as a series of articles.

THE CHAINMAKERS OF CRADLEY HEATH

From *The White Slaves of England*

The main industry of Cradley Heath is chain-making, and it may be remarked here that this industry has never been so prosperous, at least in respect of the amount of chain produced and the number of workmen employed. It appears that each week there are manufactured in the Cradley Heath district 1000 tons of chain. The chains are of every variety, from the huge 4-inch mooring cables down to No. 16 on the wire gauge, and include rigging-chains, crane-cables, mining-cables, cart and plough traces, curbs, halters, cow-ties, dog-chains, and even handcuff-links.

If chains for slaves are not made here also it is doubtless because there are no slaves in England; or it may be because hunger can bind tighter than any iron links. And chronic hunger is the experience of most of the women-workers in Cradley Heath, as any one can learn who cares to converse with them.

'We has to do with two quartern loaves a day,' said one of the woman-blacksmiths to me, 'though three such loaves wouldn't be too much for us.' This woman had six children to keep and her husband into the bargain, for he had been out of work since Christmas. She was good enough to detail to me her manner of living. A pennyworth of bits of bacon, two-pennyworth of meat from the 'chep-butcher', and a penny-worth of potatoes, all cooked together, made a dinner for the family of eight.

But such a dinner was very rarely to be obtained; most often she had to beg dripping 'off them as belongs to me,' as a relish to the insufficient bread. It appeared that she had influential relations, who could spare a cupful of dripping now and again, and who sometimes passed on some 'bits' of cast-off clothing. She showed me that she was wearing a pair of men's high-low boots, which had come to her in this way.

She 'never sees no milk', and in the matter of milk, her children, even the youngest, had 'to do the same as we'. These children, like all other children in the Cradley Heath district, had been weaned on to 'sop'. Sop is a preparation of bread and hot water, flavoured with the drippings of the tea-pot. This *plat* is much esteemed by the children, and the woman said: 'If them's got a basin of sop, them's as proud as if them'd got a beefsteak.'

In good weeks she could get a bit of margarine, and each week she bought a quarter of a pound of tea at one shilling the pound, and four pounds of sugar at a penny halfpenny. As to eggs, she said: 'By gum, I'd like one for my tea; I haven't had a egg for years.'* For clothes for her children and herself, she depended entirely on charity. None of her

* *Note.* On returning to Ambleside, where I was then living, I sent this poor woman a basket of eggs. In acknowledgment, a lady resident in Cradley Heath wrote: 'Mrs D—— has asked me if I

family had more 'nor he stood up in', and when her children's stockings wanted washing, she had to put them to bed, for none of them 'had more than one bit to his feet'. The washing was usually done on Saturday evenings, when she had finished her work.

This work consisted in making heavy chain at 5s 4d the cwt. By working incessantly for about twelve hours a day, she could make about one cwt. and a half in a week. Her hands were badly blistered, and she was burnt in different parts of the body by the flying sparks. In spite of things, she was a well-set, jovial woman, not without a rude beauty, which she explained thus:

'It's not what I gets to eat. It's me having a contented mind, and not letting nothing trouble me.'

And she asked me to compare her with a woman who sat next to her, and who was lamentably thin and worn.

'Look at my sister,' she said, 'who worrits herself.' Some money was given to this woman, and she departed joyfully

would write a few lines for her to you, and having done so, I thought I would add a little from myself, as I am sure you will pardon me for writing to you, though you are an entire stranger to me. I have known Mrs D— for nearly ten years, and have found her to be a thoroughly honest and would be a respectable woman, as she comes from a respectable family. But what with bad trade she was nearly brought to starvation some time ago. But I felt as if I could not do enough for her I am very fond of her, as she is a truthful woman, and I try as often as I can to help her. My father, and some more of the citizens of this dilapidated town, got up a Relief Committee, and we started a Bread and Tea Fund for the winter months. You would have stared had you seen her children eating the eggs which you sent; as we say in Scotland, it would do "sair een guid" to have seen them at their tea.' Mrs D—'s message ran: 'I beg to thank you for box of eggs, which came to hand quite safely, and which myself and husband and children thoroughly enjoyed. It was quite a treat for us to have such a thing in our house. The young lady who is writing this letter for me knows how hard I have had to work to make an honest living. There is eight of us in the family, and only my second son, a boy of thirteen years of age, getting 4s. a week for blowing in a chainmaker's shop, and myself, who makes chain; and after working hard from 7 a.m. till 9 p.m., from Monday till dinner time on Saturday, and receive 6s.' – R.H.S.

to pay some little debts. 'If there's anything over,' she said, 'I'll get a booster tonight.' I learnt that a 'booster' was a quartern loaf.*

This conversation took place in the Manchester Arms, which is the house of call of the chainmakers, both male and female. Beer plays a great part in the lives of the men, and even amongst the women a predilection for drink may be observed. The number of quarts of 'threepenny', or even 'twopenny', consumed by the men in the chain factories is very great. A master told me that some of his men must have a sponge beneath their belts, as they often consume three shillings-worth of beer a day at threepence the quart.

The beer chiefly drunk in Cradley is a variety known as Burton Returns, that is to say, beer which has been returned to the brewers as undrinkable by customers more fastidious than the chainmakers. A boy is attached to each factory, whose exclusive service is to run out and fetch pints for the men. The heat of the furnaces is terrible, and the work most exhausting. Men have to wring their clothes when they go home. Under these circumstances it is not surprising that they should drink such quantities; and as to their preference for alcoholic beverages, a man said to me: 'What strength is there behind six or seven quarts of water?' Some men, he admitted, seemed to manage on 'seconds', or milk which had been 'hanging about the dairy for some days'.

It was somewhat of a surprise to hear that the men could afford to spend three shillings a day on drink when at work, because it is generally understood that chainmaking is of all industries, perhaps, the worse paid, as it is certainly the most exhausting. The master, however, stated that some of his men could make as much as 10s in one day. And this investigation proved to be the case. A skilled worker can make 10s in one day, less the usual charges, but the work is so exhausting that, having worked the number of links needful

* At the time when, in the beginning of the winter of last year, the price of bread rose, I felt very anxious for Mrs D— and her seven dependents, and wrote to ask how this rise affected her. She answered that prices for chain having slightly improved, she was fortunately able to provide the same amount of bread, i.e. two-thirds of a sufficiency.

to earn that sum, he would be so fatigued that he would have 'to play' for the next two or three days. Indeed, a man who told me that he could never earn more than 20s in a week, on which he had to keep his wife and six children, added that often when he had completed a week's labour he was so knocked up that he was forced to 'mess about' for three or four days.

The work is unhealthy and dangerous. One sees few old men in Cradley. Lung disease carries the men off at an early age.

'The work affects you all over,' said a worker to me. 'When you've done a good turn, you feel like buried. You gets so cold that you shivers so you can't hold your food. The furnaces burn your insides right out of you, and a man what's got no inside is soon settled off.'

This man had burns all over his body. 'It's easier,' he explained, 'to catch a flea than a piece of red-hot iron, and the bits of red-hot iron are always flying about. Sometimes a bit gets into your boot, and puts you "on the box" for a week.' But the risk of catching cold is most dreaded, for a cold may kill a man. This worker told me of a friend of his who had walked over to Clent Hill one day, got wet, and was dead the next evening. He had also a dismal story to tell of a man who had died of clamming. The doctor had said 'his inside had gone from starvation'. This was a 'middle-handed' chainmaker (a man of middling skill), but he had got too weak to work.

Work in Cradley is done for the most part in factories, or at least in sheds where several work together. One does not see many solitary workers here as in Bromsgrove, and perhaps on this account the wretchedness of the chainmakers is not so immediately apparent, for there is a sense of comfort in gregariousness.

One may come across sheds with five or six women, each working at her anvil; they are all talking above the din of their hammers and the clanking of their chains, or they may be singing a discordant chorus; and at first, the sight of this sociability makes one overlook the misery, which, however, is only too visible, be it in the foul rags and preposterous boots that the women wear, or in their haggard faces and the faces of the wizened infants hanging to their mothers' breasts, as these ply the hammer, or sprawling in the mire on the floor, amidst the showers of fiery sparks.

Here and there in Cradley, it is true, one may come across such scenes as sadden in Bromsgrove: some woman plying her task in a cell-like shed, silent, absorbed, alone. One such a sight I particularly remember.

In a shed, fitted with forge and anvil, there was a woman at work. From a pole which ran across the room there dangled a tiny swing chair for the baby, so that whilst working her hammers, the mother could rock the child. She was working very hard at spike-making, and she told us that the previous week, her husband and herself had converted into spikes a ton of iron. These they had then packed and conveyed to the warehouse. For this ton of spikes they had received 20s, the remuneration of a week's work by the two of them, and out of these 20s there had to be deducted 3s 8d for 'breeze' (fuel). The rent of the house and shop was 3s 8d, and damage to the extent of 1s had been done to the tools. There was consequently left for the housekeeping about 11s.

This woman had five children, and she told me that she had been laughed at by her neighbours, because, in spite of her blacksmith work, she had brought each child safely into the world. The work is such that, in Cradley, Lucina is not to these female Vulcans a kindly goddess. One woman, also a blacksmith, had been seven times abandoned by her in her hour of need. It may be remarked that so pressing are the wants of the women that they will work to within an hour or two of their confinement.

A woman whom I met at the Manchester Arms was good enough to give me some particulars of the birth of 'our little Johnny'. It appears that this young gentleman was born on November 9th of last year.

'I worked up till five that day,' said his mother, 'and then I give over because I had my cleaning to do. Our little Johnny was born at a quarter past seven.'

This woman made chain-harrows, and could earn 5s a week at it, for twelve hours a day; as to which work Mr James Smith, the Secretary of the Chainmakers' Union, said, 'It's not women's work at all.'

Indeed, no part of this work is work for women, and his manhood is ashamed who sees these poor female beings swinging their heavy hammers or working the treadles of the Oliver. Oliver is here so heavy – sometimes the weight of the hammer exceeds 36 lb. – that the rebellious treadle jerks its frail mistress upwards, and a fresh ungainly effort must be hers before she can force it to its work and bring it down. As to Oliver, the name given here also to the heavy hammer which can be worked by a treadle alone, the philologist, remembering the dismantled castle of Dudley hard by, the Roundhead triumphs of the neighbouring Edge Hill, and many another spot in this land, will trace its origin to Cromwell, the heavy-hammer man; Oliver Martel, who crushed kings and castles, princes and prejudice; Oliver the democrat, whose name, by the exquisite irony of things, is now attached to an implement used by slaves most degraded, by starved mothers fighting in sweat and anguish and rags, for the sop of the weazened bairns, who in the shower of fiery sparks grovel in the mire of these shameful workshops.

The impediment of children, to mothers to whom motherhood is here a curse, is nowhere more clearly defined. The wretched woman, forging link by link the heavy chain, of which she must make 1 cwt before her weekly rent is paid, is at each moment harassed by her sons and daughters. There is one child at the breast, who hampers the swing of the arm; there is another seated on the forge, who must be watched lest the too comfortable blaze at which it warms its little naked feet, prove dangerous, whilst the swarm that cling to her tattered skirt break the instinctive movement of her weary feet.

She cannot absent herself, for as a woman told me, whose child was burned to death in her shed: 'The Crowner came down something awful on me for leaving the forge for two minutes to see to summat in the saucepan.'

The employing of a nurse to attend to the children seems impossible, according to numerous statements which were made to me. One woman told me that a nurse cost each week 2s 'to do the mother', and 3d for her pocket 'to encourage her like'; and, she added, this expense was not to be borne. She exemplified her statement by giving me an account of the earnings of the previous three days and the expenditure incurred. She had forged 728 heavy links in the three days, and for this had received 2s 2d. She had paid 7½d for firing and 1s for the nurse. Her net earnings for the 36 hours were 6½d. Her eyes reminded me of Leah, and she said:

'We'm working worse nor slaves, and getting nothing to eat into the bargain.'

Another woman who was with her told me a halfpenny-worth of oatmeal often served as a meal for her whole family. This woman's husband was in a lunatic asylum. 'Heat, worry and drink knocked my old 'un,' she said. He had left her with five children, and to feed these (Mr James Smith assured me of the truth of this statement) she used often to work from three in the morning till eleven at night, and begin again at three in the morning next day.

The work of chainmaking consists in heating the iron rods (a process which involves a number of pulls on the bellows for each link), bending the red-hot piece, cutting in on the hardy, twisting the link, inserting it into the last link of the chain, and welding, or closing it, with repeated blows of the hand hammer and the Oliver worked by a treadle. To earn 3s a woman must 'work in' forty-six rods of iron, each nine feet long, and out of these 3s she must pay for her gleeds, or fuel. This woman had to make 1 cwt of iron chain to earn 4s.

The women work on the smaller chains, and consequently use smaller rods of iron. For these less heat is necessary than for the iron worked by the men, who make the huge cables. Consequently for the women's forges the bellows which they work themselves suffices. For the men 'blast', supplied by mechanical power, is necessary. This power is supplied either by steam or by hand labour. In either case it is paid for by the men, and these complain bitterly of the rapacity of the masters in extorting for 'blast' sums the aggregate of which exceeds its cost. I know of one master in Cradley who employs men at sixty forges. Each forge brings him 3s a week for blast. The total is £9. His 'blast' is supplied by a steam-engine, the fuel for which costs him 30s a week. He has also to pay 24s a week to his engineer. His outlay each week is accordingly £2 14s, as against £9 which he receives from his men.

On the other hand this steam-engine drives the guillotine-shears (which cut the thick iron bar into the requisite lengths for the links), the brightening box, in which the chains are polished, and the testing machine, where the strength of the cables is, or more often is not, tested.*

In the smaller factories manual labour is employed to work the machines by which the forges are supplied with blast, and here also the master extorts an unjustifiable profit. I remember seeing a woman thus supplying 'blast' to four forges. She was a pitiful being, chlorotic, with hair almost white, and a stamp of imbecility – too easily comprehended – on her ravaged and anæmic face. Her work lasted twelve hours a day, and during the whole of this time she had to turn the handle of a wheel which actuated the bellows of four forges. Each worker paid 3s a week to the master for blast, whilst the anæmic Albino received for her squirrel slavery, 'when things were good', the wages of 6s a week.

Elsewhere I saw single bellows worked – at 3d a day to the

---

* Quantities of cables are exported from Cradley with bogus certificates of strength. These cables give way under the strain which they are certified to resist; ships and lives are lost, and the English chainmaking industry becomes discredited abroad. Custom falls off as a natural consequence, and the men have to suffer for the dishonesty of the masters. I have received several letters on this subject. One gentleman writes from London: 'I am a buyer for one of the large South African Export Houses, and although I was not previously ignorant of many of the facts you state, they came to me with fresh interest, as I have strong reasons for suspecting that a certain firm from whom I have been buying tested chain have been sending me false certificates. I want to get to the bottom of this matter, and it occurred to me that if you would be so kind as to put me into communication with Mr James Smith he might be able to give me some information. I presume he would be glad to do this in the interests of the class he represents, who ultimately suffer by such practices. Further, if he cared to give me a list of the Cradley and Old Hill firms who are known to be sweaters, I should be pleased to avoid them as far as I could, consistent with the interests of my colonial correspondents.' I was sorry, in view of the existing libel laws, not to be able to oblige this correspondent and others who wrote to the same effect.

worker and 6d to the employer – by very old men and women or by little boys and girls. A particular and pitiful sight was that of a sweet little lass – such as Sir John Millais would have liked to paint – dancing on a pair of bellows for 3d a day to supply 'blast' to the chainmaker at the forge, and to put 3d a day into the pocket of her employer. As she danced her golden hair flew out, and the fiery sparks which showered upon her head reminded me of fire-flies seen at night near Florence, dancing over a field of ripe wheat. Indeed this misuser of children is the most reprehensible thing that offends in the Cradley district.

There are here factories where meagre little girls and boys (to whom the youngest Ginx could give points) are put to tasks, during their apprenticeship, against which a man would revolt. I have before me an object and a vision. The object is an indenture of apprenticeship; the vision is a thing seen at Cradley, in the very factory to which the indenture refers. The indenture has been before my lords in commission assembled, and traces of Norman fingers may be recognised in the grime which besmirches this wicked document.

It refers to a girl of fourteen, who is apprenticed by 'these presents' to the art and trade of chain-making, at a wage of 2s 6d a week. The girl undertakes during her apprenticeship neither to haunt taverns nor playhouses, nor to squander what remains of her wages, after paying for 'sufficient meat, drink, medicine, clothing, lodging, and all other necessaries', in 'playing at cards or dice tables, or any other unlawful games'.

The vision is of such a girl at work in this very factory. She was fourteen by the Factory Act, by paternity she was ten. I never saw such little arms, and her hands were made to cradle dolls. She was making links for chain-harrows, and as she worked the heavy Oliver she sang a song. And I also saw her owner approach with a clenched fist, and heard him say:

'I'll give you some golden hair was hanging down her back! Why don't you get on with your work?'

Next to her was a female wisp who was forging dog-chains, for which, with swivel and ring complete, she received ¾d (three farthings) apiece. It was the chain which sells currently for eighteenpence. She worked ten hours a day, and could 'manage six chains in the day'. And from the conversation which I had with her, I do not think that she was at all the girl who would haunt playhouses and taverns, or squander her earnings at dice-tables, cards, or any such unlawful games.

The fogger flourishes in Cradley, no less than in Bromsgrove; with this difference, that in Cradley it is most often a woman who assumes the functions of the sweater. Mr James Smith introduced me to an elderly lady, who keeps a shed in the neighbourhood of a very foul slum, and employs seven girls. She 'has never forged a link of chain in her life, and gets a good living' out of the wretched women whom I saw at the forges on her premises.

Her system is a simple one. For every hundredweight of chain produced she receives 5s 4d. For every hundredweight she pays 2s 10d. The Union would admit 4s, for the Union allows 25 per cent to the fogger. Anything over 25 per cent is considered sweating. Two of the girls working in this shed were suckling babes and could work but slowly. Those who could work at their best, being unencumbered, could make a hundredweight of chain in two days and a half. Their owner walked serene and grey-haired amongst them, checking conversation, and, at times, abusive. She was but one of a numerous class of human leeches fast to a gangrened sore.

Of Anvil Yard, with its open sewers and filth and shame, one would rather not write, nor of the haggard tatterdermalions who there groaned and jumped. In fact I hardly saw them. The name 'Anvil Yard' had set me thinking of some lines of Goethe, in which he deplores the condition of the people – 'zwischen dem Ambos und Hammer' – between the anvil and the hammer.

And as these lines went through my head, whilst before my spiritual eyes there passed the pale procession of the White Slaves of England, I could see nothing but sorrow and hunger and grime, rags, foul food, open sores and movements incessant, instinctive yet laborious – an anvil and a hammer ever descending – all vague, and in a mist as yet untinged with red, a spectacle so hideous that I gladly shut it out, wondering, for my part, what in these things is right.

CHILD-SLAVERY IN BIRMINGHAM

From *The Child-Slaves of Britain*

For the sheer misery . . . of laborious and underpaid labour in which children are forced to participate as long as their little fingers can move and their eyes keep open, it is in the kitchens of the squalid homes in the courts and closes that we must look. There are a number of trades in Birmingham for which the home-labour of women and children is employed. Finding one's cotton, hemp and needles, twopence an hour may be earned by a woman assisted by one or two children in sewing the chains on to the leather for soldiers' chin-straps. But here child labour almost always fails. Government is very particular, and any strap which as to its seventy-two links (four stitches to each link) is not sewn in the best style of sempstress-ship is pitilessly refused. Deducting expenses and allowing for goods refused, 1s 8d has been earned in 2½ days by two people working for Government from 6 a.m. to 11 p.m. Where fire-men's chin-straps have to be made, the needle has to be pushed through four thicknesses of leather. It is hard work for little hands.

At wrapping up hairpins in paper, ten to the paper, with one outside to hold the package together, a light employment in which any member of the family circle may engage, as much as 2¼d may be earned by two people, or four children, in a couple of days. For this sum 1000 packages have to be made up. The goods must be fetched from the factory and carried back there besides.

One penny a day can be gained by a child in bending the tin clasp round safety-pins – 'bending safety-pins' they call it. The nimble fingers of children are apt at this work. The payment is at the rate of halfpenny a gross, but for some varieties of safety-pins as much as twopence for three gross is cheerfully paid by the manufacturers. So terrible is the competition by children in this trade that, as an old woman of ninety told me in a house 'back of Unit Street', when her husband was alive they could, by working all the week – he from 5 a.m. till 11 p.m., and she from 9 a.m. till the same hour at night –

earn two shillings a week between them.

Then there is the carding of safety-pins – that is to say, fastening safety-pins in graduated sizes on to cards. For a gross of these cards, with nine pins of different sizes on each card, the payment is 2½d. For a gross of cards with fifteen pins 4d is paid, and for a gross of eighteen-pin cards, 5d. Here children are very useful, and may after practice earn halfpenny an hour. A woman alone working her hardest can earn about twopence.

This kind of employment is much run after, and at any time of the day you may see outside the factories children waiting with perambulators to bring home their stocks of pins and cards. But trade was slack at the time of my visit to Birmingham, and many carders of safety-pins apply over and over again for the materials for their pitiful industry. In Tower Street, where I found a woman and three little children engaged in this work, I was told that 'mother' had applied twice a day at the factory for a week and that all the work she got amounted to the value of 1s 4d. Whilst this conversation was going on between us an alcoholic neighbour-woman was deriding the family energies. For her part, she insisted, rather than do such slave-work for such a price, she would ten thousand times rather go and collect horse-manure in the streets.

Three-halfpence may be earned at home by varnishing 144 penholders. Each penholder must first be rubbed with sandpaper and then varnished, five coats of the varnish being applied with a sponge. It is dirty and unpleasant work, and you may imagine the comfort of a slum-kitchen full of children in which threepennyworth of sticky penholders – 288 to wit – are lying about in the process of drying. This is reckoned skilled labour. There is a knack to be acquired, and children must serve a home apprenticeship before they can earn anything at the trade.

Papering pins and sewing buttons on to cards are two other industries where the wages per hour for child-labour may be computed by infinitesimal fractions of pence. In Birmingham the decimal system of coinage which obtains in France should speedily be introduced. One can calculate a child's hourly earnings at these miserable little trades by centimes alone.

A very general industry is the carding of hooks and eyes, and the advantage of it is that the tiniest mite can here render assistance. Mother and her little girls sew the eyes on to the cards, and then baby passes the hooks into these eyes. Mother and the girls then sew down the hooks and the card is complete. There are four dozen hooks and eyes on each card, and gross and gross of cards go to a pack. Shall we calculate the number of stitches which a pack demands? No, we have no time for mental arithmetic, but we can guess the total fairly accurately by the cotton we consume. One has to supply one's own cotton and the speed with which it is used up cannot fail to impress us.

I visited many homes where poor women and children were working at this trade. In Tower Street I found a woman who, assisted by her children out of school hours – she herself working all day – could earn eightpence. Out of this she pays a penny to a woman of the 'fogger' or 'farmer' class, who gets the work from the factory and farms it out. A reasonable woman, this fogger of Tower Street, for one hears of foggers in this city of Birmingham who will keep for themselves 50 per cent and even more of the miserable sums earned by these miserable children.

Back of Richard Street I found a woman and a little girl, who were both as white of face as is the paper upon which I trace their painful records, who were dying of starvation in the hook-and-eye trade. 'Starting,' she said, 'the two of us early on Saturday morning and working hard all day Saturday, and beginning again on Monday morning and on till dinner-time, we earned 1s 6d. You get 10d for a pack, and you find your own cotton and needles. Me and my little girl – she is the only one of my five children who can help as yet – worked yesterday from 4.30 p.m. till past 11, and we earned 4d between us.' None of these people had eaten anything all that day. There was only a little tea and sugar in the house. The babies were crying.

A miserable woman living in a 'furnished' room in Hospital Street, for which she pays 5s 3d a week, can earn, with child-help, 8d a day at this same trade.

I heard of a woman – a handless woman doubtless – in Coles-hill Street who, working with two girls, got 2s a week for herself and 2s a week for the fogger. This woman's husband was earning 18s a week, but needed most of it for himself.

There was deep pathos in all these scenes, but the spectacle which, when I think back upon these heavy hours, will always haunt me with greatest sorrow is one I saw in a kitchen, in a house off Jennens Row, in a courtyard under the lee of a common lodging. Here, late one evening, I found three little children, busy at work at a table on which were heaped up piles of cards, and a vast mass of tangled hooks and eyes. The eldest girl was eleven, the next was nine, and a little boy of five completed the companionship. They were all working as fast as their little fingers could work. The girls sewed, the baby hooked. They were too busy to raise their eyes from their tasks – the clear eyes of youth under the flare of the lamp! Here were the energy, the interest, which in our youth we all bring to our several tasks in the happy ignorance of the weight and stress of the years and years of drudgery to come.

I looked at these bright eyes, these quick and flexible fingers, and I thought of the old woman of ninety whom I had seen in the morning in Unit Street. I remembered her eyes which had the glaze of approaching dissolution upon them; I remem-bered the knotted, labour-gnarled hands. Her eyes had been bright once. She, too, had brought interest and energy to the miserable tasks in which her life began. Years had followed years, decade had added itself to decade. There had been no change brought by chance or time.

The drudgery is eternal. There is no hope of relief. One treads, firmly at first, and then with faltering steps, the mill-round of one's allotted task, until the end, which is the name-less grave. And it was because I read in the clear eyes of those children the ignorance of this cruel but indisputable postulate of the lives of the very poor, that their very bright-ness, their cheerfulness filled me with more poignant sorrow than any I had felt till then. *Quous Tandem*. How long? How long? All your life and till the grave.

B. S. Rowntree

Benjamin Seebohm Rowntree (1871–1954) was the son of a wealthy York businessman. He was educated at Owens College, Manchester, and in 1889 joined the family firm, becoming a director in 1897 and chairman 1923–41. Rowntree's interest in labour relations and the problem of poverty owes much to his Quaker background, but the direct influence on his survey of York was Booth's *Life and Labour*. From its publication in 1901 *Poverty: A Study of Town Life* was recognized as a work of great importance in pioneering new methods of social investigation. Rowntree expanded the significance of Booth's findings and refined some aspects of his approach : he also used professional specialists (physiologists and dieticians) to establish the standard of physical efficiency. In *How the Labourer Lives* (1913), written with May Kendall, Rowntree used similar methods to try to determine 'the actual economic position of the ordinary agricultural labourer'. He followed up the York survey in two subsequent volumes : *Poverty and Progress* (1941), and, in collaboration with G. R. Laver, *Poverty and the Welfare State* (1951).

WHAT 'MERELY PHYSICAL EFFICIENCY' MEANS

From *Poverty: A Study of Town Life*

. . . It is thus seen that *the wages paid for unskilled labour in York are insufficient to provide food, shelter, and clothing adequate to maintain a family of moderate size in a state of bare physical efficiency.* It will be remembered that the above estimates of necessary minimum expenditure are based upon the assumption that the diet is even less generous than that allowed to able-bodied paupers in the York Workhouse, and

that *no allowance is made for any expenditure other than
that absolutely required for the maintenance of merely physical
efficiency.*

And let us clearly understand what 'merely physical efficiency' means. A family living upon the scale allowed for in
this estimate must never spend a penny on railway fare or
omnibus. They must never go into the country unless they
walk. They must never purchase a halfpenny newspaper or
spend a penny to buy a ticket for a popular concert. They
must write no letters to absent children, for they cannot afford
to pay the postage. They must never contribute anything to
their church or chapel, or give any help to a neighbour which
costs them money. They cannot save, nor can they join sick
club or Trade Union, because they cannot pay the necessary
subscriptions. The children must have no pocket money for
dolls, marbles, or sweets. The father must smoke no tobacco,
and must drink no beer. The mother must never buy any
pretty clothes for herself or for her children, the character of
the family wardrobe as for the family diet being governed by
the regulation, 'Nothing must be bought but that which is
absolutely necessary for the maintenance of physical health,
and what is bought must be of the plainest and most
economical description.' Should a child fall ill, it must be
attended by the parish doctor; should it die, it must be buried
by the parish. Finally, the wage-earner must never be absent
from his work for a single day.

If any of these conditions are broken, the extra expenditure
involved is met, *and can only be met*, by limiting the diet;
or, in other words, by sacrificing physical efficiency.

That few York labourers receiving 20s or 21s per week
submit to these iron conditions in order to maintain physical
efficiency is obvious. And even were they to submit, physical
efficiency would be unattainable for those who had three or
more children dependent upon them. It cannot therefore be
too clearly understood, nor too emphatically repeated, *that
whenever a worker having three children dependent on him,
and receiving not more than 21s 8d per week, indulges in any
expenditure beyond that required for the barest physical needs,
he can do so only at the cost of his own physical efficiency,
or of that of some members of his family.*

If a labourer has but two children, these conditions will be better to the extent of 2s 10d; and if he has but one, they will be better to the extent of 5s 8d. And, again, as soon as his children begin to work, their earnings will raise the family above the poverty line. But the fact remains that every labourer who has as many as three children must pass through a time, probably lasting for about ten years, when he will be in a state of 'primary' poverty; in other words, when he and his family will be *underfed*.*

* Some readers may be inclined to say, upon reading the above, 'This surely is an over-statement. Look at the thousands of families with incomes of 18s to 21s, or even less, where the men *do* smoke and *do* spend money upon drink, and the women *do* spend money on dress and recreation, and yet, in spite of it all, they seem happy and contented, and the men make good workmen!' Such arguments against the actual pressure and the consequences of poverty will, however, upon closer investigation be found to be illusory. They come amongst a class of arguments against which Bastiat, the French economist, warned his readers in a series of articles entitled, 'That which is seen, and that which is not seen.' In these articles the writer pointed out the danger of forming judgments upon social and economic questions without thoroughly investigating them.

In the argument referred to above, the money spent by the poor upon drink, dress, or recreation is one of the '*things that are seen*'. There are, however, consequences of poverty which are '*not seen*'. We *see* that many a labourer, who has a wife and three or four children, is healthy and a good worker, although he only earns a pound a week. What we do *not see* is that in order to give him enough food, mother and children habitually go short, for the mother knows that all depends upon the wages of her husband.

We *see* the man go to the public-house and spend money on drink; we do *not see* the children going supperless to bed in consequence.

These unseen consequences of poverty have, however, to be reckoned with – the high death-rate among the poor, the terribly high infant mortality, the stunted stature and dulled intelligence – all these and others are not seen unless we look beneath the surface; and yet all are having their effect upon the poor, and consequently upon the whole country.

I would therefore ask any readers who think I have over-stated my case in the preceding pages to defer judgment until they read Chapter VII, where the question of 'Poverty and the Health Standard' is dealt with.

The life of a labourer is marked by five alternating periods of want and comparative plenty. During early childhood, unless his father is a skilled worker, he probably will be in poverty; this will last until he, or some of his brothers or sisters, begin to earn money and thus augment their father's wage sufficiently to raise the family above the poverty line. Then follows the period during which he is earning money and living under his parents' roof; for some portion of this period he will be earning more money than is required for lodging, food, and clothes. This is his chance to save money. If he has saved enough to pay for furnishing a cottage, this period of comparative prosperity may continue after marriage until he has two or three children, when poverty will again overtake him. This period of poverty will last perhaps for ten years, i.e. until the first child is fourteen years old and begins to earn wages; but if there are more than three children it may last longer.* While the children are earning, and before they leave the home to marry, the man enjoys another period of prosperity – possibly, however, only to sink back again into poverty when his children have married and left him, and he himself is too old to work, for his income has never permitted his saving enough for him and his wife to live upon for more than a very short time.

A labourer is thus in poverty and therefore underfed:

    (*a*) In childhood – when his constitution is being built up.

    (*b*) In early middle life – when he should be in his prime.

    (*c*) In old age.

The accompanying diagram may serve to illustrate this:

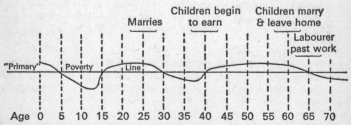

* It is to be noted that the family are in poverty, and consequently are underfed, during the first ten or more years of the children's lives.

It should be noted that the women are in poverty during the greater part of the period that they are bearing children.

We thus see that the 7230 persons shown by this inquiry to be in a state of 'primary' poverty *represent merely that section who happened to be in one of these poverty periods at the time the inquiry was made.* Many of these will, in course of time, pass on into a period of comparative prosperity; this will take place as soon as the children, now dependent, begin to earn. But their places below the poverty line will be taken by others who are at present living in that prosperous period previous to, or shortly after, marriage. Again, many now classed as above the poverty line were below it until the children began to earn. The proportion of the community who at one period or other of their lives suffer from poverty to the point of physical privation is therefore much greater, and the injurious effects of such a condition are much more widespread than would appear from a consideration of the number who can be shown to be below the poverty line at any given moment . . .

SUMMARY AND CONCLUSION

From *Poverty: A Study of Town Life*

It is proposed [here] to briefly summarise the facts set forth in the preceding pages, and to consider what conclusions regarding the problem of poverty may be drawn from them.

Method and Scope of Inquiry. As stated in the second chapter, the information regarding the numbers, occupation, and housing of the working classes was gained by direct inquiry, which practically covered every working-class family in York. In some cases direct information was also obtained regarding earnings, but in the majority of cases these were estimated, the information at the disposal of the writer enabling him to do this with considerable accuracy.

The Poverty Line. Having thus made an estimate, based upon carefully ascertained facts, of the earnings of practically every working-class family in York, the next step was to show the proportion of the total population living in poverty. Families regarded as living in poverty were grouped under two heads:

(*a*) Families whose total earnings were insufficient to obtain the minimum necessaries for the maintenance of merely physical efficiency. Poverty falling under this head was described as 'primary' poverty.

(*b*) Families whose total earnings would have been sufficient for the maintenance of merely physical efficiency were it not that some portion of it was absorbed by other expenditure, either useful or wasteful. Poverty falling under this head was described as 'secondary' poverty.

To ascertain the total number living in 'primary' poverty it was necessary to ascertain the minimum cost upon which families of various sizes could be maintained in a state of physical efficiency. This question was discussed under three heads, viz. the necessary expenditure for (1) food; (2) rent; and (3) all else.

In Chapter IV it was shown that for a family of father, mother, and three children, the minimum weekly expenditure upon which physical efficiency can be maintained in York is 21*s* 8*d*, made up as follows:

	s	d
Food	12	9
Rent (say)	4	0
Clothing, light, fuel, etc.	4	11
	21	8

The necessary expenditure for families larger or smaller than the above will be correspondingly greater or less. This estimate was based upon the assumptions that the diet is selected with a careful regard to the nutritive values of various foodstuffs, and that these are all purchased at the lowest current prices. It only allows for a diet less generous as regards variety than that supplied to able-bodied paupers in workhouses. It further assumes that no clothing is purchased which is not absolutely necessary for health, and assumes too that it is of the plainest and most economical description.

No expenditure of any kind is allowed for beyond that which

is absolutely necessary for the maintenance of *merely physical efficiency*.

The number of persons whose earnings are so low that they cannot meet the expenditure necessary for the above standard of living, stringent to severity though it is, and bare of all creature comforts, was shown to be no less than 7230, or almost exactly 10 per cent of the total population of the city. These persons, then, represent those who are in 'primary' poverty.

The number of those in 'secondary' poverty was arrived at by ascertaining the *total* number living in poverty, and subtracting those living in 'primary' poverty. The investigators, in the course of their house-to-house visitation, noted those families who were obviously living in a state of poverty, i.e. in obvious want and squalor. Sometimes they obtained definite information that the bulk of the earnings was spent in drink or otherwise squandered, sometimes the external evidence of poverty in the home was so clear as to make verbal evidence superfluous.

In this way 20,302 persons, or 27·84 per cent of the total population, were returned as living in poverty. Subtracting those whose poverty is 'primary', we arrive at the number living in 'secondary' poverty, viz. 13,072, or 17·93 per cent of the total population. The figures will be clearer if shown in tabular form:

		Proportion of total Population of York
Persons in "primary" poverty	7,230	9·91 per cent
Persons in "secondary" poverty	13,072	17·93 per cent
Total number of persons living in poverty	20,302	27·84 per cent

One naturally asks, on reading these figures, how far they represent the proportion of poverty in other towns. The only statistics which enable us to form an opinion upon this point are those collected in London by Mr Charles Booth, and set forth in his *Life and Labour of the People in London*. The objects of Mr Booth's inquiry, as explained by himself, were 'to show the numerical relation which poverty, misery, and depravity bear to regular earnings, and to describe the general conditions under which each class lives'.*

In East London Mr Booth obtained information from the School Board visitors regarding every family scheduled by the Board in which there were children of school age. These families represented about one half of the working-class population, and Mr Booth assumed that the condition of the whole population was similar to that of the part tested.

In the other districts of London Mr Booth, in order to complete his inquiry in a reasonable time, was obliged to adopt a rougher classification.

From the information thus obtained, which he checked and supplemented in various ways, Mr Booth estimated that 30·7 per cent of the total population of London were living in poverty.† *Supposing, then, that the same standard of poverty had been adopted in the two inquiries*, a comparison between the poverty in York and that of London would be possible. From the commencement of my inquiry I have had opportunities of consulting with Mr Booth, and comparing the methods of investigation and the standards of poverty adopted. As a result I feel no hesitation in regarding my estimate of the total poverty in York as comparable with Mr Booth's estimate of the total poverty in London, and in this Mr Booth agrees.

The proportions arrived at for the total population living in poverty in London and York respectively were as under:

London   30·7 per cent
York   27·84 per cent

The proportion of the population living in poverty in York may be regarded as practically the same as in London, especially when we remember that Mr Booth's information was gathered in 1887–92, a period of only *average* trade prosperity, whilst the York figures were collected in 1899, when

* *Life and Labour of the People in London*, by Charles Booth, vol. i, p. 6.

† In estimating the poverty in London Mr Booth made no attempt to differentiate between 'primary' and 'secondary' poverty.

trade was unusually prosperous.

This agreement in result is so striking that it is perhaps best to say that I did not set out upon my inquiry with the object of proving any preconceived theory, but to ascertain actual facts, and that I was myself much surprised to obtain the above result.*

We have been accustomed to look upon the poverty in London as exceptional, but when the result of careful investigation shows that the proportion of poverty in London is practically equalled in what may be regarded as a typical provincial town, we are faced by the startling probability that from 25 to 30 per cent of the town populations of the United Kingdom

---

* On this subject the present writer has received the subjoined letter from Mr Booth:

9 Adelphi Terrace, Strand, WC,
July 25, 1901.

'DEAR MR ROWNTREE – You know with what interest I have watched your investigation into the conditions of life at York, and in response to your question I certainly think that the slight difference in our methods ought in no way to prevent the possibility of a comparison being made between your results and mine.

'The methods adopted by you are more complete than those I found available for the large area of London. I made an estimate of the total proportion of the people visibly living in poverty, and from amongst these separated the cases in which the poverty appeared to be extreme and amounted to destitution, but I did not enter into the questions of economical or wasteful expenditure. You too have enumerated the cases of visible poverty, applying similar tests, and so far our estimates are fairly comparable; but you enumerate separately those whose income is such that they cannot by any means afford the expenditure which your argument sets forth as an absolutely necessary minimum. It is very possible that few of those classed by you or me as poor would pass muster as sufficiently nourished, clothed, and housed, according to this standard; but your classification separates those who conceivably might be so, from those who certainly could not.

'It is in this respect that my classification falls short of yours; but our totals may be correctly compared, and the comparison, as you have shown, is very close. At this I am not surprised. I have, indeed, long thought that other cities, if similarly tested, would show a percentage of poverty not differing greatly from that existing in London. Your most valuable inquiry confirms me in this opinion. – Yours faithfully,   CHARLES BOOTH.'

are living in poverty. If this be the fact, its grave significance may be realised when it is remembered that, in 1901, 77 per cent of the population of the United Kingdom is returned as 'urban' and only 23 per cent as 'rural'.*

The Results of Poverty. The facts regarding the *proportion* of poverty are perhaps the most important which have been dealt with in this volume, but the conditions under which the poor live, and the effects of those conditions, especially upon their physical stamina, will have also claimed the serious attention of the reader.

Housing. It has been shown that in York 4705 persons, or 6·4 per cent of the total population, are living more than two persons to a room, whilst the actual number who are living, and especially sleeping, in rooms which provide inadequate air-space for the maintenance of health is undoubtedly very much greater. Moreover, the impossibility of maintaining the decencies of life in these overcrowded houses is a factor which cannot fail to affect the morals of their inhabitants.

The close relation which exists between overcrowding and poverty is indicated by the fact that 94 per cent of the over-crowded families are in poverty either 'primary' or' secondary'.

Rent. Although rents in York are much lower than in many towns, still the proportion of total earnings spent in rent by the working classes in York is high, varying from 9 per cent in the few favoured cases where the total earnings reach or exceed 60s, to 29 per cent for those whose total family earnings fall below 18s weekly. The average proportion of total family earnings spent in rent by all sections of the working classes in

* According to the official distinction of 'urban' and 'rural' adopted by the Registrar-General, the population of England and Wales in 1901, as given in the Preliminary Report of the Census, is as follows:

Urban	25,054,268	77 per cent
Rural	7,471,242	23 per cent

If, however, the distinction between urban and rural be drawn at towns of 10,000 population, the figures are as follows:

Urban	21,946,346	67 per cent
Rural	10,579,164	33 per cent

And if drawn at towns of 20,000 population they are:

Urban	18,940,056	58 per cent
Rural	13,585,444	42 per cent

York is over 14 per cent. Although York is not a large city, and freehold land within three miles of the centre of the city may be bought for £60 to £80 an acre, it nevertheless contains slums as degradingly filthy as any to be found in London.

Relation of Poverty to Health. Turning now to the relation of poverty to health, it has been shown in the preceding pages how low is the standard of health amongst the very poor. This was tested not only by the general and infant mortality of the city, but by an examination of the physique of a large number of school children. The inferences drawn from this latter examination are corroborated by the general statistics which refer to the health standard of those who seek enlistment in the army. These indicate that a low standard of health prevails among the working classes. It therefore becomes obvious that the widespread existence of poverty in an industrial country like our own must seriously retard its development.

Workmen's Household Budgets. In the last chapter concrete evidence is advanced as to the inadequate nutrition of the poorer sections of the labouring classes. An inquiry into the diet of various sections of the community revealed the facts. (1) that the diet of the middle classes is generally more than adequate; (2) that of the well-to-do artisan is on the whole *adequate*; but (3) that of the labouring class is seriously *inadequate*. Indeed, the labouring class receive upon the average 25 per cent less food than has been proved by scientific experts to be necessary for the maintenance of physical efficiency. This statement is not intended to imply that labourers and their families are chronically hungry, but that the food which they eat (although on account of its bulk it satisfies the cravings of hunger) does not contain the nutrients necessary for normal physical efficiency. A homely illustration will make the point clear. A horse fed upon hay does not feel hungry, and may indeed grow fat, but it cannot perform hard and continuous work without a proper supply of corn. Just so the labourer, though perhaps not hungry, is unable to do the work which he could easily accomplish upon a more nutritious diet.

As the investigation into the conditions of life in this typical provincial town has proceeded, the writer has been increasingly impressed with the gravity of the facts which have unfolded themselves.

That in this land of abounding wealth, during a time of perhaps unexampled prosperity, probably more than one-fourth of the population are living in poverty, is a fact which may well cause great searchings of heart. There is surely need for a greater concentration of thought by the nation upon the well-being of its own people, for no civilisation can be sound or stable which has at its base this mass of stunted human life. The suffering may be all but voiceless, and we may long remain ignorant of its extent and severity, but when once we realise it we see that social questions of profound importance await solution. What, for instance, are the primary causes of this poverty? How far is it the result of false social and economic conditions? If it be due in part to faults in the national character, what influences can be exerted to impart to that character greater strength and thoughtfulness?

The object of the writer, however, has been to state facts rather than to suggest remedies. He desires, nevertheless, to express his belief that however difficult the path of social progress may be, a way of advance will open out before patient and penetrating thought if inspired by a true human sympathy.

The dark shadow of the Malthusian philosophy has passed away, and no view of the ultimate scheme of things would now be accepted under which multitudes of men and women are doomed by inevitable law to a struggle for existence so severe as necessarily to cripple or destroy the higher parts of their nature.

Rider Haggard

Sir Henry Rider Haggard (1856–1925), best remembered for his best-selling novels, *King Solomon's Mines* (1885), *She* (1887) and *Allan Quartermain* (1887), was passionately interested in all aspects of agriculture and emotionally committed to Norfolk, the county where he was born and later farmed. His survey of rural England was commissioned by the *Daily Express* where the letters reporting on his journey were published initially, and appeared in a two-volume book form in 1902. In this Haggard was consciously following the pattern set fifty years earlier by Sir James Caird whose reports were published by *The Times*, through 1850, and then as *English Agriculture in 1850–51* (1851). Relatively little of *Rural England* is concerned with the labourer's point of view. Haggard realized this and explained why: 'As all who are acquainted with him know, the labourer is very shy; also he is suspicious. In any case it is difficult to persuade him to talk, or to be sure, when he does talk, that he is saying what is really in his mind.' In spite of this *Rural England* is in a classic exploration mould; its concerns are central to an understanding of Edwardian England, and the approach refers back to a tradition that includes Cobbett, Arthur Young, and William Marshall, as well as Caird.

THE EXPLORER

From *Rural England*

Physically such a person must be very strong, since the work is the hardest that I have ever undertaken. Not only are the necessary correspondence and arrangements in themselves troublesome, but when these are completed, he must travel week after week and month after month, by rail, with horses, in motor-cars, on bicycles, and on foot, in order to fulfil his hundreds of engagements. He must never fall ill, or, if he does, must go on as I did, until he is well again, or collapses utterly, which I am thankful to say I did not. Every night he must be prepared, at the end of the toil of a long day, to plunge into unknown society, to make acquaintance with many new faces and listen to many fresh views or arguments, without showing signs of an exhaustion which his hosts or their guests might, not unnaturally, attribute to a lack of interest and proper gratitude. Never for one instant must he allow his attention to flag, his powers of observation to become dull, or his sight and hearing to miss anything that is of importance to his cause.

His mind should be that of a trained lawyer, able to weigh and sift evidence, discriminating between the true and the false, the weighty and the trivial. His intelligence must be of that patient and prosaic order that scorns no detail, however oft repeated, knowing that in each there is some difference from all that went before, if only it can be grasped. Vexations, disappointments, even occasional impertinences and rebuffs, should not disturb him; with a smile he must try again elsewhere. Also he must have money at his command, since such long journeyings are costly. He must learn to write accurate articles and notes under any circumstances and at any time, and, what is still more important, how to read the latter afterwards. To heat, cold, and bodily weariness he must be indifferent. Lastly, not to prolong the list, he should really know something about agriculture, and must have given adequate study to those great questions of which he proposes to treat.

Of these qualifications and others left unrecorded, I can with humility lay some claim to one – an acquaintance with my subject. I was born in a farmhouse, among high-hedged pastures near to the silence of a great wood, and I suppose the first sounds that my ears heard were the lowing of kine and the bleating of sheep. Perhaps, if there be any truth in such theories, it is to this fact that I owe my rural bent.

HOP-PICKING IN KENT

From *Rural England*

I received an interesting communication from Miss Mary L. Russell, of St John's, Sutton-at-Hone, Kent, dealing with the housing and general condition of the hop-pickers, who in the autumn of the year flock in thousands from the great towns to this county. I will quote the substance of her letter.

Miss Russell began her statement by assuring me that it was founded upon personal observations made while visiting the children of these people, and was in no wise exaggerated. She said that the habitations provided for hop-pickers are of tin, fitted with doors and iron ventilators, but without flooring or windows. One covered-in brick oven for cooking in wet weather and two or three sanitary huts are found, but there are no coppers or places for washing clothes. On some farms there is a tank to which water is brought in a cart, but at other places it must be fetched by the pickers, who sleep upon straw which is given to them, though rarely changed. The huts stand in the full sun, without any shelter from trees. They have no wells. The adult pickers can scarcely any of them read, the young men being as ignorant as the old, but the younger children can most of them read a very little, although this is not so in some cases.

The majority, both of men and women, have no thought except for the public-house and drink, and the girls are very wild. Owing to the insufficient arrangements made for personal cleanliness, the condition of the children. who are infested with insects, is extremely bad. Some of them suffer from ophthalmia, caused by dirt, and one little fellow of five, whom she knew, was covered with sores. As the doctor cannot carry on his business in such places, when children are taken ill they must be brought to him, even if their ailment is bronchitis. The condition of a woman whose child was born in one of these huts was, she said, too awful to describe to me.

Miss Russell thought that by way of remedy the Education Department should send travelling teachers to places where large numbers of children live in huts. Such children should not be allowed to pass all their time in the fruit fields, but ought to receive three hours' instruction at the beginning of the day before they were tired out. She believed that much might be done if the dwelling huts were made more suitable to their purpose, and that this could only be brought about by insisting on the local authorities building decent and sanitary tin houses and charging interest to the farmers for their use. Such houses could be moved from place to place as they were required. Miss Russell added that she knew it might be argued that, bad as these conditions were, still they are better than those of the dens in a London slum. She maintained, however, that in these country places there is a chance of improving the habits, morals, and education of a portion of our future labouring class, and that it is our duty not to allow such an opportunity to slip.

Doubtless all that Miss Russell says is true, and at any rate in a large proportion of the places which they frequent, the sanitary and moral surroundings of the hop-pickers are deplorable. But this question remains, Who is to better them? The majority of hop farmers make no more than a living; some, indeed, make less. If they were to be forced to provide respectable accommodation for the scores or hundreds of hands whom they employ for about a month of the year with their families, the workhouses of Kent would soon be overflowing. To insist upon such a thing would, I believe, in practice bring the hop industry to an end, for large tin buildings with wells, outhouses, etc., are costly. Miss Russell suggests that the work should be undertaken by the local authorities, by which I suppose she means the County or District Councils. But these bodies have to look to the rates for funds, and in Kent, as elsewhere, rates are already high enough. We may be sure that the interest which she thinks ought to be charged to the farmers, even if they did not refuse to pay it, would by no means be adequate to the capital expenditure, especially as the depreciation of movable tin buildings which must be frequently renewed, and, by the way, would be required almost everywhere at the same time, would be very heavy.

There remains the State, but the State already staggers under its load of obligations, local and imperial, like Christian beneath his sins in the Slough of Despair. How much more can its broad back carry? For my part I can see but two remedies. One – the heroic method – would be to forbid the employment of hop-pickers unless their accommodation was such as a sanitary Board would approve, which, I suppose, in most cases would mean an end of hop and fruit growing, since without ample labour at the proper season, these crops are useless. The other – a more humble expedient – is to let things go on as they are, and trust to the efforts and purses of philanthropists to better them. After all, it must be remembered that around these crowded insanitary hovels breathes the sweet, fresh air, and above them stretches the blue sky of English summer. In the festering slums of London such blessings are absent, and hop and fruit picking is the annual holiday of tens of thousands of their denizens – to them, indeed, what the autumn visit to sea or country-side is to other classes of town dwellers.

The question remains whether, with all these disadvantages which Miss Russell so movingly describes, the balance of good is not therefore still in favour of the yearly exodus to the evil-smelling shanties of the gardens of Kent, with its accompaniment of healthful labour in a pure atmosphere sweetened by the sights and sounds of Nature undefiled. After all, at the season of the year when their services are required the days are few on which the pickers or their children need pass more than eight hours out of twenty-four beneath the shelter of a roof.

LABOUR SHORTAGE IN SOMERSET

From *Rural England*

In [Mr Carter's] district labour was very scarce. The average weekly wage was about 12s, with or without a cottage; two quarts of cider per diem, the Truck Amendment Act being, he said, a dead letter which was equally ignored by master and men; and 1s a day extra in hay time and harvest, when overtime is worked. Cottage rentals are reckoned at about 1s a week, but the tenant generally gives Sunday work in lieu of the rent. Now-a-days there was not much piecework, since the labourers did not care for it unless an exorbitant price was paid, as it involves more labour. Severe labour, Mr Carter remarked, is the one thing that the modern farm-hand does not like. Since the introduction of self-binders piecework had gradually lessened, but this the men do not seem to regret. Still wages were rising, and, as he believed, within a few years would be higher by 2s the week. Meanwhile day by day the labourers became more independent.

Cottages were scarce, but, owing to the advance of de-population, were becoming more plentiful. At that time there were several to let in his village, a new thing in his experience. Nearly all these dwellings were old, and such as would not satisfy the sanitary authorities in the case of newly erected cottages. For the most part they consisted of two downstairs rooms – a living room and a wash-house – and two bedrooms. This could hardly be called decent accommodation for a mixed family; still it did not vary much; nor could such habitations be closed unless others were provided, which would never be done by private enterprise. Unless they married early and had a family, which handicapped them, the young men did not stay upon the land. From his neighbourhood they nearly all went to the Welsh coalfields, where during three or four days they earned good wages, and employed the remainder of the week in spending them. A boy who was perhaps taking 6s a week at farm work would be enticed to the mines, where he receives 15s a week, or more at a hazardous employment. Naturally he thinks it a grand thing to jump to a man's wage all at once, and on his first holiday returns home with glowing tales of the money that is to be had for the asking by those who are willing to follow his example. Is it wonderful, asked Mr Carter, that nearly all of them go away, so that a boy to drive horses on the farm cannot be procured for love or money?

The initial cause of this exodus was, he thought, our system of education. Formerly if a boy went to school, at the age of nine or ten years he left it to earn fivepence or sixpence a day by scaring birds or doing odd jobs upon the farm. Now he must remain at his lessons until he was twelve or thirteen, by which time he had lost all taste for country pursuits, and was more fit to drive a pen than to follow the plough. By all means, said Mr Carter, let a boy be taught to read and write and do the four elementary rules of arithmetic – knowledge that he could acquire by the time he was nine years of age; after which let him begin to earn his daily bread. Were they asked, this is what all boys of the labouring class would wish. Their parents would wish it also, and the plan would be approved by the common sense of the community, if this were not overruled by the dicta of educational enthusiasts and buried beneath departmental regulations. How, he asked, are the vast regions that we have recently conquered to be satisfactorily colonised? Not, he thought, by clerks and others of that ilk, but by the bone and sinew of the land, which can only be produced in perfection in the rural districts. Therefore, he said, if his parents approve, a boy should be permitted to leave school so soon as he can fairly master the three R's. Then he would take to the land naturally. In the eyes of a farm-boy scientific and technical teaching was a ridiculous fad. It was certain that a lad who migrated to the town must necessarily develope into a man of lower physique than one who stayed upon the land . . .

Mr J. D. Adams, MD, a medical officer of health for the Yeovil Rural District, gave me an interesting view on the present position of the agricultural labourer in Somersetshire, which he thought would admit of much improvement. He said that it was difficult to understand how a man earning from 14s to 16s a week could support a wife and children in a decent fashion. In the neighbourhood of Yeovil, however, the takings of a family were in most cases largely increased by gloving work, an industry in which nearly all the women and girls were more or less engaged. It was the young lads and unmarried men who became dissatisfied with farm work and wages, and migrated to the towns, or from that immediate district to the collieries in Wales. Considered from the sanitary point of view, the labourers' cottages were by no means what they should be, but in his opinion this fact was not the cause of the unpopularity of farm labour.

His experience was that the education of the boys had the effect of rendering them gregarious, and of inducing in them a distaste for farm work and an inclination for the constant society of those of their own age and class. Thus the factories in that locality found no difficulty in obtaining boys, although the hours were as long and the pay no better than on the farms, because there they found society with its pleasures, and a half holiday on Saturdays. He believed also that the fact of all the farm labourers in a district being paid the same wage, whether they were able and industrious, or idle, was disastrous in its results. Take away hope and emulation from any class, and, whether they laboured with their hands or with their brains, both the workers and their work would certainly deteriorate. The circumstance of so much land that was formerly arable having of recent years been laid down to grass had of course enabled the farmer to dispense with some of his workmen. Still the demand for farm labourers was in excess of the supply; the work was there, but the young and active men would not accept it upon the terms offered to them.

AN ESSEX LABOURER

From *Rural England*

Not far from Blunt's Hall I saw an old labourer named John Lapwood, whose life experience, which I verified by inquiry, is worth preserving. For half a century or more he worked on the Post Hall and Oliver Farms in Witham, and now, by the help of some kind friends, was spending his last days in a little cottage, where he lived with his old wife. We found him – an aged and withered but still an apple-cheeked individual – seated upon a bank, 'enjoying of the sweet air, although it be a bit draughty'. He told me that in his young days wages for horsemen used to be down to 9s a week, and for daymen to 8s, when the weather allowed them to be earned. During the Crimean War bread cost him a shilling a loaf, and other food a proportionate price. He stated that for months at a time he had existed upon nothing but a diet of bread and onions, washed down, when he was lucky, with a little small-beer. These onions he ate until they took the skin off the roof of his mouth, blistering it to whiteness, after which he was obliged to soak them in salt to draw the 'virtue' out of them. They had no tea, but his wife imitated the appear-

ance of that beverage by soaking a burnt crust of bread in
boiling water. On this diet he became so feeble that the reek
of the muck which it was his duty to turn, made him sick
and faint; and often, he said, he would walk home at night
from the patch of ground where he grew the onions and some
other vegetables, with swimming head and uncertain feet. I
asked if his children, of whom there were eight, lived on onions
also. He answered no; they had generally a little cheese and
butter in the house, but he could not put it into his own
stomach when they were hungry and cried for food. 'Things
is better now,' he added.

Well, things are better now; indeed, it is scarcely too much
to say that in many cases today, the labourer has more than
his share of the rather plumless agricultural cake. But with
such a record behind him, knowing what his fathers suffered,
is it wonderful that he should strive to drive home the nail
of opportunity, and sometimes to take advantage of the
farmers who in the past too often were so merciless?

Let us try to understand his case and be just. Think, for
instance, of this poor man Lapwood, whose condition was but
that of ten thousand others, day by day forcing his hated food
into a blistered mouth, starving that his children might be
full. Think of him with his 9s a week, and ten souls to feed,
house, and clothe, while bread stood at a shilling a loaf.
Remember, too, that from this lot there was no escape; that
labour was in overflowing supply; and that to lift his voice
against an employer, however tyrannous, meant instant dis-
missal and the hell of the poor-house – it was little better in
those days – or the roadside ditch to lie in. Is it strange that,
remembering these things, he – or rather his sons – should wax
fat and kick, that they should be haunted also by the fear
that the evil might return upon them, and bear in their hearts
resentment, cloaked but very real, against those classes at
whose hands they received that evil of which no subsequent
kindness can obliterate the memory? With the agricultural
labourer, as I believe, this resentment against past suffering,
at any rate as yet, is deeper than gratitude for present benefits.

LABOURERS' COTTAGES IN ELTISLEY

From *Rural England*

At the village of Croxton, in Cambridgeshire, on the borders of Huntingdonshire, in connection with which county I shall treat of her evidence, our host was Mr Robert Cochrane, whose daughter, Miss Constance Cochrane, is so well and honourably known for her strenuous and unselfish advocacy of the cause of the improvement of rural dwellings. In pursuit of this end Miss Cochrane has written various pamphlets, has appeared as a witness before district Councils and other authorities, and, in person or by deputy, at her own expense, has visited or collected information from scores of parishes throughout England. This is no light task for a lady to undertake, and she spoke to me with feeling of what she had suffered in its execution. To be called meddlesome and to be told to mind her own business seemed to be with her a somewhat common experience. In my view, however, it reflects great honour upon Miss Cochrane that in pursuit of a work which she knows to be good she is willing to endure much hardness.

Few questions are surrounded with greater difficulties than this of the housing of labourers in rural parishes. As a class they are not desirable tenants, and the rent that they pay is very low. To build a pair of good cottages, with three bedrooms each, at the present price of labour and materials, costs from £300 to £400, according to design and accommodation – generally nearer £400 than £300. Supposing that the average rent paid is 2s a week – and in villages it does not often amount to more, generally to less indeed – the reader can work out for himself what interest, after allowing for upkeep and repairs, this income is likely to return on the capital invested. It may be said that the erection of such necessary buildings ought not to be looked upon as an investment, but if this aspect of the case is to be disregarded, it follows that the builder must be in a position to afford the sinking of the necessary capital.

Now, taking the country through, what proportion of the owners of property are so happily placed in these times of landed depression? It may be said again – and I think with justice – that, in view of the urgent need of keeping population on the land, and of providing men and women with decent homes, this is a national rather than an individual question, and that where the individual is powerless to remedy or abate the evil, the nation, in its own interest, should come to his assistance.

Well, to a certain extent it recognises the obligation. That is to say, under the provisions of the Housing of the Working Classes Act of 1890, the Public Works Loan Commissioners are empowered to advance money for the purpose of constructing or improving dwellings for the working classes to any company, society, or private person. But consider the terms. The loan so made is to bear interest at 'not less than £3 2s 6d per cent per annum', or at such other rate of interest 'as the Treasury may from time to time authorise as being in their opinion sufficient to enable such loans to be made without loss to the Exchequer'. Moreover, it is provided amid a mass of other stipulations that 'the period for the repayment of the sums advanced shall not exceed forty years'.

It is obvious that these advantages, if they can be so called, are not sufficient to induce anybody who cannot afford to do so from his own pocket, to lay out money in building cottages.

Indeed, I believe I am right in saying that, so far as the rural districts are concerned the Act is practically a dead letter. Surely the terms ought to be widened, at any rate to the extent of lengthening the period of repayment to sixty years, making the 3½ per cent a maximum rate not variable at the option of the Commissioners, and enacting that a sufficient proportion of the interest received should go to a sinking-fund account, which at the expiration of the sixty years would extinguish the debt. That something of the sort is needed must be obvious to any who have taken the trouble to read the writings of Miss Cochrane and other authorities, and that it is needed in Cambridgeshire, Huntingdonshire, Bedfordshire, and other places that I have seen, I am prepared to bear witness from the evidence of my own eyes.

On one day of our stay with her father, Miss Cochrane conducted us to visit some dwellings at Eltisley, on the

Cambridgeshire border, a few of which I will briefly describe.

No. 1, thatched, built of cracked and ancient stud-work, contained one bedroom, one sitting-room, and one lean-to scullery. The bedroom in the roof which was stopped with rags to keep out the rain, was approached by a steep ladder, the woman who led me there crawling upon her hands and knees into the apartment, where she slept with the daughter of a neighbour, who, since Miss Cochrane stirred in these matters, passed the nights here. This girl's previous bedroom had been shared with her father, a widower, in the next cottage. I should add that she was grown up.

In the sitting-room below slept an ancient bed-ridden woman of ninety-eight and, I think, a daughter-in-law, who was staying with her. It is right to say, however, that this cottage, which belonged to one of the Cambridge colleges, was given to these people rent free until the old woman dies. In my judgment it ought not to be inhabited at all. This old lady's husband had died not long before, aged ninety-nine. I was told that Mr Terence Hooley had promised to give him £10 if he lived to 100. When he deceased a little short of the appointed age, his daughter, who showed us the cottage, said to Miss Cochrane: 'Lord! I did try hard to keep him alive to get that there £10.' I remember that this same good lady grumbled to us upon the subject of her aged mother, who lay in the bed and gave her, she said, 'a deal of trouble to look after'.

The poor are frequently somewhat callous where their sick or aged relatives are concerned. Some years ago, in the village of Ditchingham, an old woman, who was said to be 102, lived with a niece or a grand-niece. One day I passed the cottage and found this ancient dame hobbling about the garden in a great state of distress. In answer to my inquiries she informed me that her niece had put out her bit of fire – I suppose the only thing she could enjoy. Moved by compassion I interviewed the niece, who did not receive my remonstrances in a conciliatory spirit. Indeed, she became positively violent in her remarks concerning her antique relative and her ways. I rejoined that the very aged had a right to every care and attention. 'Very well,' she answered, 'if you are so fond of the nasty old thing, take and look after her yourself!'

Cottage No. 2, where lived the widower and his daughter, was, I considered, not fit for human habitation.

No. 3. – A row of cottages of small size. Until Miss Cochrane induced a neighbouring landowner to grant a strip of ground at the back, upon which the necessary outbuildings and conveniences now stand, these dwellings were confined between the main road and a large open ditch upon the edge of which their back walls were built. Into this ditch ran all the sewage and other refuse. They were known as the 'Eltisley death-trap', and their back windows could not be opened because of the stench.

No. 4 (which I did not enter). A small two-roomed cottage. Seven children were reared in the bedroom, and at one time four children slept there for a period of three months while the parents lay sick in bed. It was impossible to wash the floor, as the water ran between the boards into the sitting-room below.

No. 5 (then empty). – Two rooms and no outhouse or pantry. I measured the upstairs room. At the floor line it was 17 ft. 7 in. by 9 ft., but as the room sloped the space above was not so large. The window was 24 inches by 18 inches. In this room eight children were reared with their parents. In the sister cottage adjoining, also two-roomed, lived seven children and their parents, making for the four rooms a total of nineteen, whose water supply was a filthy hole in the garden. Now water can be fetched from a well some 600 yards away.

The occupants of one of the cottages in this village, most of whose children are now out in the world, informed me that when they told the landlord or his agent – I forget which – that Miss Cochrane said they ought to have a third room, he replied politely: 'That be d—d for a tale!'

No. 6. – Here a grown-up sister, whom I saw, and two brothers, one of them adult, slept in the same room. The law only takes notice of overcrowding, not of the mixture of the sexes, and, I may add, that the law, whatever it is, is rarely enforced – at any rate in these parts.

Of the delightful dwellings of Eltisley these samples may suffice, but Miss Cochrane informed us that at Yelling, in Huntingdonshire, where I saw some of them, they were as bad, and at Great and Little Eversden, Burrough Green, and other parishes even worse. That things had improved in Eltisley itself, was, I gathered, although she was too modest to admit it, entirely owing to her exertions. Miss Cochrane mentioned one instance of overcrowding, with which she was personally acquainted, where a house belonging to a Cambridge college was inhabited two years before my visit, by a man, his wife, and nine children, one of them a new-born baby, all sleeping in a single room. Over the bed was a shelf upon which stood uncorked bottles of honey ready for market. Probably somebody bought that honey! Miss Cochrane made representations, and ultimately new cottages were built.

LABOUR PROBLEMS IN YORKSHIRE

From *Rural England*

For labour Mr Burton said he was better off than he had been. Indeed, that harvest many Irish could not find hirers. This difference was owing to the self-binder. It was not easy, however, to secure young men, and if one went it was hard to replace him. He thought that within a few years there would be a reaction, that the towns would supply their own labour, and that the country would not be drawn upon as had been the case. Here, I am sorry to say, I must differ from Mr Burton. It is a well-known fact that cities do not and cannot breed their own manual labour, at any rate for more than one generation; after which the progeny of town folk will seldom take to hard physical work, although they may become clerks, or waiters, or shopmen, or house-porters, or drift into the great army of loafers. The actual toil of the world, as I believe, always has been and always will be done by those bred upon the land.

Mr Burton said that he allowed his men two cows each and twenty hens, with free cottages and potatoes, which brought up their wage, taking the year through, to an average value of 26s a week. He supplied the cows, fed them, and took the risk of their going wrong; but the calves belonged to him and the skim-milk was used to feed his animals. Living as he did in an 'out place', if he refused these privileges the men would not stop. In the matter of fowls, the rule was that each spring his labourers must not have more than twenty hens. If they got a little corn out of him to feed them – well, he knew nothing about it; but he did know that anyone who wished to keep a good man must overlook such small leakages. A higher wage could not be paid, but a farmer must have labour. The result of his system was that his men had never done working till six o'clock at night. In answer to my inquiries he said that the custom of his neighbours was to allow one cow to a man.

It will be observed that Mr Burton's treatment of his labourers was extraordinarily liberal, more so indeed than many farmers would be able to afford. In his case, however, the experiment seems to have answered . . .

At Lotherton I had the pleasure of meeting Mr Herbert Prater [who] . . . on the whole had a very cheerful tale to tell, the fact being that the nearness to the great market of Leeds makes land valuable and sought after . . .

Of labour he said that farmers were feeling this question very severely, but he had raised his wages, and therefore did not suffer. Also just then the coal-pits were working badly, which meant that there were more men available for the land. I have observed in various districts that wherever there are great manufactories, or much employment on railways or in mines, the rural labour conditions are apt to change very quickly in accordance with the flow and ebb of demand in these industries. It is the far country parts that are being bled to death of their men and women, since thence everyone departs and but few return.

Mr Prater paid waggoners £1 a week and gave them a row of potatoes. On the Partington farms dairymen and carters received 21s and labourers from 2s 9d to 3s a day, with good cottages at 1s 6d or 2s a week rent. He thought that farmers would be obliged to raise their rate of wage if they wanted to secure hands. There was great trouble about Sunday milking which the men would not do; indeed, he knew cases where the sons and daughters were obliged to undertake the milking. I asked Mr Prater whether milking machines would not help, but he told me that he believed them to be a failure, as they made the cows 'run their milk'. A friend of his had tried the machine and gone back to hand milking.

Mr Prater informed me that the young people were leaving the parish, although they had a village Institute on the most approved model, with two billiard tables, where many entertainments were given, to which people could belong at a subscription of 4s a year. This Institute was a comparative failure, and out of 1000 people only sixty cared to be members. He was convinced that the education which the children received unfitted them for country and domestic pursuits. Thus when Mrs Prater offered £1 1s for a sewing prize, only two girls competed, and in both cases their work was worthless. Meanwhile, like other big cities, Leeds was feeling the influx and the difficulty of housing its multitudes although an attempt was being made to relieve this pressure by the building of working men's flats.

Skilled agricultural labourers were growing scarcer, and he thought that, owing to the paucity of thatchers, Dutch barns would become a necessity. On that estate a number of cottages had been built at the high average cost of £280 each, although two 'couples' had been put up at £310 the pair. These cottages were let at 3s 6d a week, which returned 3 per cent on the outlay.

TOWN VERSUS COUNTRY

From *Rural England*

The real peril both to agriculture and, what is even more important, to the Country at large lies, however, in the fact that the supply [of labour] is being cut at its source. The results of my inquiries on this point are even worse than I feared. Everywhere the young men and women are leaving the villages where they were born and flocking into the towns. As has here been shown again and again, it is now common for only the dullards, the vicious, or the wastrels to stay upon the land, because they are unfitted for any other life; and it is this indifferent remnant who will be the parents of the next generation of rural Englishmen. It must be remembered that the census returns do not tell the whole truth of this matter,

since very often rural districts include large townships. Also
the elderly folk and many young children still remain in the
villages, the latter to be reared up at the expense of the
agricultural community for the service of the cities. As they
mature into the fulness of manhood or womanhood they leave
the home and are seen no more.

This is certain – for I have noted it several times – some parts
of England are becoming almost as lonesome as the veld of
Africa. There 'the highways lie waste, the wayfaring man
ceaseth'. The farm labourer is looked down upon, especially
by young women of his own class, and consequently looks
down upon himself. He is at the very bottom of the social
scale. Feeling this, and having no hope for the future, now-a-
days he does not, in the majority of instances, even take the
trouble to master his business. He will not learn the old finer
arts of husbandry; too often he does as little as he can, and
does that little ill.

Farming in this country is no longer what it was. In all parts
of England the land is going more and more to grass, which
means, of course, that fewer men are needed for its working;
while in many places the tendency is towards the division of
farms, until they reach a size that can conveniently be
managed by a man with the help of his own children. Also
there are always a certain number of tramps or drifters who
can be hired, to say nothing of the industrious Irishmen that
visit some of the counties in large numbers.

Therefore, great and damaging as is the present dearth of
agricultural labour, my own opinion is that more or less it
will be met in this way or in that, chiefly by the division of
holdings, the increased use of machinery, the abandonment of
the higher class of farming and of dairies which necessitate
Sunday milking, and the laying away of all but the best lands
to grass. In short, the lack of men will not kill our husbandry;
it will only change its character for the worse; with the result
that much of our soil in the future may produce perhaps one-
half of what it used to produce and, say, one-third of what
it could be made to produce.

But behind the agricultural question lies the national question. What will be the result of this desertion of the country-
side and of the crowding of its denizens into cities? That is

a point upon which it would be easy to indulge in strong words. The evils are known, and little imagination is needed to enable a writer to paint their disastrous consequence. I will, however, content myself with a moderate statement. It can mean nothing less than the progressive deterioration of the race. In the absence of new conditions which cannot be foreseen, if unchecked, it may in the end mean the ruin of the race.

Owing principally to the lowness of prices, from whatever cause arising, and the lack of labour, I take it to be proved then that in the majority of districts English agriculture is a failing industry, although at present, in the absence of serious war and want, this gradual failure does not appear materially to affect the general prosperity of the nation. Yet I maintain it is affecting it, not only by the lessening of a home-grown food supply which might be vital in the case of a European struggle, but in an even more deadly fashion by the withdrawal of the best of its population from the wholesome land into cities which are not wholesome for mind or body.

Will this movement stop? Many think so. The hopes of farmers are built for the most part on a belief, which I find to be very widespread, that the trade of the Country is threatened with imminent disaster which will send people back to the land, or at least prevent the migration of any more of them to the towns. For my own part I do not believe that anything short of actual starvation will cause those who have become accustomed to a city life – or, still more, their children – to return to labour on the soil even if they were fitted so to do. It is, however, possible that those who remain on that soil might be prevented from deserting it by the difficulty of obtaining remunerative employment in the towns. As the demand for robust country folk is at present enormous and increasing in every branch of labour – including the army, the railways, and the police – that case is however purely hypothetical. In this connection it must be remembered that the unemployed, of whom we heard so much, are not strong-limbed, sound-minded rustics, but townsmen of the second or third generation who, whatever else they can do, cannot or will not labour with their bodies. Therefore it comes to this, while there is a demand and trade flourishes the exodus must continue; and at present – with some exceptions – the demand is active and trade does flourish.

The reader may ask, Why should it continue? There are several answers. Chiefly it is a matter of wages. More money can be earned in the towns; and even if this means no real advantage, if the extra cash is more than absorbed in the extra expenses, the average man likes to have the handling of money. He does not think of the rent of the squalid rooms, of the cost of the tramcars and the music halls; he does not reck of the time when he will begin to grow old and be pushed out of his place by some new-comer from the land. Yonder it is thirty shillings; here it is only eighteen. That is what he remembers. So he goes to accomplish his destiny, whatever it may be.

But it is not solely a question of wages; he and his wife seek the change and the excitement of the streets. Nature has little meaning for most of them, and no charms; but they love a gas lamp. Nature, in my experience, only appeals to the truly educated. Our boasted system of education seems to make it detestable — a thing to flee from. Lastly, in towns there is a chance of rising; but in the country, for nineteen out of twenty, there is no hope that they will become farmers on their own account. So the countryman chooses the town, and as a consequence the character of Englishmen appears to be changing, not — as those who have observed certain recent scenes, at Waterloo Station and elsewhere, may reflect — entirely for the better . . .

People are deserting the villages wholesale, leaving behind them the mentally incompetent and the physically unfit; nor, at any rate in many parts of England — although in this matter East Anglia is perhaps better off than are most other districts — does the steady flow to the cities show signs of ceasing. Yet — and this is one of the strangest circumstances connected with the movement — those cities whither they go are full of misery. Disease, wretchedness, the last extremes of want, and the ultimate extinction of their families will be the lot of at least a large proportion of these immigrants. Has not this been shown by Mr Rowntree and others?

On the other hand, low as the wages are, it is not too much to say that in the country, or at least in that large area of it with which I am acquainted, there is in practice but little real poverty. Cases of misfortune there are, and always must be, together with cases of accidents and cases – of these a great number – where the drunkenness or other ill-behaviour of the breadwinner has brought whole families to wreck. But want, actual want of food for the stomach, of clothing for the back, and of shelter for the head, such as stalks abroad through the poorer parts of great cities, is rare today in rural England. There too those who for this cause or for that fall into its clutches can generally find a friend to help them, in nine cases out of ten the despised parson or the much-abused squire.

I know no better test of well-being than the appearance of the children of a locality. Now I venture to assert that any observer who stood at the gates of Ditchingham School, or of those of some neighbouring parish, and watched the pupils coming out to play, would find them as well and sufficiently clothed, as well fed, and in general of as happy and healthy an appearance, as it is possible for children of their class to be. If, however, he took the train to some great city and repeated his observations at the door of a large Board school, would he be able to say as much? In short, even for the very poorest, life in the country has not those horrors that in towns must be its constant companion. We complain, and rightly, of the state of our cottages; but after all, how many cases of consumption are there in them, and how, for young or old, do the rural tables of mortality compare with those of towns? Is it possible in a village for such a thing as this to happen? A lady known to the writer was district-visiting, I think in London, and in a tenement of one room found a woman nursing some children sick with I forget what complaint. Presently this poor creature opened the door of a cupboard and showed her the bodies of two more of her offspring which she had thrust away thus because there was nowhere else to put them!

Still for such homes as these, and perhaps to fates as dreadful, people flock from their wholesome, happy villages, where their labour at least brings health and in most cases sufficiency, to the towns where they believe that they are certain of higher wages and more amusement. A while ago I met a man, evidently an agricultural labourer, walking down the Strand and literally weeping. It appeared on investigation that he had come up with his family from some rural district in the hope of 'bettering' himself. The result was that at the time of our meeting he and they were learning by sharp experience the meaning of the word starvation. I have often wondered what became of that man, or if he took my advice to get him back to the country as quickly as he might.

But, as I have said, such examples do not deter those who want to go, who are young and strong and forget the day when they will be grey-headed and turned from door to door. They think that they will be among the fortunate; that they will not find themselves sick and friendless in the ward of a London hospital; that their children will devolop no disease in the crowded slums. Or perhaps they do not think even so much as this. They are weary of their lack of outlook and of working the fields that their forefathers worked before them for hundreds of years, and do not reflect that in this pursuit, humble as it seems, there is in truth great dignity; weary also of the control of village opinion and of the dulness of village life. Education has taught them to dislike manual labour, which they look down on; while newspapers, and friends who have been successful there, tell them of the glories and high wages of the town, of the music halls and the beautiful processions.

So they go and it is hard to blame them. But what will be the result upon England at large – indeed what is the result already? Again I ask, can it be denied that the national temperament is undergoing modifications subtle perhaps, but none the less profound? To 'maffick' is a very modern verb, but one of which the significance is daily widening. Moreover, the physique deteriorates. This was a fact that came home to any who, after the country-bred yeomen were exhausted, took the trouble to compare with them the crowds of town-reared men that presented themselves at the London recruiting offices to volunteer for service in South Africa. The intelligence too is changed; it is apt no longer to consider or appreciate natural things, but by preference dwells on and occupies itself with those more artificial joys and needs which are the creation of civilised, money and pleasure-seeking man.

I am convinced – and this is a very important national aspect of the question – that most of our reverses during the recent war were due to the pitting of town-bred bodies and intelligences, both of officers and men, against country-bred bodies and intelligences. We laugh at the Boer for his rude manners and his rusticity, but therein lies a strength which if he and his people are wise they will not exchange for all the gold and gems in Africa and all the most exquisite refinements of Europe. If they can resist those temptations (which for our sake it is to be hoped that they will not do); if they can continue to be content to live roughly upon their farms and produce as many children as nature gives them, then I am sure – unless we British change our ways – that whatever flag flies over it, within two generations its inhabitants of Dutch blood will, in fact, rule South Africa. Moreover, having that vast country in which to develope, within ten generations they will, I believe, be one of the great powers of the world. For in Africa the Englishman does what he does in Britain, forsakes his farm for the city, where there is more life, and more money to be made.

A well-known South African statesman writes to me:

'We see it' (i.e. the effect produced upon English people by the deterioration of our agriculture) 'in the Colonies, where it is hard indeed to get an Englishman to settle on the ground . . . even well-paid occupations cannot stem the tide that sets to the hideous collections of men they call cities. What will be the end? In a sense you may see the beginning of that end in this war: a war of city-folk against country-folk who are fortunately only a handful! You see it in the gradual domination of capital which has succeeded to the old landed privilege' – and so forth.

The 'domination of capital', the love of money and what it will bring, that is the root of the matter at home and abroad, not in one class but in all. To get more money and more pleasure the English settler and his wife leave their land in South Africa and betake themselves to Johannesburg, and to get more money and more pleasure the English labourer and his wife lock their cottage door and betake themselves to the slums of London.

Jack London

Jack London (1876–1916), the American novelist, came to write *The People of the Abyss* (1903) partly by accident. In 1902 he was commissioned by the American Press Association to report on conditions in South Africa following the Boer War. He sailed via England, intending to spend two days In London seeing the coronation of Edward VII from a working-class point of view. When the South African commission was suddenly cancelled, he took up instead a tentative agreement with a New York publisher to write a study of slum life. He spent seven weeks in the East End during which time he researched and wrote the book. It was published initially as a serial in *Wilshire's Magazine*, an American Socialist periodical with a small circulation, but London always intended the book to express in a popular way his own radical views, and this kind of popularity it has achieved. Near the end of his life London is reported as saying: 'Of all my books . . . I love most *The People of the Abyss*. No other book of mine took so much of my young heart and tears as that study of the economic degradation of the poor.'

THE DESCENT

From *The People of the Abyss*

'But you can't do it, you know,' friends said, to whom I applied for assistance in the matter of sinking myself down into the East End of London. 'You had better see the police for a guide,' they added, on second thought, painfully endeavouring to adjust themselves to the psychological processes of a madman who had come to them with better credentials than brains.

'But I don't want to see the police,' I protested. 'What I

wish to do is to go down into the East End and see things for myself. I wish to know how those people are living there, and why they are living there, and what they are living for. In short, I am going to live there myself.'

'You don't want to *live* down there!' everybody said, with disapprobation writ large upon their faces. 'Why, it is said there are places where a man's life isn't worth tu'pence.'

'The very places I wish to see,' I broke in.

'But you can't, you know,' was the unfailing rejoinder.

'Which is not what I came to see you about,' I answered brusquely, somewhat nettled by their incomprehension. 'I am a stranger here, and I want you to tell me what you know of the East End, in order that I may have something to start on.'

'But we know nothing of the East End. It is over there, somewhere.' And they waved their hands vaguely in the direction where the sun on rare occasions may be seen to rise.

'Then I shall go to Cook's,' I announced.

'Oh yes,' they said, with relief. 'Cook's will be sure to know.'

But O Cook, O Thomas Cook & Son, path-finders and trail-clearers, living sign-posts to all the world, and bestowers of first aid to bewildered travellers – unhesitatingly and instantly, with ease and celerity, could you send me to Darkest Africa or Innermost Thibet, but to the East End of London, barely a stone's throw distant from Ludgate Circus, you know not the way!

'You can't do it, you know,' said the human emporium of routes and fares at Cook's Cheapside branch. 'It is so – ahem – so unusual.'

'Consult the police,' he concluded authoritatively, when I had persisted. 'We are not accustomed to taking travellers to the East End; we receive no call to take them there, and we know nothing whatsoever about the place at all.'

'Never mind that,' I interposed, to save myself from being swept out of the office by his flood of negations. 'Here's something you can do for me. I wish you to understand in advance what I intend doing, so that in case of trouble you may be able to identify me.'

'Ah, I see! should you be murdered, we would be in position to identify the corpse.'

He said it so cheerfully and cold-bloodedly that on the instant I saw my stark and mutilated cadaver stretched upon a slab where cool waters trickle ceaselessly, and him I saw bending over and sadly and patiently identifying it as the body of the insane American who would see the East End.

'No, no,' I answered; 'merely to identify me in case I get into a scrape with the "bobbies".' This last I said with a thrill; truly, I was gripping hold of the vernacular.

'That,' he said, 'is a matter for the consideration of the Chief Office.'

'It is so unprecedented, you know,' he added apologetically.

The man at the Chief Office hemmed and hawed. 'We make it a rule,' he explained, 'to give no information concerning our clients.'

'But in this case,' I urged, 'it is the client who requests you to give the information concerning himself.'

Again he hemmed and hawed.

'Of course,' I hastily anticipated, 'I know it is unprecedented, but—'

'As I was about to remark,' he went on steadily, 'it is unprecedented, and I don't think we can do anything for you.'

However, I departed with the address of a detective who lived in the East End, and took my way to the American consul-general. And here, at last, I found a man with whom I could 'do business'. There was no hemming and hawing, no lifted brows, open incredulity, or blank amazement. In one minute I explained myself and my project, which he accepted as a matter of course. In the second minute he asked my age, height, and weight, and looked me over. And in the third minute, as we shook hands at parting, he said: 'All right, Jack. I'll remember you and keep track.'

I breathed a sigh of relief. Having burnt my ships behind me, I was now free to plunge into that human wilderness of which nobody seemed to know anything. But at once I encountered a new difficulty in the shape of my cabby, a grey-whiskered and eminently decorous personage who had imperturbably driven me for several hours about the 'City'.

'Drive me down to the East End,' I ordered, taking my seat.

'Where, sir?' he demanded with frank surprise.

'To the East End, anywhere. Go on.'

H

The hansom pursued an aimless way for several minutes, then came to a puzzled stop. The aperture above my head was uncovered, and the cabman peered down perplexedly at me.

'I say,' he said, 'wot plyce yer wanter go?'

'East End,' I repeated. 'Nowhere in particular. Just drive me around anywhere.'

'But wot's the haddress, sir?'

'See here!' I thundered. 'Drive me down to the East End, and at once!'

It was evident that he did not understand, but he withdrew his head, and grumblingly started his horse.

Nowhere in the streets of London may one escape the sight of abject poverty, while five minutes' walk from almost any point will bring one to a slum; but the region my hansom was now penetrating was one unending slum. The streets were filled with a new and different race of people, short of stature, and of wretched or beer-sodden appearance. We rolled along through miles of bricks and squalor, and from each cross street and alley flashed long vistas of bricks and misery. Here and there lurched a drunken man or woman, and the air was obscene with sounds of jangling and squabbling. At a market, tottery old men and women were searching in the garbage thrown in the mud for rotten potatoes, beans, and vegetables, while little children clustered like flies around a festering mass of fruit, thrusting their arms to the shoulders into the liquid corruption, and drawing forth morsels but partially decayed, which they devoured on the spot.

Not a hansom did I meet with in all my drive, while mine was like an apparition from another and better world, the way the children ran after it and alongside. And as far as I could see were the solid walls of brick, the slimy pavements, and the screaming streets; and for the first time in my life the fear of the crowd smote me. It was like the fear of the sea; and the miserable multitudes, street upon street, seemed so many waves of a vast and malodorous sea, lapping about me and threatening to well up and over me.

'Stepney, sir; Stepney Station,' the cabby called down.

I looked about. It was really a railroad station, and he had driven desperately to it as the one familiar spot he had ever heard of in all that wilderness.

'Well,' I said.

He spluttered unintelligibly, shook his head, and looked very miserable. 'I'm a strynger 'ere,' he managed to articulate. 'An' if yer don't want Stepney Station, I'm blessed if I know wotcher do want.'

'I'll tell you what I want,' I said. 'You drive along and keep your eye out for a shop where old clothes are sold. Now, when you see such a shop, drive right on till you turn the corner, then stop and let me out.'

I could see that he was growing dubious of his fare, but not long afterwards he pulled up to the curb and informed me that an old-clothes shop was to be found a bit of the way back.

'Won'tcher py me?' he pleaded. 'There's seven an' six owin' me.'

'Yes,' I laughed, 'and it would be the last I'd see of you.'

'Lord lumme, but it'll be the last I see of you if yer don't py me,' he retorted.

But a crowd of ragged onlookers had already gathered around the cab, and I laughed again and walked back to the old-clothes shop.

Here the chief difficulty was in making the shopman understand that I really and truly wanted old clothes. But after fruitless attempts to press upon me new and impossible coats and trousers, he began to bring to light heaps of old ones, looking mysterious the while and hinting darkly. This he did with the palpable intention of letting me know that he had 'piped my lay', in order to bulldose me, through fear of exposure, into paying heavily for my purchases. A man in trouble, or a high-class criminal from across the water, was what he took my measure for – in either case, a person anxious to avoid the police.

But I disputed with him over the outrageous difference between prices and values, till I quite disabused him of the notion, and he settled down to drive a hard bargain with a hard customer. In the end I selected a pair of stout though well-worn trousers, a frayed jacket with one remaining button, a pair of brogans which had plainly seen service where coal was shovelled, a thin leather belt, and a very dirty cloth cap. My underclothing and socks, however, were new and warm, but of the sort that any American waif, down in his luck, could acquire in the ordinary course of events.

'I must sy yer a sharp 'un,' he said, with counterfeit admiration, and I handed over the ten shillings finally agreed upon for the outfit. 'Blimey, if you ain't ben up an' down Petticut Lane afore now. Yer trouseys is wuth five bob to hany man, an' a docker 'ud give two an' six for the shoes, to sy nothin' of the coat an' cap an' new stoker's singlet an' hother things.'

'How much will you give me for them?' I demanded suddenly. 'I paid you ten bob for the lot, and I'll sell them back to you, right now, for eight. Come, it's a go!'

But he grinned and shook his head, and though I had made a good bargain, I was unpleasantly aware that he had made a better one.

I found the cabby and a policeman with their heads together, but the latter, after looking me over sharply, and particularly scrutinizing the bundle under my arm, turned away and left the cabby to wax mutinous by himself. And not a step would he budge till I paid him the seven shillings and sixpence owing him. Whereupon he was willing to drive me to the ends of the earth, apologising profusely for his insistence, and explaining that one ran across queer customers in London Town.

But he drove me only to Highbury Vale, in North London, where my luggage was waiting for me. Here, next day, I took off my shoes (not without regret for their lightness and comfort), and my soft, grey travelling suit, and, in fact, all my clothing; and proceeded to array myself in the clothes of the other and unimaginable men, who must have been indeed unfortunate to have had to part with such rags for the pitiable sums obtainable from a dealer.

Inside my stoker's singlet, in the armpit, I sewed a gold sovereign (an emergency sum certainly of modest proportions); and inside my stoker's singlet I put myself. And then I sat down and moralised upon the fair years and fat, which had made my skin soft and brought the nerves close to the surface; for the singlet was rough and raspy as a hair shirt, and I am confident that the most rigorous of ascetics suffer no more than I did in the ensuing twenty-four hours.

The remainder of my costume was fairly easy to put on, though the brogans, or brogues, were quite a problem. As stiff and hard as if made of wood, it was only after a prolonged pounding of the uppers with my fists that I was able to get my feet into them at all. Then, with a few shillings, a knife, a handkerchief, and some brown papers and flake tobacco stowed away in my pockets, I thumped down the stairs and said goodbye to my foreboding friends. As I passed out of the door, the 'help', a comely middle-aged woman, could not conquer a grin that twisted her lips and separated them till the throat, out of involuntary sympathy, made the uncouth animal noises we are wont to designate as 'laughter'.

No sooner was I out on the streets than I was impressed by the difference in status affected by my clothes. All servility vanished from the demeanour of the common people with whom I came in contact. Presto! in the twinkling of an eye, so to say, I had become one of them. My frayed and out-at-elbows jacket was the badge and advertisement of my class, which was their class. It made me of like kind, and in place of the fawning and too respectful attention I had hitherto received, I now shared with them a comradeship. The man in corduroy and dirty neckerchief no longer addressed me as 'sir' or 'governor'. It was 'mate' now – and a fine and hearty word, with a tingle to it, and a warmth and gladness, which the other term does not possess. Governor! It smacks of mastery, and power, and high authority – the tribute of the man who is under to the man on top, delivered in the hope that he will let up a bit and ease his weight, which is another way of saying that it is an appeal for alms.

This brings me to a delight I experienced in my rags and tatters which is denied the average American abroad. The European traveller from the States, who is not a Crœsus, speedily finds himself reduced to a chronic state of self-conscious sordidness by the hordes of cringing robbers who clutter his steps from dawn till dark, and deplete his pocket-book in a way that puts compound interest to the blush.

In my rags and tatters I escaped the pestilence of tipping, and encountered men on a basis of equality. Nay, before the day was out I turned the tables, and said, most gratefully, 'Thank you, sir,' to a gentleman whose horse I held, and who dropped a penny into my eager palm.

Other changes I discovered were wrought in my condition

by my new garb. In crossing crowded thoroughfares I found I had to be, if anything, more lively in avoiding vehicles, and it was strikingly impressed upon me that my life had cheapened in direct ratio with my clothes. When before I inquired the way of a policeman, I was usually asked, 'Bus or 'ansom, sir?' But now the query became, 'Walk or ride?' Also, at the railway stations, a third-class ticket was now shoved out to me as a matter of course.

But there was compensation for it all. For the first time I met the English lower classes face to face, and knew them for what they were. When loungers and workmen, at street corners and in public-houses, talked with me, they talked as one man to another, and they talked as natural men should talk, without the least idea of getting anything out of me for what they talked or the way they talked.

And when at last I made into the East End, I was gratified to find that the fear of the crowd no longer haunted me. I had become a part of it. The vast and malodorous sea had welled up and over me, or I had slipped gently into it, and there was nothing fearsome about it – with the one exception of the stoker's singlet.

ONE OF LONDON'S LUNGS

From *The People of the Abyss*

We next visited the municipal dwellings erected by the London County Council on the site of the slums where lived Arthur Morrison's 'Child of the Jago'. While the buildings housed more people than before, it was much healthier. But the dwellings were inhabited by the better-class workmen and artisans. The slum people had simply drifted on to crowd other slums or to form new slums.

'An' now,' said the sweated one, the 'earty man who worked so fast as to dazzle one's eyes, 'I'll show you one of London's lungs. This is Spitalfields Garden.' And he mouthed the word 'garden' with scorn.

The shadow of Christ's Church falls across Spitalfields Garden, and in the shadow of Christ's Church, at three o'clock

in the afternoon, I saw a sight I never wish to see again.
There are no flowers in this garden, which is smaller than my
own rose garden at home. Grass only grows here, and it is
surrounded by a sharp-spiked iron fencing, as are all the parks
of London Town, so that homeless men and women may not
come in at night and sleep upon it.

As we entered the garden, an old woman, between fifty and
sixty, passed us, striding with sturdy intention if somewhat
rickety action, with two bulky bundles, covered with sacking,
slung fore and aft upon her. She was a woman tramp, a houseless soul, too independent to drag her failing carcass through
the workhouse door. Like the snail, she carried her home with
her. In the two sacking-covered bundles were her household
goods, her wardrobe, linen, and dear feminine possessions.

We went up the narrow gravelled walk. On the benches on
either side arrayed a mass of miserable and distorted humanity,
the sight of which would have impelled Doré to more diabolical
flights of fancy than he ever succeeded in achieving. It was a
welter of rags and filth, of all manner of loathsome skin
diseases, open sores, bruises, grossness, indecency, leering
monstrosities, and bestial faces. A chill, raw wind was blowing,
and these creatures huddled there in their rags, sleeping for
the most part, or trying to sleep. Here were a dozen women,
ranging in age from twenty years to seventy. Next a babe,
possibly of nine months, lying asleep, flat on the hard bench,
with neither pillow nor covering, nor with any one looking
after it. Next half-a-dozen men, sleeping bolt upright or leaning against one another in their sleep. In one place a family
group, a child asleep in its sleeping mother's arms, and the
husband (or male mate) clumsily mending a dilapidated shoe.
On another bench a woman trimming the frayed strips of
her rags with a knife, and another woman, with thread and
needle, sewing up rents. Adjoining, a man holding a sleeping
woman in his arms. Farther on, a man, his clothing caked with
gutter mud, asleep, with head in the lap of a woman, not
more than twenty-five years old, and also asleep.

It was this sleeping that puzzled me. Why were nine out of
ten of them asleep or trying to sleep? But it was not till afterwards that I learned. *It is a law of the powers that be that
the homeless shall not sleep by night.* On the pavement, by

the portico of Christ's Church, where the stone pillars rise toward the sky in a stately row, were whole rows of men lying asleep or drowsing, and all too deep sunk in torpor to rouse or be made curious by our intrusion.

'A lung of London,' I said; 'nay, an abscess, a great putrescent sore.'

IN LINE AT THE SPIKE

From *The People of the Abyss*

First of all, I must beg forgiveness of my body for the vileness through which I have dragged it, and forgiveness of my stomach for the vileness which I have thrust into it. I have been to the spike, and slept in the spike, and eaten in the spike; also, I have run away from the spike.

After my two unsuccessful attempts to penetrate the White-chapel casual ward, I started early, and joined the desolate line before three o'clock in the afternoon. They did not 'let in' till six, but at that early hour I was number twenty, while the news had gone forth that only twenty-two were to be admitted. By four o'clock there were thirty-four in line, the last ten hanging on in the slender hope of getting in by some kind of a miracle. Many more came, looked at the line, and went away, wise to the bitter fact that the spike would be 'full up'.

Conversation was slack at first, standing there, till the man on one side of me and the man on the other side of me discovered that they had been in the smallpox hospital at the same time, though a full house of sixteen hundred patients had prevented their becoming acquainted. But they made up for it, discussing and comparing the more loathsome features of their disease in the most cold-blooded, matter-of-fact way. I learned that the average mortality was one in six, that one of them had been in three months and the other three months and a half, and that they had been 'rotten wi' it'. Whereat my flesh began to creep and crawl, and I asked them how long they had been out. One had been out two weeks, and the other three weeks. Their faces were badly pitted (though each assured the other that this was not so), and further, they showed me in their hands and under the nails the smallpox 'seeds' still working out. Nay, one of them worked a seed out for my edification, and pop it went, right out of his flesh into the air. I tried to shrink up smaller inside my clothes, and I registered a fervent though silent hope that it had not popped on me.

In both instances, I found that the smallpox was the cause of their being 'on the doss', which means on the tramp. Both had been working when smitten by the disease, and both had emerged from the hospital 'broke', with the gloomy task before them of hunting for work. So far, they had not found any, and they had come to the spike for a 'rest up' after three days and nights on the street.

It seems that not only the man who becomes old is punished for his involuntary misfortune, but likewise the man who is struck by disease or accident. Later on, I talked with another man – 'Ginger' we called him – who stood at the head of the line a sure indication that he had been waiting since one o'clock. A year before, one day, while in the employ of a fish dealer, he was carrying a heavy box of fish which was too much for him. Result: 'something broke', and there was the box on the ground, and he on the ground beside it.

At the first hospital, whither he was immediately carried, they said it was a rupture, reduced the swelling, gave him some vaseline to rub on it, kept him four hours, and told him to get along. But he was not on the streets more than two or three hours when he was down on his back again. This time he went to another hospital and was patched up. But the point is, the employer did nothing, positively nothing, for the man injured in his employment, and even refused him 'a light job now and again', when he came out. As far as Ginger is concerned, he is a broken man. His only chance to earn a living was by heavy work. He is now incapable of performing heavy work, and from now until he dies, the spike, the peg, and the streets are all he can look forward to in the way of food and shelter. The thing happened – that is all. He put his back under too great a load of fish, and his chance for happiness in life was crossed off the books.

Several men in the line had been to the United States, and they were wishing that they had remained there, and were

cursing themselves for their folly in ever having left. England
had become a prison to them, a prison from which there was
no hope of escape. It was impossible for them to get away.
They could neither scrape together the passage money, nor get
a chance to work their passage. The country was too over-
run by poor devils on that 'lay'.

I was on the seafaring-man-who-had-lost-his-clothes-and-
money tack, and they all condoled with me and gave me much
sound advice. To sum it up, the advice was something like
this : To keep out of all places like the spike. There was
nothing good in it for me. To head for the coast and bend
every effort to get away on a ship. To go to work, if possible,
and scrape together a pound or so, with which I might bribe
some steward or underling to give me chance to work my
passage. They envied me my youth and strength, which
would sooner or later get me out of the country. These they
no longer possessed. Age and English hardship had broken
them, and for them the game was played and up.

There was one, however, who was still young, and who,
I am sure, will in the end make it out. He had gone to the
United States as a young fellow, and in fourteen years'
residence the longest period he had been out of work was
twelve hours. He had saved his money, grown too prosperous,
and returned to the mother-country. Now he was standing in
line at the spike.

For the past two years, he told me, he had been working
as a cook. His hours had been from 7 a.m. to 10.30 p.m., and
on Saturday to 12.30 p.m. – ninety-five hours per week, for
which he had received twenty shillings, or five dollars.

'But the work and the long hours was killing me,' he said,
'and I had to chuck the job. I had a little money saved, but
I spent it living and looking for another place.'

This was his first night in the spike, and he had come in
only to get rested. As soon as he emerged he intended to start
for Bristol, a 110-mile walk, where he thought he would
eventually get a ship for the States.

But the men in the line were not all of this calibre. Some
were poor, wretched beasts, inarticulate and callous, but for
all of that, in many ways very human. I remember a carter,
evidently returning home after the day's work, stopping his

cart before us so that his young hopeful, who had run to meet him, could climb in. But the cart was big, the young hopeful little, and he failed in his several attempts to swarm up. Whereupon one of the most degraded-looking men stepped out of the line and hoisted him in. Now the virtue and the joy of this act lies in that it was service of love, not hire. The carter was poor, and the man knew it; and the man was standing in the spike line, and the carter knew it; and the man had done the little act, and the carter had thanked him, even as you and I would have done and thanked.

Another beautiful touch was that displayed by the 'Hopper' and his 'ole woman'. He had been in line about half an-hour when the 'ole woman' (his mate) came up to him. She was fairly clad, for her class, with a weather-worn bonnet on her grey head and a sacking-covered bundle in her arms. As she talked to him, he reached forward, caught the one stray wisp of the white hair that was flying wild, deftly twirled it between his fingers, and tucked it back properly behind her ear. From all of which one may conclude many things. He certainly liked her well enough to wish her to be neat and tidy. He was proud of her, standing there in the spike line, and it was his desire that she should look well in the eyes of the other unfortunates who stood in the spike line. But last and best, and underlying all these motives, it was a sturdy affection he bore her; for man is not prone to bother his head over neatness and tidiness in a woman for whom he does not care, nor is he likely to be proud of such a woman.

And I found myself questioning why this man and his mate, hard workers I knew from their talk, should have to seek a pauper lodging. He had his pride, pride in his old woman and pride in himself. When I asked him what he thought I, a greenhorn, might expect to earn at 'hopping', he sized me up, and said that it all depended. Plenty of people were too slow to pick hops and made a failure of it. A man, to succeed, must use his head and be quick with his fingers, must be exceeding quick with his fingers. Now he and his old woman could do very well at it, working the one bin between them and not going to sleep over it; but then, they had been at it for years.

'I 'ad a mate as went down last year,' spoke up a man. 'It was 'is fust time, but 'e come back wi' two poun' ten in 'is pockit, an' 'e was only gone a month.'

'There you are,' said the Hopper, a wealth of admiration in his voice. ''E was quick. 'E was jest nat'rally born to it, 'e was.'

Two pound ten – twelve dollars and a half – for a month's work when one is 'jest nat'rally born to it!' And in addition, sleeping out without blankets and living the Lord knows how. There are moments when I am thankful that I was not 'jest nat'rally born' a genius for anything, not even hop-picking.

In the matter of getting an outfit for 'the hops', the Hopper gave me some sterling advice, to which same give heed, you soft and tender people, in case you should ever be stranded in London Town.

'If you ain't got tins an' cookin' things, all as you can get'll be bread and cheese. No bloomin' good that! You must 'ave 'ot tea, an' wegetables, an' a bit o' meat, now an' again, if you're goin' to do work as is work. Cawn't do it on cold wittles. Tell you wot you do, lad. Run around in the mornin' an' look in the dust pans. You'll find plenty o' tins to cook in. Fine tins, wonderful good some o' them. Me an' the ole woman got ours that way.' (He pointed at the bundle she held, while she nodded proudly, beaming on me with good-nature and consciousness of success and prosperity.) 'This overcoat is as good as a blanket,' he went on, advancing the skirt of it that I might feel its thickness. 'An' 'oo knows, I may find a blanket before long.'

Again the old woman nodded and beamed, this time with the dead certainty that he _would_ find a blanket before long.

'I call it a 'oliday, 'oppin',' he concluded rapturously. 'A tidy way o' gettin' two or three pounds together an' fixin' up for winter. The only thing I don't like – 'and here was the rift within the lute – 'is paddin' the 'oof down there.'

It was plain the years were telling on this energetic pair, and while they enjoyed the quick work with the fingers, 'paddin' the 'oof', which is walking, was beginning to bear heavily upon them. And I looked at their grey hairs, and ahead into the future ten years, and wondered how it would be with them.

I noticed another man and his old woman join the line, both of them past fifty. The woman, because she was a woman, was admitted into the spike; but he was too late, and, separated from his mate, was turned away to tramp the streets all night.

The street on which we stood, from wall to wall, was barely twenty feet wide. The sidewalks were three feet wide. It was a residence street. At least workmen and their families existed in some sort of fashion in the houses across from us. And each day and every day, from one in the afternoon till six, our ragged spike line is the principal feature of the view commanded by their front doors and windows. One workman sat in his door directly opposite us, taking his rest and a breath of air after the toil of the day. His wife came to chat with him. The doorway was too small for two, so she stood up. Their babes sprawled before them. And here was the spike line, less than a score of feet away – neither privacy for the workman, nor privacy for the pauper. About our feet played the children of the neighbourhood. To them our presence was nothing unusual. We were not an intrusion. We were as natural and ordinary as the brick walls and stone curbs of their environment. They had been born to the sight of the spike line, and all their brief days they had seen it.

THE POLITICAL MACHINE

From *The People of the Abyss*

If Civilisation has increased the producing power of the average man, why has it not bettered the lot of the average man?

There can be one answer only – MISMANAGEMENT. Civilisation has made possible all manner of creature comforts and heart's delights. In these the average Englishman does not participate. If he shall be forever unable to participate, then Civilisation falls. There is no reason for the continued existence of an artifice so avowed a failure. But it is impossible that men should have reared this tremendous artifice in vain. It stuns the intellect. To acknowledge so crushing a defeat is to give the death-blow to striving and progress.

One other alternative, and one other only, presents itself. *Civilisation must be compelled to better the lot of the average man.* This accepted, it becomes at once a question of business management. Things profitable must be continued; things unprofitable must be eliminated. Either the Empire is a profit to England, or it is a loss. If it is a loss, it must be done away with. If it is a profit, it must be managed so that the average man comes in for a share of the profit.

If the struggle for commercial supremacy is profitable, continue it. If it is not, if it hurts the worker and makes his lot worse than the lot of a savage, then fling foreign markets and industrial empire overboard. For it is a patent fact that if 40,000,000 people, aided by Civilisation, possess a greater individual producing power than the Innuit, then those 40,000,000 people should enjoy more creature comforts and heart's delights than the Innuits enjoy.

If the 400,000 English gentlemen 'of no occupation', according to their own statement in the Census of 1881, are unprofitable, do away with them. Set them to work ploughing game reserves and planting potatoes. If they are profitable, continue them by all means, but let it be seen to that the average Englishman shares somewhat in the profits they produce by working at no occupation.

In short, society must be reorganised, and a capable management put at the head. That the present management is incapable, there can be no discussion. It has drained the United Kingdom of its life-blood. It has enfeebled the stay-at-home folk till they are unable longer to struggle in the van of the competing nations. It has built up a West End and an East End as large as the Kingdom is large, in which one end is riotous and rotten, the other end sickly and underfed.

A vast empire is foundering on the hands of this incapable management. And by empire is meant the political machinery which holds together the English-speaking people of the world outside of the United States. Nor is this charged in a pessimistic spirit. Blood empire is greater than political empire, and the English of the New World and the Antipodes are strong and vigorous as ever. But the political empire under which they are nominally assembled is perishing. The political machine known as the British Empire is running down. In the hands of its management it is losing momentum every day.

It is inevitable that this management, which has grossly and criminally mismanaged, shall be swept away. Not only has it been wasteful and inefficient, but it has misappropriated the funds. Every worn-out, pasty-faced pauper, every blind man, every prison babe, every man, woman and child whose belly is gnawing with hunger pangs, is hungry because the funds have been misappropriated by the management.

Nor can one member of this managing class plead not guilty before the judgment bar of Man. 'The living in their houses, and in their graves the dead', are challenged by every babe that dies of innutrition, by every girl that flees the sweater's den to the nightly promenade of Piccadilly, by every worked-out toiler that plunges into the canal. The food this managing class eats, the wine it drinks, the shows it makes, and the fine clothes it wears, are challenged by eight million mouths which have never had enough to fill them, and by twice eight million bodies which have never been sufficiently clothed and housed.

There can be no mistake. Civilisation has increased man's producing power an hundredfold, and through mismanagement the men of Civilisation live worse than the beasts, and have less to eat and wear and protect them from the elements than the savage Innuit in a frigid climate who lives today as he lived in the Stone Age ten thousand years ago.

C. F. G. Masterman

Charles Frederick Gurney Masterman (1873–1927) came from an evangelical middle-class family. He was educated at Weymouth College and Christ's College, Cambridge, where he was president of the Union, editor of *Granta*, and where he became involved in the settlement movement and social work. In April 1900, together with two friends, Reginald Bray and F. W. Head, he moved into a flat in a tenement block in Camberwell, South London, in order to live among and try to get to know the working classes. This experience provided the material for *From the Abyss* (1902) which was published anonymously, though given the significant subtitle: 'Of the Inhabitants by One of Them'. A man of outstanding talent and promise, Masterman was a Liberal MP, 1906–14, and held a succession of government posts under Asquith. He was also an active journalist and author, and a leading member of a group of young Liberals who in 1901 published a collection of essays *The Heart of Empire* which examined the social problems of modern city life. His most famous book, *The Condition of England* (1909), which develops the concerns expressed in *From the Abyss*, remains an impressive and often moving attempt to analyse the mood of a rapidly changing society.

A WEIRD AND UNCANNY PEOPLE

From *From the Abyss*

'This is Ancona,' Browning asserted after his reverie before Guercino's Angel; 'yonder is the sea.' It was necessary to apprehend hard, tangible realities after a great upheaval of spiritual emotion. This is the Strand, we have been compelled

to repeat; there is the same old crooked alley we call Fleet
Street; beyond, the gray vision of St Paul's brooding over the
busy city. For to us, too, a revelation – not entirely spiritual –
has come, and the foundations of the world have for a
moment moved. And we smile and are disturbed, and glad to
feel the solid earth again beneath our feet, and the old
accustomed things of yesterday.

At intervals during the late war events have demonstrated
the necessity for a readjustment of our outlook to an altered
environment. A change perfected in secret while men carried
on their business and their pleasure has suddenly revealed
itself with the force of a thunder-clap. The phenomenon,
deepening and intensifying by repetition, has been essentially
the same. Without warning or observation, a movement and a
sound have arisen in those unknown regions surrounding the
kindly, familiar London that we know. As the Red Indian,
putting his ear to the ground, could hear murmurs beyond the
horizon inaudible to the bystander, so the trained ear could
discern the turmoil of the coming flood and the tramp of many
footsteps. Our streets have suddenly become congested with a
weird and uncanny people. They have poured in as dense
black masses from the eastern railways; they have streamed
across the bridges from the marshes and desolate places beyond
the river; they have been hurried up in incredible number
through tubes sunk in the bowels of the earth, emerging like
rats from a drain, blinking in the sunshine. They have surged
through our streets, turbulent, cheerful, indifferent to our
assumed proprietorship; their sound has been in all ways,
their going and their coming in all men's ears. Three times at
least during these months the richest city in the world was in
the hollow of their hands. They brushed the police away like
an elephant dispersing flies. They could have looted and
destroyed, plundered and razed it to the ground. We gazed at
them in startled amazement. Whence did they all come, these
creatures with strange antics and manners, these denizens of
another universe of being? They themselves seemed half afraid
of their power, awed by unaccustomed daylight and squares
and open spaces. They drifted through the streets hoarsely
cheering, breaking into fatuous, irritating laughter, singing
quaint militant melodies. Only when night fell did their dis-

comfort drop from them. As the darkness drew on they relapsed more and more into bizarre and barbaric revelry. Where they had whispered now they shouted; where they had pushed apologetically, now they shoved and collisioned and charged. They blew trumpets; they hit each other with bladders; they tickled passers-by with feathers; they embraced ladies in the streets, laughing genially and boisterously. Later the drink got into them, and they reeled and struck and swore, walking and leaping and blaspheming God. At night we left them, a packed and sodden multitude, howling under the quiet stars. We woke in the morning, and lo! they had gone – vanished, 'as a dream when one awaketh'. We rubbed our eyes; there, once again, stood out the old familiar landmarks; the omnibuses, the respectable pedestrians, the humdrum, undisturbed London we have known so long. Silence and peace reigned along street and alley. Here was Ancona, and yonder was the sea.

All was the same, and yet all things were different. He who has once seen a ghost, said Cardinal Newman in a famous passage, can never be the same again. We have seen a ghost; we are striving to readjust our stable ideas. The newspapers stir uneasily, talk in a shamefaced manner about natural ebullitions of patriotism, police inefficiency, and other irrelevant topics; deprecate the too frequent repetition of the ceremony, and praise the humour of a modern crowd. But within there is a cloud on men's minds, and a half-stifled recognition of the presence of a new force hitherto unreckoned; the creeping into conscious existence of the quaint and innumerable populations bred in the Abyss.

Only in such striking entertainments is the observer startled into inquiry concerning the life of this new city race. To him it represents a sudden unaccountable revelation of an invasion dropped from nowhither upon his accustomed ways. Further investigation discovers the perpetual presence of an existence which only rises to menacing gaiety upon occasions of national rejoicing. One may, for example, descend a great while before civilization awakens to any of the bridges that stretch towards the chaotic regions beyond the river. The immediate impression is as of some gigantic upheaval and catastrophe in that unknown land; as if the inhabitants, like the fugitives from the cities of the plain, without time to gather up their household goods, were hurrying from a coming destruction and forbidden to look backward. A turbid river of humanity, pent up on the narrow bridge, is pouring into London; aged men in beards and bowlers shambling hastily forward; work girls, mechanics, active boys, neat little clerks in neat little high hats shining out conspicuous in the rushing stream. The pace is even lest one should fall; the general aspect is of a harassed but good-tempered energy, as of those driven along ways not clearly comprehended towards no definite goal. The Abyss is disgorging its denizens for the labour of the day.

Or one may warily venture, concealed in the fog of a November evening, to the farther side of the bridge to behold the equally astonishing spectacle of the return. Here are no militant melodies, peacocks' feathers, or voices upraised in song; but a shabby scuffle of tired people for the machinery of conveyance to their dormitories. A pool of humanity collects at the tram terminus, perpetually reinforced as the current heavily drags backward on the ebb-tide. A tram swings round the corner and draws up sharply. The crowd rolls upon it, adhering like bees, struggling with a desperate eagerness for the means of ingress. The passengers fight their way out, the toilers fight their way in; the young and the old are trampled under, a few curses arise, but the familiar work is for the most part performed in silence. In less time than it takes to recount, the vehicle within and without has become black with human beings; the superfluity are thrown out; and, while the remainder of the crowd sort themselves from each other, gather round them their dishevelled clothing and prepare with a dogged patience for the renewal of the conflict, the tram with its contented burden swings off under the arch and into the twilight.

So as if propelled by the systole and diastole of some mighty unseen heart, the wave of humanity from north, east, and south rolls daily in and out of London. It floods into every crevice, depositing its burden at every door. No street or path-way is untouched by its influence. During the working hours the hum of industry arises in workshop and counting-house and factory; a vast enterprise is perpetually fermenting; threads are being woven towards every corner of the world.

At night the gigantic machine stands idle and empty. In the unknown lands beyond, in the marshes of the South and on the hills of the North, four million people are sleeping under the stars. They have a life apart; their own existences are sharply severed asunder. The life they have made for themselves, when liberated from the forced service of others, is a life whose characteristics we are only just commencing dimly to discern.

We had thought that a city of four millions of people was merely a collection of one hundred cities of forty thousand. We find it differing not only in degree, but in kind, producing a mammoth of gigantic and unknown possibility. Hitherto it has failed to realize its power. It has counted for nothing; it has been hedged within isolated districts, each separate, apart, ignorant of the other. It has been wheedled into amiability and smoothed with honeyed words. Through the action of a benevolent autocratic Government it has now been invited to contemplate its strength. It has crept out into the daylight. At first it has moved painfully in the unaccustomed glare, as a cave bear emerging from his dark den. Now it is straightening itself and learning to gambol with heavy and grotesque antics in the sunshine. It finds the exercise pleasant; it uproots a small tree, displaces a rock, laughing with pleased good-humour. How long before, in a fit of ill-temper, it suddenly realizes its tremendous unconquerable might?

OF THE QUANTITY OF US

From *From the Abyss*

There is so much of us, and the quantity so continually increases. That is our misfortune that is costing us more than all our crime. We press in from the surrounding country in incredible number; every ship discharges a multitude from alien shores; through the gates of birth streams in the countless host. The torrent never ceases, the supply is never diminished, the river is never dry. We swarm over the adjoin-

ing land, like a locust cloud in restless movement; continual
mere pressure of numbers driving us into every corner, filling
up every vacant niche or cranny, always treading on each
other's heels, always pressing into the place of those that
have been suffocated in the swarm. We occupy factories,
and workshops, and laundries, and common lodging-houses.
We pack ourselves into small cottages and decaying mansions,
and block dwellings of gigantic and hideous architecture. We
choke up the public-houses and the few uncertain open spaces
still left to us; we overflow into canal barges, and railway
arches, and disused drains. Lines of us are pushed into the
gutters where we ply unwelcomed articles, and children's toys,
and publications obscene to the legal limit, beside the heedless stream that ever hurries past us. Others are swept into
quaint and grotesque means of livelihood; like the mobile
vegetable tissue which silently adapts itself by distorted and
abnormal mechanism to the desert, or the marshy waste, or
the sandy, barren shore. We are many, and we are struggling,
and we are silent. Our motive for the persistence of this
struggle is our continued existence; to effect this end we are
prepared to adopt any conceivable means. We convert cardboard into boots, and condemned fruit into jam, and putrid
liver into tinned delicacies for the sick. We pander with equal
readiness to the changeful fashion and the unchanging needs
of men. We are only restrained by a Government whose
designs are inscrutable from mutilating ourselves in every
form of noxious manufacture; choking ourselves with wool
dust, or rotting with phosphorus poisoning, or asphyxiating
with naphtha fumes. For the pressure of our unrealizable
number is never ceasing, and we are not greatly concerned
how or when or where we die.

All forms of habitation are alike to us so long as they
provide for a moment a resting-place, a temporary retreat
from the struggle, a place in which one can pause a moment
to take a deep breath or an untroubled sleep. To attain such
tranquillity we invade the homes of the respectable, and assail
the houses of the rich and good. Many of our streets contain
suburban terraces, every brick of which cries of middle-class
respectability, lines of three-storied houses with bow windows
and front areas and attics for the servants. Upon these we

have descended with the irresistible impulse of our number, and the original inhabitants have fled panic-stricken away. Each floor now shelters a hive of humanity, each room un-complainingly supports a family with lodgers. The street outside swarms with our children, dirty, unhealthy, happy; the houses hasten to decay; the staircases wear uneven, gaping with holes; the passages' unsavoury walls, bedaubed with grime, attest the reality and permanence of our occupation. We stay on though the ruins fall about our heads, fiercely resisting the endeavours of the sanitary authorities to eject us from our lairs. We stay on because we must; because having once elbowed our way in we turn at bay in the one spot where we can remain unhustled; because the water fills the bottle and the cork is sealed.

This, then, is the first thing to note of us, not our virtue or vices, beauty, apathy, or knowledge; but our overwhelming, inconceivable number – number continually increasing, multi-plying without a pause, coming not with observation, choking up the streets of the great city, and silently flowing over the dismal wastes beyond. We occupy with equal alacrity mansions once built by the wealthy and wise, who dreamt not of a perishable home, and tenements of damp cardboard thrown up in the night by the assiduous jerry-builder upon foundations of broken bottles, and the refuse of the city. Sanitary or unsanitary, attic or condemned cellar, disused factory or corrugated iron washhouse – all are equally welcome. In tropical forests a box suspended from a bough will in a few days be found filled with strange and gorgeous vegetable and insect life. Place a disused sentry-box upon any piece of waste ground in South or East London, and in a few hours it will be occupied by a man and his wife and family, inundated by applications from would-be lodgers.

And this continual rush of our numbers which is our greatest enemy overshadows all our existence. Behind our stolid faces can be traced the glance of the harassed and the hunted. We fight for places in the tardy tram which bears us to the north in the morning; we fight for similar places on our return from the long day's toil. Forced from our dwellings by swarms of sleepy children, at even we crowd into the public-houses, never able to get at arm's length from our fellow-men. All around us stretches the evidence of our perpetual increase. Gigantic erections continually arise into which are swept our children for certain periods of each day; no sooner is one completed than it is filled and another begun. We jostle each other on the pavements; we choke up our main streets with our markets, openly trafficking before all men; we fill every conceivable space in London except our churches. And neither day nor night, summer nor winter, seed time nor harvest, yield any check to our impetuous increase . . . The speculative builder builds up and down hill; waste or marsh, valley or plain, prove no obstacles to his all-conquering progress; he fills up a swamp with refuse, and covers with innumerable houses the dwelling-places of the dead. When all England has become converted into a Bermondsey or a Camberwell, will he be able successfully to overcome the hitherto untameable sea? These things are too hard for us, and we have no time to ponder them; should we pause for such a purpose we should drop out of the stream, or be trampled under by those swooping down upon us; the never-ending generations of the future; the new generations continually knocking at our doors.

Whither is this tending, and what is to be the end of it all? That is the one unanswerable question. Remember, again, the South American forest. Tall trees insolently rise to heaven; surrounding them is the mass of tangled, choking vegetation; gorgeous colours of unequalled beauty; ceaseless, silent strife. Below are all forms of life driven under, forced to adapt themselves to unnatural surroundings, distorted into repulsive, twisted, grotesque forms of existence; each seemingly prepared for any monstrous change if only it can preserve its life and propagate its kind. Some, as parasites, cling to the tall trees in order that they, too, may see the sun, finally throttling their protectors in their deadly embrace. Others take fresh root on the ledges of boughs, or support themselves by slimy suckers or clinging thorns. Everywhere exuberant, many-featured life, struggling under the tropical sun; a struggle continued ardently year after year, through innumerable succeeding generations. Only always at length the end. Some inexplicable change; slowly, imperceptibly, the torrent of life has overreached itself; the struggle has become too terrific; the vitality is gradually dying. And then, as the whole mass festers in all the gorgeous, wonderful beauty of decay, comes the mangrove — dark-leafed, dank, slippery, unlovely, sign and symbol of the inevitable end. And with the mangrove the black-marsh and the reeking, pestilential mud. Until at length all the glory and life and struggle of the tropical forest has passed away for ever; and in its place stretch the wide spaces of sullen swamp, and dull, gnarled, fruitless trees, and the silence of stagnant, scum-coated pools, and the salt, interminable, tideless sea.

OF THE SILENCE OF US

From From the Abyss

If the first thing to note is our quantity, the second is our silence — a silence that becomes the more weird and uncanny with the increasing immensity of our number. That one or a few should pass through life dumb is nothing noteworthy; when the same mysterious stillness falls upon hundreds of thousands the imagination is perplexed and baffled. In some forms of disturbed dream a crowded panorama occupies the scene; each figure acts his part in dumb show; there is apparent activity and motion, but no sound discernible. And the terror of the situation is somehow interwoven with this silence; it weighs down as with a sense of physical oppression; could one only once cry aloud, it appears, the fantastic vision would vanish away. A similar feeling is experienced in the contemplation of the moving crowds of the abyss; could they but in a moment of illumination be stimulated to a united utterance, one feels that strange events would follow. Yet the moment of illumination never comes. The stream of life flows ever onward, continuous, rapid, noiseless; the drops change from moment to moment, but the current is persistent, and the channel never dry. And all with a mysterious stillness; the river singing no secrets of its origin in the far-off region of the hills; nor of the rocks and eddies and shallows which lie beneath its smooth surface; nor of the vast tides of the ocean to which it is ever hurrying, the spaciousness and depth of the infinite sea.

Daily there rises from our streets and crowded dwellings

the noises of a varied activity, the tramp of the interminable procession of human life pent up in narrow ways, the confused mysterious turmoil of a troubled people crushed together beneath the stars. Never is there complete unbroken stillness; disturbed as with uneasy dreams, the city slumbers heavily. The cries of the belated reveller have scarcely died away when there arises the sound of man going forth to his work and to his labour until the evening. During the daytime boys and girls playing in the streets thereof foreshadow the fulfilment of the coming millennium. But, always noisy, we rarely speak; always resonant with the din of many-voiced existence, we never reach the level of ordered articulate utterance; never attain a language that the world beyond can hear. We boast no leaders, no interpreters, no recognised channels of expression; inquiring for new ideas or suggestions fertile for the future, no one but a maniac would burrow in the block dwellings of London. There are hundreds of thousands of us. Large provincial cities, capitals of foreign states, whole countries and colonies could be rent from us without anyone noting the difference; every year we quietly add a great city to our population. We have developed a quaint and specialized life of our own, sharply divided from the life of men who live in the sunshine. Yet we have no meeting-place, no newspaper, no common centre of government; we drift to our work daily, dumbly contented if work is easy and lucrative, dumbly resentful if the reverse conditions prevail, but dumb always, happy or miserable, poor or prosperous, living for the most part with no articulate expression, and passing without a cry 'to the Eternal Silence'.

At intervals, indeed, desperate and heroic attempts are essayed to galvanize us into utterance; as, for example, when we are called upon to demonstrate in favour of some social panacea, or to protest against some organized wrong. At such times we discover our walls and hoardings bedaubed with hysteric exhortation to exhibit our unconquerable will by demonstration in some neighbouring park or square. We gaze blear-eyedly at these discomforting invitations as we hurry in the morning for the tardy tram. The great day arrives that is to settle the fate of nations. An infinitesimal modicum drifts to the appointed place of meeting, exhibiting every aspect of dumb disgust. A few unhealthy and discoloured children congregate around the platform anticipating with unquenchable hope a distribution of apples or buns. We contemplate with fish-like eyes the excited speakers, marvelling in a dull, dim way at their unaccountable vivacity. Should one slip when mounting the platform, we chuckle with pleased approbation. Should another at the conclusion of his impassioned oration sit down upon his hat, we dissolve in ecstasy. At the conclusion we drift out into the neighbouring public-houses, thankful again to attain silence. In our Sunday paper we read of a monster demonstration in South London, and scarcely realize this was we.

For our silence is only paralleled by our distrust of the speech of others. Our first inquiry of any would-be reformer is not What does he want? but What does he get? Kindly and enthusiastic millionaires build for us art galleries, collections of paintings and statuary, museums filled with stuffed beasts and the products of foreign lands. We gaze on their imposing façades as we hurry to work in the morning, or hurry at even to rest. Amiable young men elevate us by frequent lectures on the ethics of Dante, the poetry of the Renaissance, and similar pleasing topics. We have occasionally descried notices of these on our hoardings sandwiched between the sprawling invitations of some philanthropist's unattainable butter or unspeakable pills. On Sunday nights every street corner discloses the gathered group of women, the dim, evil-smelling oil-lamp, the quavering chorus, the perspiring preacher; past them all flows perpetually the stream of life and the tramp of many footsteps. Lectures, sermons, the charms of oratory, impassioned debate, the _obiter dicta_ of great and suave politicians, preachers and philanthropists, art, science, foreign diplomacy, the ways and manners of men and nations, the vastness and variety of the universe – all these to us who work and devour and rest, and rest and devour and work, pass by us and over us and beyond us, the mere shadow of a dream.

Sometimes, indeed, there are those of us who suddenly have been awakened to the fact that beyond the water, in a world but dimly realized by our dwellers, we are the subjects of lengthy and acrimonious controversy. Novelists jaded with battues of blacks in unknown lands, select as heroes the denizens of lands still more unknown at their very doors; relate of their travels into our dangerous and desolate regions, of the life and manners and habits of the aborigines. Social reformers hotly contest as to the better methods of improving us. Lines of statistics, volumes of reports, fiery controversy rages; heaven and earth are called to attest to the futility of one method, the demoralization incident to a second, the obvious success of a third. Rival Churches expend all the energy of imagination in claiming from amongst us varied infinitesimal proportions of adherents. In a strange world, where people have leisure to think and energy to argue, such discussions doubtless provide a welcome relief to ennui and jaded intellect. Never, alas! do we sufficiently realize the process as to be fully awakened to the humour of it. For, doubtless, in a combat of rival ants on an ant-heap, could the busy creatures awaken to the fact that beyond them were intelligences discussing their feelings, dissecting their desires, and heatedly thwarting each other's efforts to aid them, they might pause at least for a moment in their struggle to give vent to their emotion in inextinguishable laughter.

Over our heads pass the forces that make and unmake empires. International combats wage in South Africa or the Behring Sea; the Church is torn asunder by grave questions of the use of incense or the lighting of wax candles; great problems agitate the minds of nations, and loom large in the history of the times. To us these are nothing, less than nothing and vanity; echoes faint, indeed, as if coming from another world; like a tale of little meaning, though the words are strong. We are very many, so many, indeed, that it seems incredible that each individual should count for anything at all in the sight of man or of God. And we are very silent, so silent that no one to this hour knows what we think on any subject, or why we think it. We are born into a world already too full, that exhibits no manifest delight at our advent. We cease to be children before we have ever known childhood. We take up the burden of silent work through long years of silent endurance. We rear up others to compete against us in a similar life. At length, at the closing of the day, we pass to a silent grave. Of the meaning of this dim, silent life existence we have no power to ascertain; we have almost ceased to wonder; we have never capacity or leisure persistently to inquire. Men and nations rise and fall, and today is never the same as yesterday; but the quantity of us and the silence of us remains unchanged, the permanent elements where all other things are transitory.

That no voice should remain from the crowded warren of the medieval town seems strange to the present-day student. That no voice will pass to posterity from the million-peopled ghetto of London will assuredly appear to the future historian a more inexplicable mystery. What manner of life peopled that monstrous ruin? What strange race choked up those gigantic and hideous dwellings? What motives impelled their continual striving? What aspirations did they cherish? What temptations did they wrestle with? What hope sustained them through the unchanging monotonous days? These are questions that will remain for ever unanswered. No future historical novelist will be able to reconstitute from contemporary documents the inner life of Pentonville or Camberwell. The obscure monuments of them will alone remain as a protest, an object-lesson to future moralists, the products of a wave of humanity that silently heaped itself up into a menacing aggregation, and as silently fell away. That they struggled to manhood or womanhood in dusty and crowded ways; that they rose to shabby success or sank to shabby failure; that they vanished into the interminable acreage of the forgotten, unknown dead; these skeleton facts will remain. The rest will merge into a kind of confused 'alarm of struggle and flight'; a vision of a 'long battle in the mist', where 'friend slew friend, not knowing whom he slew'; and 'all of high and holy dies away'. A riddle whose solution is dark and obscure, and presents no obvious meaning. A picture in which the waste and scattering and crushing out of the possibilities of life in the ordinary undistinguished multitude will, to the eyes of the future, thrust a black smudge across the background of the civilization of the twentieth century, softening the loud plaudits of its contemporary acclaimers into a minor melody, at once humorous, pathetic, and sorrowful.

INVADING THE SUBURBS

From *From the Abyss*

South of the Abyss stretches a tangled maze of suburbs. The ground rises from the old marshes now choked up with crowded life. Up the hills emerge the great roads flanked by white houses embedded in a wealth of greenery, discernible in the distance from our uppermost windows. And over the crest and down the slopes beyond expands all that quaint detached suburban life, not unbeautiful; a population for the most part parasitic on the city of London, filled with the strangest ideals. Each little house stands in its little garden; each little householder leaves at regular times, black-coated and top-hatted, for the London train; each little wife pilgrimages at intervals up to Victoria for the wild excitement of an afternoon's shopping. The young men of the district are early apprenticed in the counting-houses employing their fathers. The young women, too genteel to work, find time hang heavy on their hands till the evening. But in the evening, especially in the summer evening, all is life and merriment. Trees hang over the pathway from the little gardens, the long avenues of gas-lamps stretch out like fairy lights, the scent of the lilac and laburnum is in the air; little tennis-courts, little croquet lawns, little garden tea parties yield satisfaction intensified by the long afternoon at the office stool. As these disperse in the gloaming and boys and girls in white depart homewards, the glare over the hills to the northward, streaming up beyond the villas and gardens, alone reveals the nearness of the hot troubled life in the Abyss.

The very proximity in class as in area creates a spirit of placid hostility; just as the 'loyalists' in South Africa are the most ferociously bitter towards the men of alien race. No intercourse or traffic takes place across the border line of the Abyss. The suburban race is hurried through our territory high on embankments or buried deep in tubes. Our visitors come from the far away West, from provincial towns, from universities of uncertain position; an armed neutrality ranges along the limits of our region, guarded by jealous spies. Occasionally a suburban dweller gazing around him in an attitude of discomfort is found pilgrimaging through our territory; occasionally the forlorn sight of a child of the Abyss, trailing behind it a line of youthful companions, inflames with disordered visions of smallpox and virulent fevers the respectabilities of some quiet suburban avenue. But on the whole the tacit agreement has been faithfully maintained on both sides; the frontier being recognised as the southern limit for the wandering of our children and the boundary north of which suburbandom cannot penetrate without peril to its soul.

Yet though individual exploration is thus firmly discouraged, the continual multiplication of our impetuous increase is ever beating against the barriers; and a persistent irresistible pressure is destined eventually to overwhelm and outswarm the present abysmal limitations. The process is a subtle one, not uninstructive; a movement which creates forces in the rear of fortifications still offering a bold front to the invader and leaves them suddenly useless. Here the tired waves vainly breaking seem no sudden inch to gain; far off to the southward, through creeks and inlets, has silently flooded in the Abyss.

The process, in rough typical form, is somewhat as follows: beyond, in the outer ring of suburbandom, some ancient house or well-wooded estate, is being offered for sale; the owner having attained poverty and collapsed, or attained riches and migrated to Kensington seeking advancement and enlightened society. The speculative builder purchases, borrowed money is advanced, perhaps from South African millionaires impatient for high interest and quick returns; and the Belle Vue or Fair Light estate is in process of development.

Here is the whole change laid bare in successive layers of completion. From the shady villa-studded lane we suddenly emerge into energetic rude activity. The great trees are falling, grass is being torn up, shrubs and flowers are disappearing. A little further, and a huddled plan of narrow streets has appeared, traced as if by miracle on the damp ground; next we light on builder's chaos, weird skeletons of houses, growing visibly from day to day. Beyond, the houses have already been completed, and the bricks and mortar are being painted on in red and white. The stubborn material things have as it were become plastic before our eyes. A moment more and we are in populated streets; roads labelled, curtains in little bow-windows, a little packed maze of little packed houses all leaning up against each other lest they should fall down, cut into cubes, with tiny backyards in which a woman can just turn round. At a central site appears a clean, attractive gin palace; along one side extends a raw row of new red shops; at a corner sprawls a gigantic elementary school, erected at the cost of some thirty or forty thousand pounds, model of latest educational efficiency; in a less favoured site rises a tiny corrugated iron edifice with the legend 'Site for the permanent Church of St Aloysius. £5000 required', brooding over it. And then, suddenly ended as suddenly began, we pass outward again into a different universe of being; the suburban lane, the detached houses, the lilacs and syringa, silence and peace.

The Abyss has budded. And the bud detached from the parent stalk has fallen into the midst of a matrix of suburbs. Here, at least, one might hope all is for the best. The houses, though tiny, are clean and respectable, inhabited by the best type of artizan. The numbers cannot yet overwhelm the neighbouring denizens. Behold, the hopeful spectator might observe, the happy abolition of the segregation of classes; men and women of diverse rank mingling together as citizens of the same great community; the rich and the poor meeting together, and God the maker of them all.

Alas for the best-laid schemes of mice and men! That tiny bud is destined to prove a canker which will eat out the heart of the peaceful township into which it has fallen. Here is no condition of stable equilibrium; and the subsequent development is being written at this moment in letters which he that runs may read. One day the dwellers on the highroad between the bud and its parent awaken early in the morning to find cable trams down their thoroughfares, and cable cars, closely packed with men outside and in, smoking short pipes or reading pink papers, hurtling past their very front gardens. With blanched faces they gather up their household goods and flee away; and the tram travellers behold at morn and even long lines of notice-boards advertising as 'To let' dingy white houses embedded in decaying and desolate gardens. Meanwhile the immediate neighbours of the bomb so suddenly dropped into their midst, as if fearing a premature explosion, gradually edge away; a vacant ring of isolation develops round the bud. In the bud itself internal changes are fermenting. The original promoters have sold their holdings as rapidly as may be, and cleared off to find fresh fields for their maleficient energy. The purchasers have been the occupiers themselves, desiring a permanent rent-free home; or small house-farmers seeking speedy returns; or persons with savings just enough to live on if invested at a high rate of interest. None of these have capital to spend on the repairs speedily necessary. Ceilings bulge in; walls bulge out; paint peels off; windows break and remain unmended; water-supply and sanitary apparatus fall permanently out of repair. Houses run up in three months for a 15 per cent return are not likely to prove an abiding city.

Small jobbers raise the rents, the most effective way – such is the paradoxical law of the Abyss – of ensuring the creation of a slum. The original respectable emigrants move off again southward, seeking, as always, a new house, hitherto un-occupied, which will not fall into decay.

Stephen Reynolds

Stephen Reynolds (1881–1919) was born in Devizes, Wiltshire, and educated at Manchester University where he
took a degree in chemistry. He spent a brief spell in Paris
trying to make a living as a writer, but after an illness
moved to Devon. As he explains in an autobiographical
fragment: 'Made my home with a fisherman's family and,
as a general thing, threw up middle-class society. Can't
say I feel much loss.' He later acted as a government
adviser on Inshore Fisheries and, in 1914, became Resident
Inspector of Fisheries for the South West Area. Although
now remembered for his studies of working-class life,
Reynolds attached great importance to an early novel
The Holy Mountain which he was unable to get published.
When *A Poor Man's House* (1909) was accepted, he insisted
that both books be published together. Following the
success of *A Poor Man's House*, he wrote, together with
two of his fishermen friends Bob and Tom Woolley,
Seems So! A Working-Class View of Politics (1911).

A DEVONSHIRE KITCHEN

From *A Poor Man's House*

This morning, when I arrived downstairs, the kitchen was all
of a caddle. Children were bolting their breakfast, seated and
afoot; were washing themselves and being washed; were
getting ready and being got ready for school. Mrs Widger
looked up from stitching the seat of a small boy's breeches
in situ. 'I've a-laid your breakfast in the front room.'

Thither I went with a book and no uncertain feeling of
disappointment.

The front room looks out upon Alexandra Square. It is, at
once, parlour, lumber room, sail and rope store, portrait gallery

of relatives and ships, and larder. It is a veritable museum of the household treasures not in constant use, and represents pretty accurately, I imagine, the extent to which Mrs Widger's house-pride is able to indulge itself. But I have had enough at Salisbury of eating my meals among best furniture and in the (printed) company of great minds. The noise in the kitchen sounded jolly. Now or never, I thought. So after breakfast, I returned to the kitchen and asked for what bad behaviour I was banished to the front room.

'Lor'! If yu don't mind this. On'y 'tis all up an' down here . . .'

The Widgers' kitchen is an extraordinary room – fit shrine for that household symbol, the big enamelled tin teapot. At the NW corner is the door to the scullery and to the small walled-in garden which contains – in order of importance – flotsam and jetsam for firewood, old masts, spars and rudders, and some weedy, grub-eaten vegetables. At the top of the garden is a tumble-down cat-haunted linhay, crammed to its leaky roof with fishing gear. No doubt it is the presence everywhere of boat and fishing gear which gives such a singular unity to the whole place.

The kitchen is not a very light room: its low small-paned window is in the N. wall. Then, going round the room, the courting chair stands in the NE corner, below some shelves laden with fancy china and souvenirs – and tackle. The kitchener, which opens out into quite a comforting fireplace, is let into the E. wall, and close beside it is the provision cupboard, so situated that the cockroaches, having ample food and warmth, shall wax fat and multiply. Next, behind a low dirty door in the S. wall, is the coalhole, then the high dresser, and then the door to the narrow front passage, beneath the ceiling of which are lodged masts, spars and sails. The W. wall of the kitchen is decorated with Tony's Oddfellow 'cistificate' with old almanacs and with a number of small pictures, all more or less askew.

There is an abundance of chairs, most of them with an old cushion on the seat, all of them more or less broken by the children's racket. Over the pictures on the warm W. wall –

against which, on the other side, the neighbour's kitchener stands – is a line of clean underclothing, hung there to air. The dresser is littered with fishing lines as well as with dry provisions and its proper complement of odd pieces of china. Beneath the table and each of the larger chairs are boots and slippers in various stages of polish or decay. Every jug not in daily use, every pot and vase, and half the many drawers, contain lines, copper nails, sail-thimbles and needles, spare blocks and pulleys, rope ends and twins. But most characteristic of the kitchen (the household teapot excepted) are the navy-blue garments and jerseys, drying along the line and flung over chairs, together with innumerable photographs of Tony and all his kin, the greater number of them in seafaring rig.

Specially do I like the bluejacket photographs; magnificent men, some of them, though one strong fellow looks more than comical, seated amid the photographer's rustic properties with a wreath of artificial fern leaves around him and a broadly smiling Jolly-Jack-Tar face protruding from the foliage. Some battleships, pitching and tossing in fearful photographers' gales* and one or two framed memorial cards complete the kitchen picture gallery.

It is a place of many smells which, however, form a not disagreeable blend.

An untidy room – yes. An undignified room – no. Kitchen; scullery (the scullery proper is cramped and its damp floor bad for the feet); eating room; sitting room; reception room; storeroom; treasure-house; and at times a wash-house – it is an epitome of the household's activities and a reflexion of the family's world-wide seafaring.

* Composite pictures apparently; made from a photograph of a ship and of a bad painting of a hurricane.

ACCUMULATED WISDOM

From *A Poor Man's House*

Everything, and nothing, is prosaic. 'Tis *all according*. But it is startling indeed how suddenly sometimes the earth takes on a new wonderfulness, and Saint Prosaic a new halo. What, to put it in the plainest manner possible, am I doing here? Merely fishing and sailing on the cheap (not so very cheaply); roughing it – pigging it, as one would say – with people who are not my people and do not live as I have been accustomed to do. Yet, as I know well *all* the time, this change from one prosaic life to another has brought about a revelation which, like great music, sanctifies things, makes one thankful, and in a sense very humble; incapable of fitting speech, incapable of silence.

Astonishment at, and zest in, these Under Town lives; the discovery of so much beauty hitherto unsuspected and, indeed, not to be caught sight of without exceptional opportunity, sets one watching and waiting in order to find out the real difference of their minds from the minds of us who have been through the educational mill; also to find out where and how they have the advantage of us. For I can feel rather than see, here, the presence of a wisdom that I know nothing about, not even by hearsay, and that I suspect to be largely the traditional wisdom of the folk, gained from contact with hard fact, slowly accumulated and handed on through centuries – the wisdom from which education cuts us off, which education teaches us to pooh-pooh.

Such wisdom is difficult to grasp; very shy. My chance of observing it lies precisely in this : that I am neither a sky-pilot, nor a district visitor, nor a reformer, nor a philanthropist, nor any sort of 'worker', useful or impertinent; but simply a sponge to absorb and, so far as can be, an understander to sympathize. It is hard entirely to share another people's life, to give oneself up to it, to be received into it. They know intuitively (their intuitions are extraordinarily acute) that one is thinking more than one gives voice to; putting two and two together; which keeps alive a lingering involuntary distrust and a certain amount, however little, of ill-grounded respectfulness. (Respectfulness is less a tribute to real or fancied superiority, than an armour to defend the poor man's private life.) Besides which, these people are necessary to, or at least their intimacy is greatly desired by, myself, whereas their own life is complete and rounded without me. I am tangential merely. They owe me nothing; I owe them much. It is I who am the client, they the patrons.

THE LANGUAGE OF CLASS

From *A Poor Man's House*

It is stupid, at present, to ignore the existence of class distinctions; though they do not perhaps operate over so large a segment of life as formerly, they still exist in ancient strength, notwithstanding the fashionable cant – lip-service only to democratic ideals – about the whole world kin. There is not one high wall, but two high walls between the classes and the masses, so-called, and that erected in self-defence by the exploited is the higher and more difficult to climb. On the one side is a disciplined, fortified Gibraltar, held by the gentry; then comes a singularly barren and unstable neutral zone; and on the other side is the vast chaotic mass. In Under Town, I notice, a gentleman is always *gen'leman*, a workman or tramp is *man*, but the fringers, the inhabitants of the neutral zone, are called *persons*. For example : 'That man what used to work for the council is driving about the *gen'leman* as stays with Mrs Smith – the *person* what used to keep the green-grocery shop to the top of High Street afore she took the lodging house on East Cliff.' It is, in fact, strange how undemocratic the poor man is. (Not so strange when one realises that far from having everything to gain and nothing to lose by a levelling process, he has a deal to lose and his gains are problematical.) I am not sure that he doesn't prefer to regard the gen'leman as another species of animal. Jimmy and Tommy have a name of their own for the little rock-cakes their mother cooks. They call them *gentry-cakes* because such morsels are fitted for the – as Jimmy and Tommy imagine – smaller mouths of ladies and gentlemen. The other afternoon Mabel told me that a boat she had found belonged not to a boy but to a *gentry-boy*. Some time ago I begged Tony not to *sir* me; threatened to punch his head if he did. It discomforted me to be belaboured with a title of respect which I could not reasonably claim from him. Rather I should *sir* him, for he is older and at least my equal in character; he has begotten healthy children for his country and he works hard 'to raise 'em vitty'. Against my book-knowledge he can set a whole stock of information and experience more directly derived from and bearing upon life. I don't consider myself unfit to survive, but he is fitter, and up to the present has done more to justify his survival – which after all is the ultimate test of a man's position in the race. At all events, he did cease *sir-ing* me except on ceremonial occasions. At ordinary times the detested word is unheard, but it is still: 'Gude morning, sir!' 'Gude night, sir!' And sometimes: 'Your health, sir!' At that the matter must rest, I suppose, though the *sir* is a symbol of class difference, and to do away with the symbol is to weaken the difference.

But at the same time, I am lucky enough to possess certain advantages. I have, for instance, managed to preserve the ability to speak dialect in spite of all the efforts of my pastors and masters to make me talk the stereotyped, comparatively inexpressive compromise which goes by the name of King's English. Tony is hard of hearing, catches the meaning of dialect far quicker than that of standard English, and I notice that the damn'd spot *sir* seldom blots our conversation when it is carried on in dialect. Finally there is the great problem of self-expression. There, at any rate, I am well to windward.

The cause of the uneducated man's use of the word *like* is interesting. He makes a statement, uses an adjective, and – especially if the statement relates to his own feelings or to something unfamiliar – he tacks on the word *like*, spoken in a peculiarly explanatory tone of voice. What does the word mean there? Is it merely a habit, a 'gyte', as Tony would say? And why the word *like*? . . .

Drummond of Hawthornden exclaims:

> *This Life, which seems so fair,*
> *Is like a bubble blown up in the air*
> *By sporting children's breath . . .*

Bacon speaks more boldly and concisely. He forsakes simile for metaphor, leaving the word *like* to be understood.

> *The World's a bubble, and the Life of Man*
> *Less than a span . . .*

Were Tony to try and express himself by the same means, he would say: 'The world's a bubble, like, and the life of man less than a span, like.'

Like, in fact, with the poor man as with the poet, connotes simile and metaphor. The poor man's vocabulary, like the poet's, is quite inadequate to express his thoughts. Both, in their several ways, are driven to the use of unhackneyed words and simile and metaphor; both use a language of great flexibility;* for which reason we find that after the poet himself, the poor man speaks most poetically. Witness the beautiful description: 'All at once the nor'easter springed out from the land, an' afore us could down-haul the mainsail, the sea wer feather-white an' skatting in over the bows.' New words are eagerly seized; hence the malapropisms and solecisms so frequently made fun of, without appreciation of their cause. *Obsolete* has come hereto from the Navy, through

---

* The flexibility and expressiveness of dialect lies largely in its ability to change its verbal form and pronunciation from a speech very broad indeed to something approaching standard English. For example, 'You'm a fool,' is playful; 'You'm a fule,' less so. 'You're a fool,' asserts the fact without blame; while 'Thee't a fule,' or 'Thee a't a fule!' would be spoken in temper, and the second is the more emphatic. The real differences between 'I an't got nothing,' 'I an't got ort,' and 'I an't got nort,' – 'Oo't?' 'Casn'?' 'Will 'ee?' and 'Will you?' – 'You'm not,' 'You ain't,' 'You bain't' and 'Thee a'tn't,' – are hardly to be appreciated by those who speak only standard English. *Thee* and *thou* are used between intimates, as in French. *Thee* is usual from a mother to her children, but is disrespectful from children to their mother.

sons who are bluejackets. Now, when Tony wishes to sum
up in one word the two facts that he is older and also less
vigorous than formerly, he says: 'Tony's getting obsolete, like.'
A soulless word, borrowed from official papers, has acquired
for us a poetic wealth of meaning in which the pathos of
the old ship, of declining years, and of Tony's own ageing, are
all present with one knows not what other suggestions besides.
And when *obsolete* is fully domesticated here, the *like* will
be struck off . . .

ART THAT IS LIVED

From *A Poor Man's House*

There is something about this singing of sea-songs by a sea-
farer which makes them grip one extraordinarily. They are far
from perfect in execution, they are not always quite in tune,
especially on Tony's high notes, yet, I am certain, they are as
artistic in the best sense as any of the fine music I have heard.
Tony sings with imagination: he sees, *lives* what he is singing. Between this sort of song and most, there is much the
same difference as between going abroad, and reading a book
of travels; or between singing folk-songs with the folk and
twittering bowdlerised versions in a drawing-room. However
imperfect technically, Tony's songs are an expression of the
life he lives, rather than an excursion into the realms of art –
into the expression of other kinds of life – with temporarily
stimulated and projected imagination. His art is perpetual
creation, not repetition of a thing created once and for all.
The art that is *lived*, howsoever imperfect, has an advantage
over the most finished art that is merely repeated. Next after
the music of, as one might say, superhuman creative force –
like Bach's and Beethoven's – comes this kind, of Tony's.

Cultured people talk about the artistic tastes of the poor,
would have them read – well, they don't quite know what –
something 'good', something namely that appeals to the
cultured. It has always been my experience in much lending
of books, that the poor will read the literature of life's funda-

mental daily realities quickly enough, once they know of its existence. What they will not read, what in the struggle for existence they cannot waste time over, is the literature of the etceteras of life, the decorations, the vapourings. Sane minds, like healthy bodies, crave strong meats, and the strong meats of literature are usually the worst cooked. I am inclined to think that the taste of the poor, the uneducated, is on the right lines, though undeveloped, whilst the taste of the educated consists of beautifully developed wrongness, an exquisite secession from reality. As Nietzsche pointed out, degenerates love narcotics; something to make them forget life, not face it. Their meats must be strange and peptonized. Therefore they hate, they are afraid of, the greatest things in life – the commonplace. Much culture has debilitated them. Rank life would kill them – or save them.

GAMBLING WITH THE SEA

From *A Poor Man's House*

News has come along from Plymouth that the boats there have fallen in with large shoals of herring. The air here has since been charged with excitement – the excitement of men who earn their livelihood by gambling with the sea. The drifters have fitted out. Most of the boats are up over – lying on the sea wall – but a few days ago many busy blue men slid the big brown drifters down their shoots to the beach. Looking along, one saw a couple of men standing in each drifter and, with the leisurely haste of seamen, drawing in their nets. It gave a peculiar savour, a hopeful animation, to the blank wintry sea. It was as if the spring had come to us human beings prematurely, before it was ready to seize on nature.

Yesterday afternoon I felt too unwell to lend a hand in shoving off the boats. So I climbed to the top of the East Cliff. The air was cool and still – so still that all the Seacombe smoke hung in the valley and drifted slowly to seawards and faded there. While the sun was setting behind a bank of sulky dull clouds, some woolpacks, faintly outlined in white against the grey, rose almost imperceptibly in the western sky. Everything, the sea itself, seemed very dry. Nothing moved on the cliffs, except some small birds which flittered homelessly among the black and twisted burnt gorse. They were very tiny and pitiful against, or indeed amid, the solemn gathering of the great slow clouds. On looking down from the edge of the cliff, a slight mistiness of the air gave one the impression that there was, lying level above the sea, a sheet of glass that dulled the sound of the water yet allowed one to discern every half-formed ripple, and even the purple of the rocks beneath. Five hundred feet below and a quarter of a mile out, were three boats. They also, like the birds, seemed pitifully tiny. But, unlike the birds, they did not seem purposeless. It was evident they were moving, though one could not see rowers, oars, or splashes, for they progressed in short jumps and above the dulled rattle of a billow breaking on the pebbles, the faint click-thud of oars between thole-pins was plainly audible. I had an odd fancy that the six men were rowing through immensity, into eternity, to meet God; and that they would so continue rowing, eternally.

This morning, very early, the crackle of burning wood in the kitchen fireplace awoke me. Then I heard the sea roaring; then Tony's bare feet on the stairs. 'Wind's backed an' come on to blow,' he said. 'They've a-had to hard up an' urn for it. Two on 'em's in, an' one have a-losted two nets. I told 'em 'twasn't vitty when they shoved off. 'Tis blowing hard. I be going out along to see w'er t'other on 'em's in eet.'

The sea was angry, the moon obscure. The dead-asleep town stood up motionless before the madly-living breakers. It seemed as if a horrible fight was in progress; loud rage and dumb treachery face to face in the semi-darkness; and between the livelong combatants, little men ran to and fro, peering out to sea.

Presently the third boat ran ashore. Its bellied sail hid everything from us who waited at the water's edge. It was hoisted on a high wave, and cast on land. The sea did not want it then. The sea spewed it up. The sea can afford to wait, even until the clean bright little town is a ruin on a salt marsh.

Returning in house, we made hot tea, and laughed.

We had, as it were, said *Good-Night* to the town, though it was only half-past three in the afternoon. Most lazy we must have looked as we sailed off to the fishing ground with a light fair wind, NNW. John's young muscular frame was leaning against the mainmast, like a magnificent statue dressed for the moment in fishermen's rig. Tony aft was lounging across the tiller. He fits the tiller, for he is older and bent and his eyes are deeply crowsfooted with watching. Both of them showed the same splendid contrast of navy-blue jerseys against sea eyes and spray-stung red and russet skins. I was lying full length along the midship thwart. We lopped along lazily, about three knots to the hour.

As we lounged and smoked, each of us sang a different song, more or less in tune. It sounded not unmelodious upon the large waters. At intervals we asked one another where the 'gert bullies of herrings' had gone off to. Eastwards, westwards, to the offing, or down to the bottom to spawn?

So near the land we were, yet so far from it in feeling. There, to the NE, was the little town, sunlit and brilliantly white, with the church tower rising in the middle and the heather-topped cloud-capped hills behind. There around the bay, were the red cliffs, crossed by deep shadows and splotched with dark green bushes. The land was there. We were to sea. The water, which barely gurgled beneath the bows of the drifter, was rushing up the beaches under the cliffs with a myriad-sounding rattle. Gulls, bright pearly white or black as cormorants, according as the light struck them, were our only companions. The little craft our kingdom was – twenty-two foot long by eight in the beam – and a pretty pickle of a kingdom!

Mixed up together in the stern were spare cork buoys, rope ends, sacks of ballast, and Tony. Midships were the piled up nets and buoys. For'ard were more ballast bags and rope ends, some cordage, old clothes, sacks, paper bags of supper, four bottles of cold tea, two of paraffin oil and one of water, the riding lamp and a very old fish-box, half full of pebbles, for cooking on. All over the boat were herring scales and smelly blobs of roe. It's some time now since the old craft was scraped and painted.

But the golden light of the sunset gilded everything, and the probable catch was what concerned us.

We chose our berth among the other drifters that were on the ground. We shot two hundred and forty fathom of net with a swishing plash of the yarn and a smack-smack-splutter of the buoys. We had our supper of sandwiches and tatie-cake and hotted-up tea.

'Can 'ee smell ort?' asked John, sniffing out over the bows.

'Herring!' said I. 'I can smell 'em plainly.'

'Then there's fish about.'

Tony however remarked the absence of birds, and declared that the water didn't look so fishy as when they had their last big haul. 'They herrings be gone east,' he repeated.

'G'out! What did 'ee come west for then? I told yu to du as yu was minded, an' yu did, didn' 'ee? Us'll haul up in a couple o' hours an' see w'er us got any.'

We didn't turn in. We piled on clothes and stayed drinking, smoking, chatting, singing – a boat-full of life swinging gently to the nets in an immense dark silence, an immense sea-whisper.

About nine o'clock we hauled in for not more than nine dozen of fish. The sea-fire glimmered on the rising net, glittered in the boat, and then, with an almost painful suddenness, snuffed out. 'They be so full as eggs,' said John every minute or two, holding out fish to Tony, who felt them and answered, 'Iss, they'm no scanters [spawned or undersized fish]. *They* bain't here alone.'

Nets inboard, we rowed a little east of another boat, to shoot a second time. John said, 'Hoist the sail, can't 'ee.' Tony said, 'What's the need?'

Before eleven we were foul of the other boat's nets and had again to haul in. Tony puffed and panted with the double weight; John disentangled the mesh and swore.

'If we'd a-hoisted the sail . . .' he grumbled.

'There wasn't no need if we'd a-pulled a bit farther.'

'What's the good o' pulling yer arms out?'

'I knowed where to go, on'y yu said we was far enough.'

'No I didn't!'

'S'thee think I don' know where to shute a fleet o' nets?'

'Well, we'm foul, anyhow.'

'I was herring drifting afore yu was born. I knows well enough.'

'Why don' 'ee hae yer own way then, if yu knows? Yu'm s'posed to be skipper here.'

'If I'd had me own way . . .'

'Hould thy bloody row, casn'!'

It sounded like murder gathering up; but Tony calls it their brotherly love-talk, and they are no worse friends for it all. The better the catch, the more exciting the work, and the livelier the love-talk. They say, therefore, that it brings luck to a boat.

A third time we shot nets, safely to the east of every other craft. Then John with his legs in a sack and a fearnought jacket round him, snored in the cutty, whilst Tony nodded sleepily outside. The sky eastwards had already in it the weird whitish light of the coming moon. The risen wind was piping out from land. I could see the bobbing lights of the other drifters to westward, and the glint of the Seacombe lamps on the water. Every now and then a broken wave came up to the boat with a confidential hiss. I had a constant impression that out of the dark flood some great voice was going to speak to me – speak quite softly.

'Shall us hot some more tea?' said Tony. 'My feet be dead wi' cold.'

We took the old fish-box and placed on the pebbles in it an old saucepan half full of oakum soaked in paraffin. Across the saucepan we ledged a sooty swivel, and on the swivel a black tin kettle which leaked slowly into the flame. Tony and myself lay with our four feet cocked along the edge of the box for warmth. The smoke stank in our nostrils, but the flame was cheery. By that flickering light the boat looked a great deep place, full of lumber and the blackest shadows. The herring scales glittered and the worn-out varnish was like rich brown velvet. And how good the tea, though it tasted of nothing but sugar, smoke, paraffin and herring.

It was nearly midnight. Tony suggested forty winks.

John was still sprawling beneath the cutty. Tony and I snoozed under the mainsail, huddled up together for the sake of warmth, like animals in a nest. At intervals we got up to peep over the gunwale or to bale the boat out. Then with comic sighs we coiled down together again. It was bitterly cold in the small hours. We pooled our vitality, as it were, and shared and shared alike. When we finally awoke, about five in the morning, the wind had died down, the sky and moon were clouded, and a dull mist was creeping over the sea.

We hauled in the net – fathoms of it for scarcely a fish.

'Have 'ee got anything to eat?' asked Tony.

'No.'

'Have yu got ort to drink?' asked John.

'No.'

'Got a cigarette?' I asked.

'Not one.'

'If we was to go a bit farther out and shute . . .' said Tony.

'G'out! Hould yer row!'

'All very well for yu. Yu been sleeping there for all the world like a gert duncow [dog-fish]. Why didn' 'ee wake up an' hae a yarn for to keep things merry like?'

John was leaning out over the bows. He rose up; stretched himself. 'Shute again!' he said with scorn. 'Us an't got nort to eat, nort to drink, nort to smoke, nor nort to talk about, an' us an't catched nort. Gimme thic sweep there, an' let's get in out o' it, I say.'

It was foggy. I steered the boat by compass over a sea that, under the smudged moon, was in colour and curve like pale violently-shaken liquid mud. In time we glimpsed the cliffs with the mist creeping up over them. Day was beginning to break, and with a breath of wind that had sprung up from the SE, we glided like a phantom ship on a phantom sea towards a phantom town between whose blind houses the wisps of the fog writhed tortuously.

Sixteen hours to sea in an open boat – for three hundred herrings – and the price three shillings a hundred!

It is nothing to fishermen, that; but we were all glad of our breakfast, a smoke and our beds.

WHY LIVE WITH THE POOR?

From *A Poor Man's House*

I am often asked why I have forsaken the society of educated people, and have made my home among 'rough uneducated' people, in a poor man's house. The briefest answer is, that it is good to live among those who, on the whole, are one's superiors.

It is pointed out with considerable care what ill effects such a life has, or is likely to have, upon a man. It is looked upon as a kind of relapse. But to settle down in a poor man's house is by no means to adopt a way of life that is less trouble. On the contrary, it is more trouble.

It is true that most of what schoolmasters call one's accomplishments have to be dropped. One cannot keep up everything anywhere.

It is true that one goes to the theatre less and reads less. Life, lived with a will, is play enough, and closer acquaintance with life's sterner realities renders one singularly impatient with the literature of life's frillings. I do not notice, however, that it makes one less susceptible to the really fine and strong things of literature and art.

It is true that one drops into dialect when excited; that one's manners suffer in conventional correctness. I suppose I know how to behave fairly correctly; I was well taught at all events; but my manners never have been and never will be so good, so considerate as Tony's. 'Tisn't in me.

It is true that one becomes much coarser. One acquires a habit of talking with scandalous freedom about vital matters which among the unscientific educated are kept hid in the dark – and go fusty there. But I do not think there is much vulgarity to be infected with here. Coarseness and vulgarity are incompatibles. It was well said in a book written not long ago, that 'Coarseness reveals but vulgarity hides.' Vulgarity is chiefly characteristic of the non-courageous who are everlastingly bent on climbing up the social stairs. Poor people are hardly ever vulgar, until they begin to 'rise' into the middle class.

It is true that, so far as knowledge goes, one is bound to be cock o' the walk among uneducated people – which, alone, is bad for a man. But knowledge is not everything, nor even the main thing. Wisdom is more than knowledge: it is *Knowledge applied to life, the ability to make use of the knowledge well.* In that respect I often have here to eat a slice of humble-pie. For all my elaborate education and painfully gained stock of knowledge, I find myself silenced time after time by the direct wisdom of these so-called ignorant people. They have preserved better, between knowledge and experience, that balance which makes for wisdom. They have less knowledge (less mental dyspepsy too) and use it to better purpose. It occurs to one finally that, according to our current standards, the great wise men whom we honour – Christ, Plato, Shakespeare, to name no more – were very ignorant fellows. Possibly the standards are wrong.

To live with the poor is to feel oneself in contact with a greater continuity of tradition and to share in a greater stability of life.

Mary Higgs

Mary Higgs (1854–1937) was born in Devizes, Wiltshire, the daughter of a Congregational minister, but moved to the North of England as a child when her father became minister of College Chapel, Bradford. She was educated at a private school and the newly founded Girton College, Cambridge, where she was the first woman to study for the Natural Science Tripos. She afterwards became a school-teacher in Bradford. In 1879 she married Thomas Higgs and moved to Oldham, the town with which her name was always to be associated, when her husband became minister of the Greenacres Congregational Church. She was connected with a wide range of religious and philanthropic organizations, being Secretary of the Ladies Committee visiting the Union Workhouse, Oldham, and organizer of a home for destitute women. It was through this work that she began her personal study of tramps and lodging-houses on which she became an acknowledged authority. On the death of her husband she devoted herself to social work in Oldham and was awarded the OBE for this in 1937. *Three Nights in Women's Lodging Houses* was published as a pamphlet in 1905, and collected into book form with other similar pamphlets as *Glimpses Into the Abyss* (1906), from which the present extract is taken.

THREE NIGHTS IN WOMEN'S LODGING HOUSES

From *Glimpses into the Abyss*

I. THE FIRST NIGHT

On a bright evening in May, when the trees were fresh with Nature's tracery, and the sky glowed with colour, my friend and I found our way by train and tram to a house, which was professedly a lodging-house for all sorts and conditions of women. The building, a large, tall, better-class dwelling-house, set back in a front garden, looked almost too respectable for us, as we had donned our tramp's attire. Some children were playing in the passage, and called 'the missus', who made no objection to our engaging two beds at sixpence each, warning us we should have to share a room with strangers. She then showed us into a small kitchen, clean and comfortable, but with little accommodation – two short forms and a dresser were the furniture, with shelves in the wall and a sink. A door gave access to a yard with sanitary convenience, and there was a good fire and plenty of boiling water. We sat a little while to rest, and to listen to one or two inmates – a woman who smelt of liquor, an elderly woman who appeared to help the person in charge, and a rather handsome dark girl, nicely dressed and clean, who told us she had been married a few months, and was deserted by her husband. We learnt afterwards that she had been in hotel and restaurant service. We soon decided to go out and buy some provisions, and to have a walk round. We had only expected the beds to be fourpence a night, so were rather short of money. We laid out our scanty resources as follows: Tea 1d, sugar 1d, bread 3d, butter 2d (and 1d we paid for the loan of a knife to be afterwards returned). With these we went back, but not being hungry yet we decided to go to the common sitting-room. This we found in possession of several women, mostly young. It was now nearing 10 p.m., and they were all busy tidying themselves, rouging their faces, blacking their eyelids, and preparing to go on the streets. All this was done perfectly openly, and their hair was curled by the fireside. It was wonderful how speedily they emerged from slatterns into good-looking young women. Each then sallied forth, and, being left alone, we returned to the kitchen and prepared to make tea and cut ourselves some bread and butter. Meanwhile various women passed and re-passed. Three cats were on the hearth – one, a tabby, was called 'Spot'. A Scotch woman was rather genteel in appearance, about forty, but who openly boasted she had been drunk every day for more than a week; she came in and went out more than once. She sat on the

form and related *apropos* of 'Spot', that she got a situation as
housekeeper, 'though she could not say she had not a spot
on her character'. A widower with several grown-up sons
wished to engage her as housekeeper. He asked about her
character, she said: 'Without thinking, I replied, "I am afraid
it will not bear too strict an investigation," and, by Jove!
if he didn't engage me at once!' She said it was a good place,
and she might have been in it all the time but for 'a bit of
temper'. 'Yes, and married the master!' added another. A
considerable flurry was caused by the advent in the corner
of two or three huge black beetles, or 'blackjacks' as they were
called, which made everybody draw up their skirts. The form
was removed to the middle of the room. The dark young lady
told us a good deal about her past; how she had an old
mistress who died in her chair and 'looked heavenly', and
how her daughter wished to take her to London, and even sent
her fare, but she would not go. She sighed over it, and said,
when we asked her if she was not sorry, that she had wished
many times she had gone; 'but,' she added, 'I was young and
foolish, and had no one to advise me.' A nice, bright-looking
young girl, who had come in looking very weary, and who had
a bad cough, interested us much. She had been out since eight,
but obtained no money. She said she had been out all one
night, and so got her cough. Later we learned her story. She
had been out late one night when in service on a gala day, and,
having a strict mistress, she was afraid of returning to her
place. A companion persuaded her to take train to N—. The
girls had just enough money, and were landed as strangers in
a strange town. They walked about and found this lodging-
house. They entered, and, being destitute, fell at once into
prostitution.

By this time we thoroughly understood the character of the
house. It may be there were exceptions, but they would be
but few. The inmates, probably about sixty, young and old,
were living a life of sin, and we were told that the proprietor
of this lodging-house owned fifteen others. We learnt that a
house could be taken for £2 11s a week, and 8s for a servant.
We learnt that most of the girls came home very late – many
as late as two o'clock – and in such a state that they kept the
others awake, singing and talking, drunk or maudlin. The

house was open till two at any rate every night.

We stayed up till twelve o'clock to learn as much as we could; then, as the proprietress seemed rather anxious for us to go to bed, we went upstairs and were shown into a fair-sized room with seven beds, low iron bedsteads with wire mattresses, and fairly clean mattress, sheets, and pillows. A woman who had a terrible cold and cough and our Scotch friend came to bed, the latter being comparatively sober, though she had had many drinks that day. Later on the other beds were filled. One had had over eleven shillings in the morning, but seemed to have 'got without it'. The woman with a cold insisted on having the window closed, and the room was very stifling, otherwise clean and comfortable (compared with some of our experiences); but our companions, some of them, had on filthy underclothing when seen by daylight.

The woman of the house called us about nine o'clock, and we had to get up 'willy-nilly'. There was a bath-room, with wash-basins and hot and cold water, and we learnt there were some 1s beds with separate washing accommodation.

A woman whose hair was going grey ascribed it to constant dyeing. A young girl had to go to see the doctor.

We found our way to the kitchen and prepared breakfast, securing our knife once more which we had returned. We took our breakfast to the dining-room, where a number of dissolute girls – some handsome, almost all slatternly – were already collected. We saw our young acquaintance of the night before, apparently breakfastless, and invited her to join us, which she gladly did. We learnt that she had had no food the day before, except a drink of tea and a little bread and butter, having had 'no luck'. Evidently she was starved into prostitution, about which she was still very shamefaced. She had been in several lodging-houses. The town ones were 'ten times worse'. A private one she had been in one night had had no lavatory accommodation; she had to go and wash at the station, paying twopence. She was afraid to solicit in town; the 'bobbies' kept a sharp look-out, and sometimes were in plain clothes. One had stopped her when she was only walking, told her she was on the streets, asked her where she came from, and advised her to go home to her mother. He asked why she was 'on the town', and when she told him she had got no work, he said, 'You all say that.' As she was afraid in the town, she was in the habit of going out to the suburbs. Her friend had quarrelled with her, and even struck her in the street. She was in another lodging-house, and 'doing well' on the town.

This forlorn girl had tried in vain to find a true friend among the others. One had borrowed and not repaid, one had been friendly and cast her off. We promised to try and help her.

Breakfast over, we sat and watched the scene, being three times moved to make room at the tables. Round the fire was a group of girls far gone in dissipation; good-looking girls most of them, but shameless; smoking cigarettes, boasting of drinks, or drinking, using foul language, singing music-hall songs, or talking vileness. The room grew full, and breakfasts were about, onions, bacon, beefsteak, tea, etc., filling the air with mingled odours. A girl called 'Dot' and another danced 'the cake-walk' in the middle of the floor.

On this scene entered the girl who had to go to the doctor. She was condemned to the Lock Hospital, and cried bitterly. An animated conversation took place about the whereabouts and merits of various lock wards or hospitals, and everyone tried to cheer her up. 'Never mind, Ivy, you'll soon be through with it!'

Later entered a distressed mother. Her girl was wrongly accused of stealing. She had traced her to another lodging-house, but it was closed. She spoke to say that 'she was her child whatever she had done, and she would see her through and take her home if she could find her, as she was her best friend'. 'Tell her if you come across her that the back door is always open, and she will be welcome.' Several girls cried, thinking of their mothers, and a woman offered to take her and search for her daughter later on. This scene brought tears to the eyes of our young friend, and I said, 'That's what your mother will say.' We had now to leave her, under promise not to go out until we returned. We left our tea and bread and solitary penny, and gladly escaped to the fresh air.

During the time these scenes had gone on several girls received notes. One was packing up to go somewhere; one was told 'the landlord wanted her' . . .

II. THE SECOND NIGHT

Returning at ten o'clock, we purchased, at the little shop which caters for this lodging-house, a loaf of bread for 2¼d, two ounces of boiled ham, a penny tin of condensed milk, and a pennyworth of sugar; tea and butter we had with us. Armed with these, in the kitchen we speedily obtained hot water and made our tea-supper. We took it into the dining-room for cool-ness' sake, and established ourselves at a table. This room had three long wooden tables and forms. It was an oblong room with one fire-place, and out of it was another kitchen with fireplace and gas stove . . .

The proprietress as we entered had told us not to mind a woman who was 'gone dotty' with drink. She also was in this room, properly maudlin. She had a chemise, which she kept tucking into her breast, pulling up her under-garments, and examining her stockings. She was taking more drink still, brought in in a bottle, and though warned, I believe she insisted presently on sallying forth, and would probably fall into the hands of the police. The other women present humoured her to avoid a quarrel.

By this time we felt quite 'at home', knowing the faces of a good many of the inmates. Most were out, but one and another we recollected came dropping in, in some cases to go out again. Our dark friend came and questioned us as to how we had got on. We told her we had done very well. She said, 'I suppose you have been round the town?' Evidently she was fishing for our occupation, and I fear she would gather the wrong impression from our affirmative reply; but we really had been about and could not 'give ourselves away'. This little person seemed to keep from drink, though she told us she had lost her last place through buying, with her own money, bottles of stout, and so horrifying her mistress, who, she said, was 'a religious woman, but a regular pig'. This mistress took drink herself, but 'would not own it', and 'suffered from indigestion'. She had the doctor, and he recommended change, society, etc., but she lazed about most of the day and drank. Little Dark Hair said she could have stood it if the woman had been straight, if she had told her she took drink and it wasn't good for her; but to call it 'indigestion', and dismiss her servant for buying in a few bottles of stout out of her own money, it was too disgusting! She left, and didn't feel like asking for a character, as what she said was regarded as cheek! She was evidently very low-spirited, for she said she wished she was 'in a bandbox', and then explained she meant her coffin. She said she would get out of this if she had a home; but she had no home, no friends. She was soon to become a mother – she would soon have to go to the workhouse. We gave her the address of a friend who would help her, but could not ourselves do so because of our *incognito*.

There was a great difference in the characters and appearance of the various women. One old woman apparently got her living by running errands and doing odd jobs for the girls. I think one woman was a pedlar. The former woman showed by her conversation that she had lived an immoral life. There were several women about thirty or forty, who behaved quietly and were dressed comparatively modestly and cleanly. Some looked quite superior to their position, but I believe they had only acquired the wisdom. of reticence, as they dressed themselves up and went out like the others, and one I thought particularly quiet, who seemed to watch us a good deal, smoked like the others, after she had been out. Some explanation of the probable life of these elder women was afforded next morning by a woman, rather stout, and more talkative. She had gone out overnight, setting off from her regular place, which was apparently some way off in a suburb. A 'toff' took her to have a drink, and promised her money to go with him to an hotel. He afterwards gave her the slip, leaving her penniless. Another girl, young and pretty, said she was given in the dark two pennies silvered over! A dark girl told her she 'wasn't so soft; she always felt the edges of her money in the dark and knew by that' . . .

III. THE THIRD NIGHT

. . . We set out once more to search for lodgings, intending to make straight for a street we had heard of by name. We took a penny tram-ride to the heart of the town, and asking directions of a woman, got a very bad impression from her of the street whither we were bound, a mild recommendation to one lodging-house, and a warm one, coupled with an invitation, to the one whither she was going. However, we 'preferred the worst', and so with thanks we left her. When, however, after a long walk we found the street, it was narrow and unsavoury, and the lodging-houses were all small cottages. We looked through open doors at a few interiors – and flinched! We knew what they would be like only too well! Besides, as we wanted to see as much 'life' as possible, we preferred a larger one. We could be *sure* of what these low-class ones were, if a slightly better one was unsatisfactory. So we sought a street near by, which we had also heard mentioned, and which, being a principal thoroughfare, was flanked by houses of a larger type, once inhabited by the well-to-do, but which now had descended to be lodging-houses.

A female lodging-house (next door to a men's lodging-house) looked clean and respectable, although through the open door we caught a glimpse of a girl who was dressing, and who attracted some attention from passers-by by her condition of half-undress. We paid sixpence each, and secured two beds in the same room. We then were 'free of the house', which consisted of a long passage leading to a small kitchen. Leading from the passage was a front parlour occupied by the 'deputy' and her husband, a larger dining-table furnished as usual with tables and forms, and a door leading to a yard with sanitary conveniences. A stairway with oak balustrading led above; a door which could be locked had been placed at the bottom, and no one was allowed upstairs till they went to bed – a good precaution for cleanliness and decency.

In the kitchen there was a fire, and hot water in a boiler by the side. A couple of tables and two forms, accommodating each about four people, were the only furniture besides a rack in the wall and some shelves filled with hats and other clothes. There was no room for more, as a small sink with hot and cold water occupied the corner by the fire. There were a few pots in much request, and two large tins. These formed the only apparatus for washing of all kinds. We saw them used overnight for bathing the feet, etc., one girl washing her feet in them; we knew they were used for washing clothes, and we saw them full of dirty pots in the morning. As we heard the state of one girl alluded to as contagious, 'but she won't go to hospital', it is easy to be imagined that we could not bring ourselves to eat and drink there. Nor did we consider it safe to use any sanitary convenience except upstairs, for it was easy to see the character of the house. We sat on the form in the kitchen for nearly an hour, while the girl we had seen made her elaborate toilet. She had a most severe cough, and could hardly speak, yet she sat, often in full view of the front door, in a low chemise and skirt, both of good quality if they had only been *clean*, which they were not. She had finished her washing process, but there were many others. She powdered her face and breast, she rouged herself with great care (being chaffed meanwhile by some of her companions), she burnt a match and blackened her eyebrows, and then by slow degrees she did her hair in numerous rolls, finishing up by curling the little ends and putting a net over all. Then, after some discussion as to which hat suited her (apparently hats, though they had owners, were common property), she put on first a very thin muslin blouse with a hole at the shoulder, then a clean skirt and a costume skirt and jacket (the latter very open at the neck), and finally the selected hat. She looked, when thus disguised, a handsome young woman, but her face was really thin and wan, and it was almost death to her to go out, as she did, into the cold night air with only a thin tie to protect her chest. She returned in the morning, saying she had been at the C— Hotel all night, and had been drinking all the time, and had not slept at all. She looked very weary, and rolled up some clothes and lay full length on a form to attempt to sleep. She could not long survive such a life. One girl had died the previous week there . . .

I have before had occasion to notice the harm done by hospital authorities in sending friendless girls, without sufficient enquiry (or even though knowing they are quite friendless), back to their native town. Girls such as this should be passed on to some agency that would 'mother' them. It is easy to see how a little indecision, and the pressure of hunger, might anchor a girl to sin. For most of those who entered were openly leading a life of shame. Girl after girl came in, rested, and went out. We learnt their 'by-names', and those of others. 'Red Jinny', distinguished from 'Scotch Jinny' and other Jinnies, was living with a companion in prostitution.

The pathetic history of a young woman who began her toilet by having a foot-bath (in one of the tins), her legs being swollen with varicose veins, will illustrate this life. She had a good home, a kind and strict father. The way home was always open to her, for her parents had not the slightest idea she was living in sin. They thought she was in service. She had actually been home over the week-end, and thoroughly enjoyed herself, going on Sunday to church and Sunday school. ('I wish I was as good!' sighed one when she heard it.) Yet for two or three years she had really led the life of a prostitute. Her history was a sad one. She kept company five years, and then her young man betrayed her. She managed to conceal this from her parents, and in order to maintain her baby she went on the streets. For two and a half years she lived with a prostitute friend, and worked and struggled for her little one, coming home one day to find her scalded and her companion 'blind drunk'. However, the child survived, only to perish of bronchitis and pneumonia. Her mother had worked for her and clothed her with her own fingers, making all her clothes herself. She was clever, for as she talked she unpicked a hat and twisted and turned it to new account. After her child died she left her companion – or was deserted by her – and now for some months she had been living here, except for home visits. She found it hard to get out of 'the life', because she had kept up the deception that she was entangled in. 'Her father would die' if he knew she was in such a place! But he must get to know in the long run unless she got out of 'the life'. Already she had been twice in the hands of the police – once for drink, and once for accosting. The second time she got off for 'first offence'. She gave an assumed name and paid the fine, but next time she would have to 'go down'. We got a good opportunity to press her to go where we knew she would find friends, as she was the only one in bed in our room by twelve o'clock. She did not go out because of a superstitious feeling that 'something was going to happen', which, she said, had also preceded her being taken up. She said she wished she was at home in her own good bed, which was always kept for her; but she was getting to drink and swear, and this life would soon kill her. We placed before her as strongly as we could the path to safety, and urged her to struggle free for the sake of father and child. It made one long to go and *live* continuously with these girls, gradually acquiring influence, and being able to speak to them as a Christian woman, and save them from the web in which they were entangled. Such work would be difficult and delicate, for it would be necessary to live quietly, maintaining oneself among them and acting by character, not by profession.

But surely something more is possible. There should be large, well-ventilated, well-provided women's lodging-houses, open even to the prostitute, but under the care of wise, motherly women. Here it was impossible for a girl even to keep her own property; there was not a locker or any place to put anything away. Girls slept with their hats on their beds for security. Everything was 'borrowed' or 'made off with'. A little care would keep a decent girl steady and safe, and bring many a wanderer back to goodness. Here everything tended to demoralisation. The sanitary arrangements were deficient. I cannot defend the shameless toilet in full view of an open door to the street, which we saw repeated, even to half-nudity, several times over. But this kitchen was the only place in which to wash and dress, and the door must needs be open. The constant talk was filthy – not on the part of all, but on that of many – and the life most were leading not in the least disguised. The more successful girls were sometimes out all night. Two or three came in very drunk and were piloted to bed by friends. Shameless expressions which cannot be repeated were used with regard to actions which decency conceals. Yet listening were other girls not so far gone in sin . . .

I have tried to tell a plain, unvarnished tale – in which nevertheless much is left out that would not bear printing – of the way in which these our young sisters live. The pity of it is that though some may from sheer wickedness seek it, more – perhaps most – are drawn in by frivolity and misfortune. It may be exceedingly difficult to rescue them when contaminated, surrounded as they are by all those invisible ties of friendship which chain a woman's heart. We make elaborate institutions to *rescue* them, which are often surrounded by such restrictions that they defeat their own end.

Can we not do something to solve the problem by providing

suitable and sufficient women's lodging-houses under good management, where freedom is not interfered with unduly, but influence for good is steady?

In Christian England a friendless girl should never want a friend and a home. And to guard our girls is to preserve our nation from the worst of evils – the corruption of a 'trade' based on greed and dishonour. Yet how else can a destitute girl get her living without a friend?

When all else is sold she sells herself to live!

Lady Bell

Lady Florence Bell (1851–1930) was born in Paris, the daughter of a fashionable doctor, Sir Joseph Olliffe. In 1876 she married Sir Hugh Bell, a wealthy ironmaster, colliery owner, and businessman. *At the Works* (1907), which was dedicated to Charles Booth, developed out of Lady Bell's close involvement in the lives of the workers at her husband's Middlesbrough iron foundry and focuses notably on the domestic and cultural aspects of working-class life. Although now remembered mainly as the author of this one book, Lady Bell also published essays, novels, and plays, and many books especially for children. In 1927 she produced a successful edition of the letters of her step-daughter Gertrude Bell, the Arabic scholar and explorer.

READING HABITS IN MIDDLESBROUGH

From *At the Works*

In these days when books are cheaper and libraries more plentiful, the workman, no doubt, has more opportunities for study than he used to have: a great many more books are accessible to him than in former times. There are a certain number of born readers among the workpeople in the town described, as there are, happily, in every layer of society, who not only devour omnivorously the books that come under their hand, but also go further afield and find more for themselves. But these are but a small proportion of the total number. Reading, perhaps, is not so prevalent a habit in any class of society as we try to think; but there is such a pressure of opinion in favour of it that it is difficult for the most candid to admit that they do not care about it. All the same, I believe that these are in a much larger proportion than we imagine. Learning to read does not necessarily lead to the enjoyment of literature. It is, no doubt, an absolutely necessary step in that direction, but I cannot help thinking, on looking at the results all round, and not only among the workmen, that the knowledge and practice of reading make nearly as often for waste of time as for edification. We are apt, even those among us whose habitual reading by no means constitutes a liberal education, to exclaim with genuine surprise and dismay when we realize what the working classes are in the habit of reading, or when we find that they do not read at all. We then solace ourselves by bringing out one of those comforting easy phrases which we carry about ready to apply to any place in the social fabric that seems to need it, and we say: 'With the spread of education the working classes will read something better worth reading.' But will they? The spread of education has a broad back. It is made to bear the burden of many unrealized, if not unrealizable, projects. Education is being spread very thin indeed for the people who are in question, and I will venture to say, judging from what I have observed of the reading of men and women who have been what is called 'educated', and of those who have not, that it is not the spread of education that will alter the reading of the great mass of the community, those who swell the tables of statistics and bring down the average of the enlightened. On the whole, I think it may be stated that a large majority of people of both sexes, in every walk in life, read, with hardly any selection of their own, what comes under their hand, what is suggested to them, and what they see being read by the person next door.

The reading that comes under the hand of the workman consists chiefly of the newspapers hawked about the streets, and those supplied by the small composite shops found in the poorer quarters. These shops, which sell various other goods – groceries, haberdashery – put before the public an unfailing supply of daily and weekly newspapers suited to their tastes, and penny novelettes. Roughly speaking, more than a quarter of the workmen read books as well as newspapers; nearly half of them read the paper only, and a quarter do not read at all. Of these, some only read a daily paper, the favourite being a local halfpenny evening paper, which seems to be in the hands of every man and woman, and almost every child. It contains a summary of general news, a serial story, a good deal of sporting information, also gossip and commercial news. Many workmen read in addition to this paper the weekly Sunday papers, containing several sheets, and providing a good deal of miscellaneous information. These are great favourites, and help to make the Sunday pass quite harmlessly, at any rate, for many among the workmen, who spend the day in bed, reading and smoking. The Sunday papers are a very special feature in the literature of the working classes. They are provided in view of the fact that the Sunday is the principal day on which both men and women are likely to read, and they consist of special papers, such as *The Umpire, The People, Reynolds's Weekly, Lloyd's News, Weekly Despatch, The Week, News of the World, The Sunday Chronicle*. And it is interesting to note that, even in households where each penny is an important item of expenditure, 1d, 2d, 3d, and sometimes as much as 6d, is set apart for this delectable Sunday reading.

As might perhaps be expected, the workman reads, as a rule, more than his wife, not only because his interest on the whole is more likely to be stimulated by intercourse with his fellows widening his horizon, but because he has more definite times of leisure in which he feels he is amply justified in 'sitting down with a book'. About a quarter of the men do not read at all: that is to say, if there is anything coming off in the way of sport that they are interested in, they buy a paper to see the result. That hardly comes under the head of reading. The boys read papers that make them laugh, *Comic Cuts* and the like. I have seen a large number of comic illustrated papers, compared with which *Answers* and *Tit-Bits* are the very aristocracy of the press. The *Winning Post* and other sporting papers, which represent the whole world as governed by the huge spirit of betting, are more and more in the hands of readers of all ages, with very undesirable results. The question of betting literature, for which there is an ever-increasing demand, is too wide to go into here. The *Illustrated Police Budget* is a sensational and much-read paper. In a number which has lately come into my hand there is a special double-page illustration headed 'Father Murders Six Children'. Outside the page, on one cover, is a picture of a man cutting his wife's throat, on the other of an actress being thrashed by an irate wife, the counterpart, in a cruder form, of the detective stories revelled in by readers of more education and a wider field of choice, such stories as 'Monsieur Lecoq' and 'Sherlock Holmes'.

The above publications, which make so large a part of the reading of the men and boys, are something between a pamphlet and a newspaper. Their reading of books comprises novels, sometimes travels, hardly any poetry, a few essays, books relating to their work, and one or two biographies.

I give here, taken haphazard and, where it is possible, in the very wording, the replies made in 200 houses visited to questions respecting the reading of the inmates. These replies speak for themselves. The weekly wages are inserted, where known, as a guide to the standing of the man; the calling of the men quoted has not been given for fear of identification. They are all people employed in various capacities at the ironworks.

1. Husband and wife cannot read. Youngest girl reads the paper to them sometimes, but 'she has a tiresome temper and will not always go on'. (Wages, 18s per week.)

2. Does not care very much for reading – 'just the newspapers'. (Wages, £2 10s to £3 per week.)

3. Fond of reading.

4. Tries to teach himself German.

5. Husband reads newspapers only, particularly racing news. Wife spends much time in reading penny dreadfuls, illustrated papers which she considers 'thrilling, as they give such a good account of "high life and elopements".' Husband disapproves of his wife's tastes.

6. Wife very fond of reading, particularly children's books. Husband dislikes reading anything.

7. Likes reading the Parliamentary news, and doesn't approve of 'local nonsense'. Wife fond of reading stories of country life. (Wages, 25s per week.)

8. Fond of reading, especially history. (Wages, 30s per week.)

9. Great reader, particularly of history, 'sea battles and their results'. His wife reads Shakespeare and revels in 'Hamlet' 'For lighter reading' likes Marie Corelli and Miss Braddon. (Wages, 36s per week.)

10. Very fond of reading books relating to his work, which he borrows from his brother. Wife does not care for reading. (Wages, 37s 6d per week.)

11. Great reader, saved up his money to buy engineering and theological books. (Wages, 28s.)

12. Brother does not care to read. Sister very fond of reading, and reads Mrs Henry Wood and Shakespeare to the rest of the family.

13. This man's wife never learnt to read, as she was brought up in some remote country village, and the 'school-dame had a spite against her'. (Wages, 9d per hour.)

14. Reads everything he can get hold of. (Wages £3 per week.)

15. Very fond of reading books relating to his work. (Wages, 36s per week.)

16. Husband cannot read. Wife only time to read on Sunday and then reads the *Sunday Magazine.*

17. Great reader, particularly seafaring tales. Wife does not care to read except on Sundays, when she prefers the *News of the World*, which she considers 'a great paper for enlarging the mind'.

18. Great reader; prefers above all to read of wars, in which he takes the greatest interest. He has 'often been mistaken for a soldier from his conversation and great knowledge of battles'. Wife very energetic woman, doing her own baking, washing, papering, etc., and no time to read. (Wages, £2 10s per week.)

19. Fond of reading romances. Wife does not care for reading at all, prefers sewing.

20. Only cares to read about sports, anything else he considers trash. Wife cannot read.

21. Husband cannot read. He says when he was young he was tongue-tied and no trouble was taken with him; he still has impediment in his speech. Wife always reads to him in the evenings, and by this means keeps him at home, but he will listen to nothing but romances.

22. Husband's chief delight is in reading detective stories. Wife cannot read.

23. Neither husband nor wife can read. The wife was brought up by an aunt who would not allow her to go to

I.U.E.   K school. Her boy is going to teach her to read.

24. Fond of reading 'downright exciting stories after his work is done to get his mind into another groove'.

25. Husband very fond of reading – novels only – so is his wife. (Wages, £2 10s to £3.)

26. Both husband and wife are great readers – novels – which they get from the Free Library and borrow from their neighbours. Husband reads aloud to wife. (Wages, 3s 3d to 3s 9d per day.)

27. Neither he nor his wife can read. (Wages, 21s to 25s per week.)

28. Reads newspapers, evening paper chiefly. (Wages, 25s per week – varying.)

29. Does not read much, as his eyes were burnt in an accident at the works. Wife no time to read, and prefers to 'be lazy on Sundays'. (Wages, £3 per week.)

30. Great reader, and has quite a collection of books on various subjects, which he has bought cheaply at the market.

31. Neither he nor his wife care in the least for reading: they occasionally 'pick up a paper'. (Wages, 30s per week and overtime.)

32. Reads newspapers only.

33. Is devoted to books, spends all his spare time reading. Is a member of the International Library of Famous Literature, and has a small bookcase full of splendid books which he pores over every night to his intense enjoyment. He also gets books from the Free Library on science, blast-furnaces, etc. His wife cannot read and refuses to learn, although he is most anxious to teach her. (Wages, 5s 11d to 6s 3d per day.)

34. Husband cannot read, but likes pictures, and his wife reads to him.

35. Neither he nor his wife cares for reading: occasionally they 'pick up a paper'. (Wages, 23s per week – varying.)

36. Is fond of reading and interested in Parliamentary news.

37. Is a great reader, and has 'taught himself mostly, as he was only at school two years'.

38. Reads to his wife, as she is nearly blind. (Wages, 4s 9d per day.)

39. Both fond of reading – husband, sentimental stories; wife, biographies. (Wages, 4s 6d to 5s 6d per day.)

40. Not readers. (Wages, 5s per day.)

41. Husband reads sporting papers only; wife, boys' tales of adventure.

42. Neither fond of reading.

43. Reads a great deal at the workmen's club to which he goes, but will not bring any books home.

44. Reads aloud to his wife, chiefly Mrs Henry Wood's books.

45. Both fond of reading nice novels. (Wages, £2 10s per week.)

46. Reads paper only. Wife can neither write nor read. (Wages, 26s per week.)

47. Is a very great reader. (Wages, 26s per week.)

48. Talks intelligently about current events, and reads all the newspapers he can get hold of to his wife at home.

49. A great reader of fiction; wife would be, but has not time. (Wages, 3s 4d per day.)

50. Wife fond of reading exciting novels, which the husband considers waste of time. (Wages 5s 6d per day.)

51. Wife fond of reading, but comic papers only. (Wages, 23s per week.)

52. Wife never reads anything – all her spare time is taken up sewing. (Wages, 21s to 23s per week.)

53. Husband reads daily paper to his wife, and enjoys a good novel.

54. Great reader of seafaring tales. Wife no time for reading.

55. Never reads. Sons fond of reading papers – sporting news. (Wages, 5s 3d per day.)

56. Does not care for reading. (Wages, £2 10s to £3 per week.)

57. Both fond of reading novels. (Wages, 4s 9d per day.)

58. Whole family fond of reading, especially fairy tales. They all read aloud in the evening, and the children repeat the stories to their playmates. (Wages, 4s 9d per day.)

59. All fond of reading. Wife likes Mrs Henry Wood; the men prefer travels. Nephew is a good French scholar.

60. Both fond of reading – wife, novels; husband, chemistry.

61. Do not read.

62. Never read books. Husband reads daily paper. (Wages

30s to 35s per week.)

63. All fond of reading. Boy reads books of adventure.

64. Read paper only. (Wages, 25s per week.)

65. Both fond of reading, especially the *Sunday Magazine*. (Wages, 23s per week.)

66. Both fond of reading, and prefer novels. (Wages, 36s per week.)

67. Mother and son both fond of reading – she tales of adventure, he novels.

68. Daughters fond of reading: prefer novels.

69. All fond of reading books of travel and adventure. Husband prefers Parliamentary news.

70. Family do not care for reading.

71. Both fond of reading.

72. Fond of reading novels.

73. Not great readers; wife prefers knitting and sewing. (Wages, 50s per week.)

74. Do not care for reading.

75. Husband fond of fiction. Wife likes sewing best.

76. Mother cannot read. Son prefers newspapers.

77. All the men, three lodgers, are fond of reading, and get books from the news-room library.

78. Do not read much; think it a waste of time.

79. Goes frequently to Free Library and reads all the better magazines, also Plato, Aristotle, etc.; considers their works 'such splendid food for man's mind'. Has learnt a little French.

80. Prefer daily papers.

81. Fond of reading novels.

82. Both fond of reading.

83. Read very little, chiefly newspapers.

84. Not a reading family at all.

85. Reads books and magazines relating to his work. (Wages, £2 15s weekly.)

86. Buys books referring to his work. (Wages, £3 10s per week.)

87. All the family are fond of reading. (Wages, £3 15s per week.)

88. Great reader. (Wages, £2 per week.)

89. Husband and son read novels and papers. Wife never reads.

90. Wife very fond of reading, and prefers Mrs Henry Wood.

91. None of the family ever read, which the old grandmother thinks 'a sad pity'.

92. Husband does not care for reading.

93. None of the family ever read at all, except the daily paper. (Wages £3 per week.)

94. No readers.

95. Fond of reading 'good stories' and papers. (Wages, 3s 3d per day.)

96. A great reader, especially travels and biographies.

97. Daughter's husband reads aloud to the family in the evening.

98. Read only the papers. (Wages, 38s per week.)

99. Reads a great deal — everything he can get hold of. (Wages, 36s per week.)

100. Do not care to read at all. (Wages, £2 10s per week.)

101. Mother and son both fond of reading novels.

102. Does not care for reading, except the newspapers. (Wages, 5s.)

103. Great reader. (Wages, 36s per week.)

104. Husband great reader. Wife never been taught to read.

105. None of the family care in the least for reading.

106. Both fond of reading, especially Mrs Henry Wood. (Wages, £2 10s per week.)

107. Not a reading family, but like to hear the news. (Wages, 5s per day.)

108. Wife 'puts in the days reading and sewing'. (Wages, 26s per week.)

109. Wife very fond of reading. As a rule the men do not read many books, but they nearly all read an evening paper. (Wages, 30s to 45s per week.)

110. Always reads an evening paper, but does not 'bother with books'.

111. Read evening paper.

112. All very fond of reading, and get books from library every week. (Wages, £2 per week.)

113. Spends Sunday in bed and reads all day. (Wages, £2 per week.)

114. Son reads all his spare time, *Tit-Bits* and *Answers*, and

goes in for the competitions, especially those to do with football. (Father's wages, 3s 6d per day; son's, 5s 6d per day.)

115. Wife can neither read nor write.

116. Not fond of reading. Wife likes reading story-books of every description – 'nice ones'. (Wages, 35s to £2 per week.)

117. Boys great readers.

118. Neither husband nor wife very fond of reading. He reads *News of the World* and the *Gazette*, and she reads the *Sunday Companion* on Sundays.

119. Apparently fond of reading, as there were several penny books lying about.

120. Cannot read, and his wife has no time for it. (Wages, 23s per week.)

121. Never cared for reading much, and wife cannot read.

122. Husband very fond of reading – anything he can lay hands on.

123. Great reader; novels and newspapers chiefly – 'nothing deep'. (Wages, 30s to £2 per week.)

124. Reads sporting papers. (Wages, 30s to £2 per week.)

125. Very fond of reading, especially anything about his work.

126. Does not care to read anything but the newspapers. Wife prefers to sew.

127. Do not read anything.

128. Neither he nor his wife can read, as, though they were respectably brought up, they were sent out to work very young. (Wages, 25s 6d per week.)

129. Both very fond of reading – she *Horniman's Magazine*, he the papers, as he likes to know what is going on in the world. (Wages, £2 10s per week.)

130. Neither he nor his wife care in the least for reading – she prefers sewing, he plays with the children or sleeps over the fire.

131. Wife a good scholar and likes reading story-books. Husband can hardly read at all, but listens to his wife reading. (Wages, 27s to 30s per week.)

132. Very fond of reading stories of sea adventures. (Wages, 30s per week.)

133. Reads the evening paper, but never books. (Wages, 3s 9d per day.)

134. Reads a great deal, but only books on 'religious disbeliefs'. (Wages varying from 23s per week.)

135. Not a reading family. Man reads the papers.

136. Likes to read everything he can find; nothing comes amiss, as he is a really good scholar. (Wages, 27s per week.)

137. Does not care for reading at all. Wife likes reading Mrs Henry Wood's books. (Wages, 36s per week.)

138. Both fond of reading, especially Rider Haggard's books. (Wages, 36s to 39s per week.)

139. No scholars. Eldest boy tells them 'all the news he hears'. (Wages, 27s to 29s per week.)

140. Wife cannot read. Husband reads aloud to her in the evening while she mends.

141. Single man, not fond of reading.

142. Wife very fond of reading histories and the customs and modes of living in other lands.

143. Both very fond of reading 'stories about other people's lives, without any murders in them'. (Wages, 22s per week.)

144. Single men. Very fond of reading, especially biographies.

145. Son is very fond of reading 'books of adventure' and 'wild escapes'.

146. Reads the newspaper 'without much interest' – never reads a book. (Wages, 4s 6d per day.)

147. Does not care for reading. (Wages, 30s to 36s per week.)

148. Both are fond of reading nice tales of home-life. Girl-wife appreciates poetry. (Wages, 4s 9d per day.)

149. Wife has never learnt to read. Husband reads to her nearly every evening, chiefly religious books.

150. Reads books on his work whenever he can get them, as he is most interested in it.

151. Reads the paper intelligently, and can talk about what he reads. Wife says she is 'not struck on reading at all, and could never see any interest in it'. She thinks her husband reads too much, as he always reads the evening paper. (Wages, £2 per week.)

152. None of the family care for reading. (Wages, £3 per week.)

153. Neither care to read. (Wages, about £2 per week.)

154. Reads the papers.

155. Served in Boer War; reads eagerly all accounts of the war; fond of books of adventure and the lives of explorers. Wife hardly ever reads, not caring for it. (Wages, about £3 per week.)

156. Reads newspapers only. (Wages, £2 per week.)

157. Never reads anything, not even the newspaper. (Wages, 5s daily.)

158. Cannot read. Wife suffers with her eyes, or would read a good deal.

159. Does not read much, as he is 'too tired' after his work. Wife would read more than she does, as she is very fond of it, but she does not like the sewing to get behindhand. (Wages, £2 and over per week.)

160. Whole family fond of reading novels. (Wages, £2 per week.)

161. Does not care in the least for reading of any kind. Wife has 'too much to do' to be able to read.

162. Neither he nor his wife can read. (Wages, 23s per week.)

163. Does not like his wife to read – thinks she might 'get hold of wrong notions'.

164. Both man and wife fond of reading 'all nice tale-books'. (Wages, 36s per week.)

165. Not fond of reading.

166. Only reads daily papers. Wife 'very poor scholar'. (Wages, 36s per week.)

167. Great reader, particularly fond of Dickens and *Chambers's Journal*. Wife thinks reading *most uninteresting*; 'it always sends her to sleep'.

168. He reads aloud to his wife in the evening Mrs Henry Wood's books and Dickens. Wife too busy to read. (Wages, 21s per week.)

169. The second son in this family is 'very intellectual', and a great and enthusiastic reader of what his mother calls 'such dreadfully hard books'. He is a Greek scholar, and possesses numerous Greek books, besides Ruskin, Browning, Shakespeare, biographies, etc.

170. A great reader, and borrows novels at the club he goes to.

171. Both man and wife fond of reading novels, and he also likes travels.

172. Reads the daily papers assiduously. (Wages, 36s per week.)

173. Both he and his wife read a good many novels during the winter evenings.

174. Both fond of reading 'good novels – the old-fashioned sort'. (Wages, 36s per week.)

175. Only reads evening paper.

176. Fond of reading about travels; very loath to lend his new books to the neighbours. (Wages, £3 per week.)

177. Both he and his wife read newspapers and magazines, but 'cannot be bothered with a book'.

178. Both very fond of reading. (Wages, 36s per week.)

179. None of the family care in the least for reading.

180. Both fond of reading; he reads aloud to her while she makes the children's clothes. (Wages, £4 per week.)

181. Reads paper only.

182. Reads 'good novels' to his wife.

183. Very keen politician, and reads all Parliamentary news.

184. Neither he nor his wife ever read a book. (Wages, 25s per week.)

185. This woman, at the age of fifty, made a desperate attempt to learn to read, and, being asked what sort of books she would prefer, said, 'Something with a little love and a little murder.'

186. This woman, asked what she liked to read, replied: 'Something that will take one away from oneself.'

187. Husband and wife read daily local paper – nothing else.

188. This family never 'wastes time' over reading books, but the father and son take an interest in the political news in the papers.

189. Parents fond of reading penny novelettes. Son prefers sporting papers.

190. The husband does not care to read more than the evening paper. Wife cannot read or write, but she gets her husband to read to her all that is going on in the world.

191. A rather delicate young man, fond of reading, especially books about his work; explaining his love for it by the fact that his 'father was the same, and had more brains than he

knew what to do with'.

192. Husband reads.

193. Husband 'sits down with a paper or book' after his supper every evening.

194. Reads only newspapers. 'No time' for books.

195. Young man, very ill, likes the picture papers, and is especially interested in sports, cricket and football.

196. This woman, when asked if she never read, answered she 'was no scholar', and she was often glad she had never learnt to read, as if she had she might have 'put off' – i.e. wasted – the time, instead of doing needlework.

197. The husband much interested in reading, especially anything about Japan.

198. Husband takes evening paper, reads Dickens and Thackeray, and 'always has a book going'. (Wages, 22s per week.)

199. Husband does not read books, but reads many of the papers. Takes in football papers and *Answers*.

200. Husband and wife have a Canadian paper sent them every week by relatives, and read every word of it.

The above number (200) is perhaps hardly enough to generalize from, but still it is interesting to see that of that number there are:

17 women who cannot read.
 8 men who cannot read.
28 houses where no one cares to read.
 8 men who actually dislike reading.
 3 women who actually dislike reading.
 7 women who say they 'have no time for it'.
50 houses where they only read novels.
58 houses where they read the newspapers only.
37 houses where they are 'fond of reading' or 'great readers'.
25 houses where they read books that are absolutely worth reading (this includes the men who read books about their work).

Some of the readers among the above are men of the very keenest intelligence, reading the best books that they can lay hands on, and eagerly availing themselves of the very good Free Library belonging to the town in question. The population of the town is over 100,000; the number of borrowers from the Free Library is 4500, that is, 4½ people out of every 100 take out a book. In many cases, of course, this represents a larger number of readers than borrowers, as books may be passed on to other members of the family; but it does not represent, as may be seen, a great number of the public. Statistics of the mere number of volumes taken out may be misleading, as the same people take out books over and over again. Most of what is taken out of the Free Library is fiction. The Library is used by many of the better class of workmen, but not much by the very poor. It is quite possible that some of these are deterred by the mere ceremonies that have to be gone through to take out a book. A woman who lives in a distant part of the town, whose outer garment is probably a ragged shawl fastened with a pin, may not like going up an imposing flight of stairs, getting a ticket, giving a name, looking through a catalogue, having the book entered, etc.; whereas many of these would read the book if it were actually put into their hands. Women, at any rate, of all classes know how often our actions are governed by our clothes, and how the fact of being unsuitably clad for a given course of conduct may be enough to prevent us from embarking on it. The establishment in recent years of children's libraries connected with the schools is giving admirable results. The children get into the habit of borrowing books and taking them home, and are more likely to frequent other libraries as they grow up.

The people who, for one reason or another, do not use the Free Library, will sometimes be willing to frequent smaller and less imposing centres of improvement. In two small lending libraries connected with ironworks, the one standing actually in the midst of the works, the other in a workmen's club in the town, the reading-rooms are well frequented, and give the impression of a goodly number of readers; but, as a matter of fact, on the works' library list there are about 70 borrowers out of a possible 1000 or more, and at the workmen's club 60 out of a possible 600. There are here, again, however, more readers than there are borrowers on the list, as each book is handed round and read by several people.

These somewhat unambitious libraries have been gradually provided with books, on the principle not so much of directing a course of reading as of providing a course that would be acceptable to the readers. They contain children's books, most of Dickens, most of Scott, some of Miss Yonge, Hall Caine, Bulwer Lytton, a good many of Mrs Henry Wood, a number of miscellaneous tales of a harmless kind, and also some books that may be grouped together as 'improving', such as – I quote at random from the catalogue – *A Chapter on Science, Voyages of Columbus, A Dash from Khartoum, The Great Boer War, The Great Invasion of 1813*, some poets, some Shakespeare, and some essays. The latter books are not much taken out; again here, what is chiefly required is fiction. This need not surprise us. The town we are speaking of exists for the iron trade, and is inhabited mainly by workmen engaged in strenuous physical labour; they are not very likely at the conclusion of a day's work to wish to read anything that involves an effort of attention. Many busy hard-working men in other walks of life read when they come in from their day's work, I believe, just about the same thing, with a difference, as the hard-working man of the artisan class : that is, they read the papers and they read novels, or at any rate something that is purely recreative : and the desirable thing, no doubt, is to have something recreative, more or less interesting, available at the right moment.

It often happens in a workmen's club that a man will take up and read a book that he finds on the table, when he would not even ask to have it got out of a cupboard in the same room. And this also is quite natural. A working-man seeking diversion may be willing to read the things that he finds under his hand, but he may not have purpose and zest enough to take definite steps to procure anything else, let alone the fact that he may not know what to procure, since he has not the opportunities enjoyed by the better off of compiling lists of books from the literary columns of the newspapers.

It will be interesting to observe that of the authors mentioned in the above list the name of Mrs Henry Wood occurs seven times, Shakespeare twice, Dickens twice, Marie Corelli once, Miss Braddon once, Rider Haggard once. The chief favourite, therefore, as may also be gathered from the books taken out of the libraries, is Mrs Henry Wood. It is interesting to consider the reason of this. Mrs Henry Wood has doubtless delighted many of the educated when they were younger, that is, before their experience had shown what we will call the unlikelihood of some of her combinations. What makes her so popular among the working classes is probably, first of all, the admirable compound of the goody and the sensational: the skill in handling which enables her to present her material in the most telling form, and a certain directness and obvious sentiment that they can understand, while at the same time it is just enough above their usual standard of possibilities to give an agreeable sense of stimulus. *East Lynne* is perhaps the book whose name one most often hears from men and women both. A poor woman, the widow of a workman, who had gone away to a distant part of the country, and was being supported by the parish, wrote to some one in her former town to say that she thought that if she had 'that beautiful book *East Lynne* it would be a comfort to her'. And on another occasion a workman, wishing to add to the library of a club he frequented, brought a copy of *East Lynne*, saying it was the book he liked best.

The working-men's wives read less than their husbands. They have no definite intervals of leisure, and not so many of them care to read. Among those who do, most of them, I am told, prefer something about love, with a dash of religion in it. This is the character of most of the penny stories which form the bulk of the literature accessible to them. They like some relief to the greyness of their lives, some suggestion of other possibilities; but for many of them anything that excites laughter goes too far in the other direction, although they are usually ready to laugh at something humorous if read to them more than if they read it themselves. But they generally prefer something emotional and not laughable. More than one would expect of the women between fifty and sixty cannot read: even some of those of forty. And they nearly all of them seem to have a feeling that it is wrong to sit down with a book. If there is anything more practical to do, is there not some truth in this view? Even among the well-to-do this idea persists a great deal more than one would at the first blush admit.

The women who never read during their leisure usually gossip. It is not so much that what they read is beneficial to them as that it keeps them from doing something less beneficial. Also, and this is an important factor, it puts them at a disadvantage with their children, and prevents them, even if they were disposed to do so, which does not happen very often, from exercising any check over the children's reading or taking an interest in it. There are a certain proportion among the women who are book-lovers, who will read anything that comes in their way; and heavy is the responsibility, therefore, of those who should help to provide them with books. I was told by one of the nurses at a Home that a working woman she was nursing had seventeen penny papers, which she used to conceal under her pillow. Other reading was provided for her of a rather better character, which she devoured. She could hardly be taken as a type, as she was of the genus omnivorous reader.

I have looked through a number of the penny stories that the women mostly read. They are irreproachable, and they have the most curious resemblance of plot. In four that I read, one after another, the poor and virtuous young man turned out to be a long-lost son, and became rich and powerful. One thing to be deplored is the very small print of these publications. One can hardly expect for a penny to get a complete novel in pica; but there is no doubt that the very bad print of these books, read often by imperfect light, is largely responsible for the damaged eyesight and headaches among the women, as they grow older. It would be, to my mind, a public benefaction if it were possible to organize some distribution of books on hire, in good print – wholesome, harmless fiction, of the kind that would interest the cottage readers – literally a circulating library for the people. A hawker with a barrow might carry these round the poorer streets, and offer them on hire at the cottage doors, as so many things of other kinds, that are absolutely useless to boot, are now carried round and offered. If such books, published at sixpence or even ninepence, were let out at a penny or twopence a week, according to their size and price, the hawker would probably drive a good trade. The selection of books, of course, would not be left to him, and, at the beginning, he would have to be guaranteed against possible loss. He would certainly find customers; for, as we have shown, the working-man's wife, as a rule, is ready to hire anything that is offered to her.

The born readers, men and women both, are of course not so dependent upon what is put into their hands: but the great majority are hopelessly dependent on it in this class as in any other. It is perhaps worth adding here that on finding what were the results of the inquiry made respecting reading among the workmen, a similar investigation was attempted among people who were better off, and the result of this inquiry among those whom we may call 'drawing-room readers' is curiously instructive. The first fifty who were asked had all during the previous six months been reading the same books. On all their tables there were five or six large biographies, a book of essays, some letters that had attracted attention, one or two novels by personal friends, one or two novels by writers of position: that is, all these educated people had been reading, exactly like the uneducated, the books that came under their hand or that other people had talked to them about. In very few cases had the average reader who had not the temperament of the student, gone beyond this to strike out some line indicated by a particular bent, aptitude, or special course of study.

In the face of this very hand-to-mouth course of reading of the well-to-do, we can hardly wonder that the average working-man and his wife, who do not hear much talk of books or of writers, should not eagerly seek for the masterpieces of literature, or gravitate, as we seem to expect them to do, towards the very best. It seems undeniable that for the great majority of people reading means recreation, not study: it is a pity we have only the one word to designate the two pursuits. And we may well rejoice, and not seek for anything further, if the working-man, and especially the working-woman, whose daily outlook is more cramped and cheerless than that of the man, should find in reading fiction a stimulus and change of thought.

Mrs Pember Reeves

Magdalene Stuart Reeves (1865–1946?) was born in Australia where her father was a bank manager in New South Wales, but moved to New Zealand as a child. She married William Pember Reeves, a prominent journalist and politician, who later became High Commissioner for New Zealand, 1905–8, and Director of the London School of Economics, 1908–19. Mrs Reeves, herself a journalist and active feminist, joined the Fabians in 1904, served on the executive until 1919, and through the Fabian Women's Group carried out the research which was published first as a Fabian tract *Family Life on a Pound a Week* (1912) and later as *Round About a Pound a Week* (1913).

A HORRIBLE PROBLEM

From *Round About a Pound a Week*

One of the criticisms levelled at these respectable, hard-working, independent people is that they do like to squander money on funerals. It is a view held by everyone who does not know the real circumstances. It is also held by many who do know them, but who confuse the fact that poor people show a great interest in one another's funerals with the erroneous idea that they could bury their dead for half the amount if they liked. Sometimes, in the case of adult men, this may be so. When alive, the man, perhaps, was a member of a society for burial benefit, and at his death the club or society bury him with much pomp and ceremony. In the case of the young children of people living on from 18s to 30s a week, the parents do not squander money on funerals which might be undertaken for half the price.

A working man and his wife who have a family are confronted with the problem of burial at once. They are likely to lose one or more of their children. The poorer they are, the more likely are they to lose them. Shall they run the risk of burial by the parish, or shall they take Time by the forelock and insure each child as it is born, at the rate of a penny a week? If they decide not to insure, and they lose a child, the question resolves itself into one of borrowing the sum necessary to pay the funeral expenses, or of undergoing the disgrace of a pauper funeral. The pauper funeral carries with it the pauperization of the father of the child – a humiliation which adds disgrace to the natural grief of the parents. More than that, they declare that the pauper funeral is wanting in dignity and in respect to their dead. One woman expressed the feeling of many more when she said she would as soon have the dust-cart call for the body of her child as that 'there Black Mariar'. This may be sheer prejudice on the part of poor parents, but it is a prejudice which richer parents – even the most educated and highly born of them – if confronted with the same problem when burying their own children, would fully share. Refusing, then, if uninsured, to accept the pauper burial, with its consequent political and social degradation of a perfectly respectable family, the parents try to borrow the money needed. Up and down the street sums are collected in pence and sixpences, until the price of a child's funeral on the cheapest scale is secured. Funerals are not run on credit; but the neighbours, who may be absolute strangers, will contribute rather than suffer the degradation to pauperism of one of themselves. For months afterwards the mother and remaining children will eat less in order to pay back the money borrowed. The father of the family cannot eat less. He is already eating as little as will enable him to earn the family wage. To starve him would be bad economy. He must fare as usual. The rest of the family can eat less without bothering anybody – and do.

What is the sum necessary to stand between a working man and pauperdom should he suffer the loss of a child? Inquiry among undertakers in Lambeth and Kennington resulted in the discovery that a very young baby could be buried by one undertaker for 18s, and by a dozen others for 20s. To this must be added the fee of 10s to the cemetery paid by the undertaker, which brought his charges up to 28s or 30s. No firm could be discovered who would do it for less. When a child's body is too long to go under the box-seat of the driver, the price of the funeral goes up. A sort of age scale is roughly in action, which makes a funeral of a child of three more expensive than that of a child of six months. Thirty shillings, then, is the lowest sum to be faced by the grieving parents. But how is a man whose whole weekly income may be but two-thirds of that amount to produce at sight 30s or more? Of course he cannot. Sheer dread of the horrible problem drives his wife to pay out 10d, 11d, or 1s a week year after year – money which, as far as the welfare of the children themselves go, might as well be thrown into the sea.

A penny a week paid from birth just barely pays the funeral expenses as the child grows older. It does not completely pay them in early infancy. Thirteen weekly pennies must be paid before any benefit is due, and the first sum due is not sufficient; but it is a help. As each child must be insured separately, the money paid for the child who does not die is no relief when a death occurs. Insurance, whether State or other insurance, is always a gamble, and people on £1 a week cannot afford a gamble. A peculiar hardship attaches to burial insurance. A man may have paid regularly for years, may fall out of work through illness or other misfortune, and may lose all benefit. When out of work his children are more likely to die, and he may have to suffer the disgrace of a pauper funeral after five years or more of regular payment for burial insurance.

Great numbers of premature confinements occur among women who live the lives these wives and mothers do. A premature confinement, if the child breathes, means an uninsured funeral. True, an undertaker will sometimes provide a coffin which he slips into another funeral, evade the cemetery fee, and only charge 10s; but even 10s is a terrible sum to produce at the moment. Great is the anxiety on the part of the mother to be able to prove that her child was stillborn.

The three-year-old daughter of a carter out of work died of tuberculosis. The father, whose policies had lapsed, borrowed the sum of £2 5s necessary to bury the child. The mother was four months paying the debt off by reducing the food of herself and of the five other children. The funeral cortège consisted of one vehicle, in which the little coffin went under the driver's seat. The parents and a neighbour sat in the back part of the vehicle. They saw the child buried in a common grave with twelve other coffins of all sizes. 'We 'ad to keep a sharp eye out for Edie,' they said; 'she were so little she were almost 'id.'

The following is an account kept of the funeral of a child of six months who died of infantile cholera in the deadly month of August 1911. The parents had insured her for 2d a week, being unusually careful people. The sum received was £2.

	£	s	d
Funeral	1	12	0
Death certificate	0	1	3
Gravediggers	0	2	0
Hearse attendants	0	2	0
Woman to lay her out	0	2	0
Insurance agent	0	1	0
Flowers	0	0	6
Black tie for father	0	1	0
	2	1	9

The child was buried in a common grave with three others. There is no display and no extravagance in this list. The tips to the gravediggers, hearse attendants, and insurance agent, were all urgently applied for, though not in every case by the person who received the money. The cost of the child's illness had amounted to 10s, chiefly spent on special food. The survivors lived on reduced rations for two weeks in order to get square again. The father's wage was 24s, every penny of which he always handed over to his wife.

The usual amount paid for burial insurance is 1d a week for each child, 2d for the mother, and 3d for the father, making 11d a week for a family with six children, though some over-cautious women make the sum more.

Another form of thrift is some sort of paying-out club. Usually payments of this kind come out of the father's pocket-money, but a few instances where the women made them came within the experience of the investigators. One club was named a 'didly club'. Its method seemed to consist in each member paying a certain woman ¼d the first week, ½d the next week, ¾d the next week, and so on, always adding ¼d to the previous payment. The money was to be divided at

Christmas. It was a mere way of saving, as no interest of any kind was to be paid. Needless to relate, about October the woman to whom the money had been paid disappeared. Stocking clubs, crockery clubs, and Christmas dinner clubs, make short appearances in the budgets. They usually entail a weekly payment of 3d or 4d, and when the object – the children's winter stockings, the new plates, or the Christmas dinner – has been attained, the payments cease.

One form of money transaction which is hardly regarded as justifiable when poor people resort to it, but which at the same time is the ordinary, laudable, business custom of rich men – namely, borrowing – is carried on by the poor under very distressing conditions. When no friend or friends can be found to help at a crisis, many a woman has been driven – perhaps to pay the rent – to go to what she calls a lender. A few shillings are borrowed – perhaps five or six. The terms are a penny a week on every shilling borrowed, with, it may be, a kind of tip of half a crown at the end when all the principle and interest has been paid off. A woman borrowing 6s pays 6d a week in sheer interest – that is, £1 6s a year – without reducing her debt a penny. She is paying 433 per cent on her loan. She does not know the law, and she could not afford to invoke its aid if she did know it. She goes on being bled because it is the local accepted rate of a 'lender'. Only one of the women whose budgets appear in these pages has had recourse to this kind of borrowing, but the custom is well known by them all.

Such is the passion for weekly regular payments among these women that, had the Post Office initiated regular collection of pennies instead of the industrial insurance companies doing so, either the Post Office would now be in possession of the enormous accumulated capital of these companies, or the people on 20s a week would have been much better off. The great bulk of the pennies so urgently needed for other purposes, and paid for burial insurance, is never returned in any form whatsoever to the people who pay them. The small proportion which does come to them is swallowed up in a burial, and no one but the undertaker is the better for it. As a form of thrift which shall help the future, or be a standby if misfortune should befall, burial insurance is a calamitous blunder. Yet the respectable poor man is forced to resort to it unless he is to run the risk of being made a pauper by any bereavement which may happen to him. It is a terrible object lesson in how not to manage. If the sum of £11,000,000 a year stated to be paid in weekly pennies by the poor to the industrial burial insurance companies were to be spent on better house room and better food if, in fact, the one great universal thrift of the poor were not for death, but were for life—we should have a stronger nation. The only real solution of this horrible problem would seem to be the making of decent burial a free and honourable public service.

THE POOR AND MARRIAGE

From *Round About a Pound a Week*

So many strictures are made on the improvident marriages of the poor that it is necessary to look at the matter from the point of view of the poor themselves.

If the poor were not improvident, they would hardly dare to live their lives at all. There is no security for them. Any work which they do may stop at a week's notice. Much work may be, and is, stopped with no notice of any kind. The man is paid daily, and one evening he is paid as usual, but told that he will not be needed again. Such a system breeds improvidence; and if casual labour and daily-paid labour are necessary to society, then society must excuse the faults which are the obvious outcome of such a system.

In the case of marriage, as things now are, the moment a man's money approaches a figure which seems to him a possible one he marries. For the first year or even two years he may have less ready money but more comfort. The wife keeps their one room clean and pleasant, and cooks, none too well perhaps, but possibly with more attention to his special needs than his former landlady did, or than his mother did, who had her own husband as well as her other children to cater for. The wage may be £1 a week. He gives the wife 18s and retains 2s for himself. The result of her management may closely approach the following budget of two actual young people who came within the investigation.

Mr W., aged twenty, a toy-packer in City warehouse —
wages 20s; allows 18s. He has been married eighteen months,
and when this budget was drawn up a baby was expected
any day. His wages were raised from 18s a year ago. His wife
before marriage was a machinist on piece-work, and could earn
10s a week. She worked for six months after marriage, and paid
for most of the furniture in their own room; also she provided
the coming baby's clothes. She is clean and thrifty, writes a
good hand, and keeps excellent accounts. She is nineteen.

Out of the 2s retained by the husband, he pays 6d a week
into a clothing club, and of course his 4d is deducted for State
Insurance. With the rest 'he does what he likes'. Sometimes he
likes to give the wife an extra penny for her housekeeping.
The menu, from the list of food purchases given on next page,
appears to consist of a sufficiency of bread, of meat, of
potatoes, and perhaps of greens, as the husband's dinners eaten
away from home probably include greens for him. Some cold
meat, with bread and butter and tea, would be provided for
the evening meal; bread, butter, and tea would be the
invariable breakfast.

Date of budget, 16 January 1913:

	s	d
Rent (one good room upstairs; two windows)	5	0
Burial insurance	0	3
Boot club	0	6
Coal (1 cwt. stove coal for foreign stove, which stands out in the room, and will be very dangerous when the baby begins to crawl)	1	3
Gas	0	8
Soap	0	3
Oil	0	2
Matches	0	1½
	8	2½

Left for food 9s 9½d

	s	d
Six loaves	1	4½

Husband's dinners (he is given 6d daily by his wife for his dinner, which he eats away from home)	3	0
Meat	3	2½
½ lb. butter	0	6
1 lb. flour	0	1½
1 tin of milk	0	4
4 oz. tea	0	4
1 lb. moist sugar	0	2
½ lb. dripping	0	3
8 lb. potatoes	0	4
4 lb. greens	0	2
	9	9½

An average per head of 4s 10¾d a week for food

If the wages never rise, and if the family grows larger, the amounts spent on burial insurance, soap, coal, gas, and, later on, rent will increase, leaving less and less for food, with more people to feed on the less amount. Extra bedding will eventually have to be bought, though the parents will naturally put off that moment as long as possible. Should the wage rise gradually to 24s, or even 25s, it would not all go upon the general living. The man would naturally take a larger amount of pocket-money, and out of the extra sum which he might allow the wife, he would certainly expect better living. A 'relish to his tea', costing 2d a day, mounts up to 1s a week, and a 'rasher to his breakfast' costs the same. So an increase of 2s might be completely swallowed up in extra food for the worker. And it would be really needed by him, as his proportion of the money spent would tend to diminish with more mouths to fill.

Another instance of a young couple starting on £1 a week is that of Mr H., who is twenty-two, and works in a brewery. Every third week he has night work. He allows his wife his whole wage. There is one child of six months. The wife is twenty. She worked in a polish factory until marriage, when she was dismissed, with a small bonus, as the firm does not employ married women. With the bonus she helped to furnish. She is an excellent housewife, and keeps her room comfortable.

Date of budget, 16 January 1913:

	s	d
Rent (one room, small; one window, upstairs)	3	6
Husband's fares	1	0
Husband's pocket-money	1	0
State sickness insurance	0	4
Four week's burial insurance (Mr H. had been ill on half pay, and burial insurance had stood over)	1	0
Soap, soda	0	3½
1 cwt coal	1	6
Gas	0	6
Wood	0	2
Newspaper	0	1
Boracic powder	0	1
Cotton	0	2
Needles	0	0½
Buttons	0	1
Paid off loan (5s borrowed from a brother during husband's illness)	1	0
	10	9

This leaves for food, 9s 3d between three people, or an average of 3s 1d a head.

	s	d
9 loaves	1	10½
8 oz. tea	0	8
2 lb. moist sugar	0	4
1 tin of milk (a smaller tin than Mrs W.'s)	0	3½
½ lb. butter (slightly better than Mrs W.'s)	0	7
2 lb. flour	0	3
8 lb. potatoes	0	4
Vegetables	0	7
Salt, mustard, sauce	0	2½
Fruit	0	6
Fish	1	0
Bacon	0	4½

Mineral water (recommended by doctor for Mr H. during his illness)	0	3
Meat	2	0
	9	3

Owing to Mr H. getting home to his meals, there is more elasticity in this menu. Much less meat is eaten, and fish and bacon appear instead. More bread, more tea, more vegetables are eaten, and fruit is added. The usual breakfast is bread, butter, and tea; the dinner a small amount of meat, with potatoes and vegetables; the evening meal, fish or bacon, with potatoes, as well as the eternal bread, butter, and tea. All these four young people are steady and intelligent. They have enough to eat, but they are put to it for proper clothing already. The H.'s will have to move sooner than the W.'s if their family increases, as their room, though a pleasant one, is not above half the size of the other.

It is obvious that with both these young men marriage is, so far, both pleasant and successful. It is worth the sacrifice in pocket-money which it must entail upon them. Their working life is much the same as it was during their bachelorhood, while their free time is more comfortable and more interesting. Should they have waited to marry until later in life, they would probably have lived no cheaper as bachelors, though the money would have been spent differently, and they would have been less wholesomely comfortable.

The young women's lives are far more changed. They tell you that, though they are a bit lonely at times, and miss the companionship of the factory life and the money of their own to spend, and are rather frightened at the swift approach of motherhood, 'You get accustomed to it,' and 'It won't be so lonely when the baby comes,' and 'He's very handy when he's at home.' The first baby is a source of great interest and pleasure to both parents, especially if it is well managed and does not cry at night, though one young father who was accustomed to a restless baby said he 'missed it ter'ble at night' when it was away in hospital. It is different when the children multiply and the room becomes crowded and food is less plentiful. Then the case of the man is hard and unattractive; the amount of self-sacrifice demanded of him, if he be at all tender-hearted towards his family, is outrageous. He must never smoke, he must never take a glass of ale; he must walk to and from his work in all weathers; he must have no recreations but the continual mending of his children's boots; he must neither read nor go to picture palaces nor take holidays, if he is to do all that social reformers expect of him when they theoretically parcel out his tiny income. Needless to say, the poorly paid man is not so immeasurably superior to the middle-class man in the matter of self-denial and self-control as he seems expected to be. He does smoke, he does sometimes take a glass of ale; he does, in fact, appropriate a proportion of the money he earns to his own pleasure. It is not a large proportion as a rule, but it upsets the nice calculations which are based upon the supposition that a man earning 25s a week spends every penny of it in the support of his family. He is, most probably, a hard-working, steady, sober man; but he may spend perhaps 2d a day on beer, 1d a day on tobacco, and 2d a day on tram fares, and that without being a monster of selfishness, or wishing to deprive his children of their food. In most budgets he keeps from 2s to 2s 6d for himself, in some 5s or 6s, and in some nothing. He varies as his brethren vary in other classes. Sometimes he walks to and from work; sometimes he pays his fares out of the money he keeps; and sometimes he gets them paid out of the money with which he supplies his wife. Though fond of the children when they are there, this life of stress and strain makes the women dread nothing so much as the conviction that there is to be still another baby with its inevitable consequences – more crowding, more illness, more worry, more work, and less food, less strength, less time to manage with.

There are people who argue that marriage should be put off by the poor until they have saved up enough to secure their economic independence, and that it would not hurt young men on £1 a week to put off marriage till they are thirty, they, meantime, saving hard during those ten years. Should the poorly paid workman overcome his young impulse to marry the moment his wage reaches £1 a week, and should he remain a bachelor until thirty, it is quite certain that he would not marry at all. This may be a good thing or a bad thing, but it would be so. A man who for ten years had had the spending of 20s a week – and it is a sum which is soon spent without providing luxuries – would not, at thirty, when perhaps cold reason would direct his impulse, feel inclined to share his £1 a week with an uncertain number of other people. His present bent is towards married life. It provides him for the first year or two with attention to his comfort and with privacy and freedom for his personality, as well as satisfying his natural craving for sex-relationship. Should he thwart that impulse, he, being an average, normal man, will have to find other ways of dealing with these desires of his. He is not likely to starve every instinct for ten years in order, perhaps, to save a sum which might bring in an income of a couple of shillings a week to add to his weekly wage. He would know, by the time he was thirty, that even 22s a week does not guarantee a family against misery and want. The self-sacrifice demanded of the father of even a small family on such an income would appal him.

The young couple who marry and live contentedly on 20s a week are usually members of families of at least four or five persons, and have struggled through their childhood on their share of an income which may have been anything from 20s to 25s or 26s a week. Their standard of comfort is disastrously low, and they do not for the first year or two realise that even two or three children will develop into a burden which is too great for their strength. It is not the greater number of children alone: it is the greater cost of accommodating, feeding, and clothing boys and girls as they get older which increases the strain. Moreover, the separation of interests soon begins to show itself. The husband goes to the same work – hard, long, and monotonous – but at least a change from the growing discomfort of the home. He gets accustomed to seeing his wife slave, and she gets accustomed to seeing him appear and disappear on his daily round of work, which gradually appeals less and less to her imagination, till, at thirty, she hardly knows what his duties are – so overwhelmed is she in the flood of her own most absorbing duties and economies. Her economies interfere with his comfort, and are irksome to him; so he gets out of touch with her point of view. He cannot see why the cooking should be less satisfactory than it used to be, and says so. She knows she needs a new saucepan, but cannot possibly afford to buy one, and says so. He makes his wife the same allowance, and expects the same amount of food. She has more mouths to fill, and grows impatient because he does not understand that, though their first baby did not seem to make much difference, a boy of three, plus a baby, makes the old problem into quite a new one.

One of her questions is the balance between rent and food, which is of enormous importance. Yet she never can feel certain that she has found the right solution. Shall they all live in one room? Or shall they take two basement rooms at an equally low rent, but spend more on gas and coal, and suffer more from damp and cold? Or shall they take two rooms above stairs and take the extra rent out of the food? Her own appetite may not be very large, so she decides perhaps on the two better rooms upstairs. She may decide wisely, as we think, but the sacrifice in food is not to be ignored in its results on the health of the children.

Another of her problems is, How is she to keep her husband, the bread-winner, in full efficiency out of the few shillings she can spend on food, and at the same time satisfy the appetites of the children? She decides to feed him sufficiently and to make what is over do for herself and the children. This is not considered and thought-out self-sacrifice on her part. It is the pressure of circumstances. The wage-earner must be fed. The arrangement made between husband and wife in cases where the man's work is at a distance – that 6d a day, or 3s a week, should be allowed by her for his dinners – may have begun, as in the case already quoted, before any children had appeared, and may continue when there are six children. Even if the wage has increased, and if, instead of 20s, the worker is getting 23s or 24s, he probably keeps an extra shilling for himself. Instead of allowing his wife 18s a week, he allows her 20s or 21s. If she has several children, the father's weekly 3s for dinner is far harder to compass than when she managed for two only on 18s. Rent, instead of being from 3s 6d to 5s for one 'good' upstairs room, amounts to from 6s to 7s for two upstairs rooms, or, if house-room be sacrificed to food, rent may be 5s 6d for two deadly basement rooms. Insurance has mounted from 3d a week to 9d a week.

Gas which was 6d is now 1s, on account of the extra cooking. Soap and other cleaning materials have increased in quantity, and therefore in expense from 2d to 5½d. Clothing is a problem for which very few weekly figures are available. It must be covered by payments to clothing and boot clubs, or each article must be bought when needed. In any case the expense is greater and the amount of money available for food grows less. The unvarying amount paid for the bread-winner's necessary daily food becomes a greater proportion of the food bill, and leaves all the increasing deficit to be met out of the food of the mother and children. It is unavoidable that it should be so; nobody wastes time thinking about it; but the fact that it is so forces the mother to take a different point of view from that of the father. So each of them gradually grows to understand the other less.

Both parents are probably devoted to the children. The husband, who is sick of his wife's complaints, and can't be bothered with her story of how she has no boots to wear, listens with sympathy and understanding to her tale of woe about Tommy having no boots to his feet. The boy who cannot speak at three years of age, or the girl who is deficient in weight, in height, and in wits, often is the father's special pet, for whom he will sacrifice both food and sleep, while the mother's whole life is spent in a dreary effort to do her best for them all round.

Much has been said and written, and much more will be said and written, on the question of the poor and large families. We wrangle as to whether their numerous children are an improvidence and an insult to the community, or whether, on the contrary, the poorest class is the only class which, in that respect, does its duty to the nation. One thing is quite certain, and it is that it would be as unthinkable as impossible to bring compulsion to bear on the poor because they are poor. For those who deplore large families in the case of poor people, it must be a comfort to remember a fact which experience shews us, that as poverty decreases, and as the standard of comfort rises, so does the size of the family diminish. Should we be able to conquer the problem of poverty, we should automatically solve the problem of the excessively large family.

Bibliography

PRIMARY

THOMAS ARCHER *The Pauper, The Thief, and the Convict* (1865)

THOMAS BEAMES *The Rookeries of London* (1850)

LADY FLORENCE BELL *At the Works* (1907)

Landmarks (1929)

CHARLES BOOTH *Condition and Occupations of the People of The Tower Hamlets 1886–7* (1887)

Life and Labour of the People in London (1 volume 1889; 2 volumes 1891; 9 volumes 1892–7; 17 volumes 1902–3)

Charles Booth's London (1969), edited by Albert Fried and Richard Elman. Selections from *Life and Labour.*

The Aged Poor in England and Wales (1894)

Old Age Pensions and the Aged Poor (1899)

WILLIAM BOOTH *In Darkest England and the Way Out* (1890)

A. L. BOWLEY and A. R. BURNETT-HURST *Livelihood and Poverty* (1915)

REGINALD BRAY *The Town Child* (1907)

Boy Labour and Apprenticeship (1911)

MAUDE F. DAVIES *Life in an English Village* (1909)

EDWARD DENISON *Letters and Other Writings* (1872) edited by Sir Baldwyn Leighton

FREDERICK ENGELS *The Condition of the Working-Class in England* (1845). In *Marx and Engels On Britain* (Moscow 1962); and translated by W. O. Henderson and W. H. Chaloner (Oxford 1958)

JOSIAH FLYNT *Tramping With Tramps* (1900)

JOHN GARWOOD *The Million-Peopled City* (1853)

WILLIAM GODWIN *London Shadows* (1854)

Town Swamps and Social Bridges (1859)

JAMES GREENWOOD *A Night in a Workhouse* (1866)

The Seven Curses of London (1869)

In Strange Company (1873)

The Wilds of London (1874)

Low-Life Deeps (1876)

Tag, Rag & Co. (1883)

On Tramp (1883)

H. RIDER HAGGARD *Rural England* (2 vols. 1902)

MARY HIGGS *The Tramp Ward* (1904)

Three Nights in Women's Lodging Houses (1905)

Glimpses Into the Abyss (1906)

JOHN HOLLINGSHEAD *Ragged London in 1861* (1861)

EDWARD G. HOWARTH and MONA WILSON *West Ham* (1907)
M. E. LOANE *The Queen's Poor* (1905)
   The Next Street But One (1907)
   From Their Point of View (1908)
   Neighbours and Friends (1910)
JACK LONDON *The People of the Abyss* (1903)
OLIVE MALVERY *The Soul Market* (1906)
C. F. G. MASTERMAN (ed.) *The Heart of Empire* (1901)
   From the Abyss (1902)
   In Peril of Change (1905)
   The Condition of England (1909)
HENRY MAYHEW *London Labour and the London Poor* (4 vols. 1861)
   The Unknown Mayhew (1971), edited with introductory essays
    by E. P. Thompson and Eileen Yeo.
   The Victorian Working Class (1973), edited by P. E. Razzell and
    R. W. Wainwright. Selections from the *Morning Chronicle*
    survey by Mayhew and other contributors.
ANDREW MEARNS *The Bitter Cry of Outcast London* (1883); edited
   by Anthony S. Wohl (Leicester 1970)
   London and Its Teeming Toilers (1886)
MRS PEMBER REEVES *Round About a Pound a Week* (1913)
STEPHEN REYNOLDS *A Poor Man's House* (1909)
   Seems So! A Working-Class View of Politics (1911). Written with
    Bob and Tom Woolley.
   Letters of Stephen Reynolds (1923), edited by Harold Wright.
B. S. ROWNTREE *Poverty: A Study of Town Life* (1901)
   How the Labourer Lives (1913). Written with May Kendall.
G. A. SALA *Twice Round the Clock* (1858); edited by Philip Collins
   (Leicester 1971)
ROBERT SHERARD *The Cry of the Poor* (1901)
   The Child-Slaves of Britain (1905)
   The White Slaves of England (1897)
GEORGE R. SIMS *How the Poor Live* (1883)
   How the Poor Live and Horrible London (1889)
   Glances Back (1917)
EVERARD WYVALL *'The Spike': An Account of the Workhouse
   Casual Ward* (1909)
JAMES YEAMES *Life in London Alleys* (1877)

SECONDARY

HENRIETTA BARNETT *Canon Barnett* (2 vols. 1918)
MARY BOOTH *Charles Booth: A Memoir* (1918)
ASA BRIGGS *Social Thought and Social Action: A Study of the Work
   of Seebohm Rowntree* (1961)
   Victorian Cities (1963)

M. BRUCE *The Coming of the Welfare State* (1961)

JOHN BURNETT *Plenty and Want: A Social History of Diet in England from 1815 to the Present Day* (1966)
   (Ed.) *Useful Toil: Autobiographies of Working People from the 1820s to the 1920s* (1974)

ARTHUR CALDER-MARSHALL *Prepare to Shed them Now: The Ballads of George R. Sims* (1968)

MORTON COHEN *Rider Haggard: His Life and Work* (1960)

H. J. DYOS 'The Slums of Victorian London', *Victorian Studies*, XI (1967)

H. J. DYOS and MICHAEL WOLFF (eds.) *The Victorian City: Images and Realities* (2 vols. 1973)

BENTLEY B. GILBERT *The Evolution of National Insurance in Great Britain* (1966)

RUTH GLASS 'Urban Sociology in Great Britain: A Trend Report', *Current Sociology*, IV (1955)

M. K. HIGGS *Mary Higgs of Oldham* (Oldham 1954)

SAMUEL HYNES *The Edwardian Turn of Mind* (1968)

K. S. INGLIS *Churches and the Working Classes in Victorian England* (1963)

D. CARADOG JONES *Social Surveys* (1949)

GARETH STEDMAN JONES *Outcast London: A Study in the Relationship Between Classes in Victorian Society* (1971)

P. J. KEATING *The Working Classes in Victorian Fiction* (1971)
   'The East End in Fact and Fiction', in Dyos and Wolff (eds.) *The Victorian City*

ROYSTON LAMBERT *Sir John Simon and English Social Administration* (1963)

NORMAN LONGMATE *The Workhouse* (1974)

H. M. LYND *England in the 1880s* (1945)

STEVEN MARCUS *Engels, Manchester and the Working Class* (1974)

LUCY MASTERMAN *C. F. G. Masterman: A Biography* (1939)

C. L. MOWAT *The Charity Organisation Society* (1961)

DAVID OWEN *English Philanthropy 1660–1960* (1965)

M. RICHTER *The Politics of Conscience: T. H. Green and His Age* (1964)

MICHAEL E. ROSE *The Relief of Poverty 1834–1914* (1972)

J. W. ROBERTSON SCOTT *The Story of the Pall Mall Gazette* (1950)

M. B. SIMEY *Charitable Effort in Liverpool in the Nineteenth Century* (Liverpool 1951)

T. S. and M. B. SIMEY *Charles Booth: Social Scientist* (1960)

ANTHONY S. WOHL 'The Bitter Cry of Outcast London', *International Review of Social History*, XIII (1968)

BEATRICE WEBB *My Apprenticeship* (1926)